Hossein
Bidgeli

BUSINESS BASIC

Brooks/Cole Series in Computer Science

BUSINESS BASIC
Robert J. Bent and George C. Sethares

BASIC: AN INTRODUCTION TO COMPUTER PROGRAMMING
Robert J. Bent and George C. Sethares

BEGINNING BASIC
D. K. Carver

BUSINESS BASIC

Robert J. Bent
George C. Sethares
BRIDGEWATER STATE COLLEGE

Brooks/Cole Publishing Company
Monterey, California
A Division of Wadsworth, Inc.

Printed in the United States of America

10 9 8 7 6 5 4 3 2

Library of Congress Cataloging in Publication Data

Bent, Robert J   1934–
  Business BASIC.

  Includes index.
  1. Basic (Computer program language)   2. Business
—Data processing.   I. Sethares, George C., 1930–
joint author.   II. Title.
QA76.73.B3B47   001.6′424   79–18502
ISBN 0-8185-0359-9

Acquisition Editor: *James F. Leisy, Jr.*
Production Editor: *Micky Lawler*
Interior and Cover Design: *Katherine Minerva*
Illustrations: *Tom Nix, Creative Graphics; Katherine Minerva*
Typesetting: *Instant Type, Monterey, California*

To the children:

Bob
Cathie
Eileen
Ellen
Gary
George
Greg
Jeff
John
Kerry
Lisa
Mark
Patti
Steve

PREFACE

This book is intended for an audience with no prior programming experience. A working knowledge of elementary algebra is the only mathematics needed to understand the material and complete the assignments successfully. The many worked-out examples illustrate how the BASIC programming language can be used in a data-processing environment (as opposed to a scientific environment). Both the examples and the numerous problem sets are drawn from a wide range of application areas, including business, economics, personal finance, and the social sciences.

We wrote this book with two principal goals in mind. First, we felt it important to present the elements of BASIC so that meaningful computer programs could be written at the earliest possible time. We adhere to the notion that one learns by doing. As a result, problem solving is emphasized from the beginning, and the various aspects of the BASIC language are introduced only as needed. Our second goal was to write a book that would serve as a general introduction to computer programming, not just to a programming language. Simply describing a variety of computer applications and ways to go about writing BASIC programs for these applications does not constitute an introduction to programming. What is required is a consideration of the entire programming process. The approach we have taken toward this objective is to introduce programming principles only as they can be understood and appreciated in the context of the applications being considered. For example, a beginner can easily appreciate the necessity of choosing variable names and determining how they are related. Hence, this step is introduced very early. On the other hand, the value of modularization—that is, breaking down a long and possibly complex task into more manageable subtasks—is not so easily grasped in the context of the straightforward programming problems first encountered. As natural as modularization may appear to an experienced programmer, a beginner must "see" its usefulness before being convinced of its value. Therefore, this programming principle is not introduced until later in the book.

Throughout the text we have attempted to conform to the most common BASIC usage. BASIC is not a static language. It seems that each new BASIC implementation contains what the designers consider to be "improvements." In an attempt to standardize the most common BASIC features, the American National Standards Institute (ANSI) prepared a document, dated December 1, 1976, entitled "Proposed American National Standard for Minimal BASIC." In all but two instances, which are clearly identified, our presentation of minimal BASIC conforms to the proposed ANSI standard.

Those BASIC features not described in the proposed ANSI standard are referred to as extended BASIC. Extended BASIC features that have been widely implemented and whose implementations differ only slightly are introduced along with the minimal BASIC. Phrases such as "Your BASIC system may allow you to . . ." indicate that the BASIC feature to be described is not a part of minimal BASIC. The material contained in this text, including the problem sets, has been carefully organized so that topics that are not a part of minimal BASIC may be omitted with no loss of continuity.

A few remarks are appropriate concerning the order in which we have introduced the elements of BASIC. The INPUT statement is introduced early and before the READ and DATA statements to emphasize the interactive nature of BASIC. The GO TO statement is presented with the INPUT statement so that the nature of the computer as a fast and sophisticated calculator can be shown early. The IF statement is introduced in the very next chapter so that certain difficulties arising from the use of GO TO statements can quickly be resolved. Selecting an order in which to present the remaining BASIC instructions was not so simple. It is our feeling that certain BASIC instructions become more meaningful if they can be described in terms of other BASIC instructions. For example, in data-processing applications, the automatic FOR/NEXT loops are especially useful for processing large quantities of data; hence, the FOR/NEXT loops (Chapter 8) are presented just after the READ/DATA statements (Chapter 7) that are used to present such large quantities of data to the computer for processing. The introductory material for the remaining BASIC instructions is presented in such a way that these instructions can easily be taken up in some other order.

Section 7.4, which describes the method of top-down programming, must not be skipped, for in many respects it is the most important section in the book. It brings together many of the programming principles stressed in the first seven chapters and should serve as a model for all subsequent programming endeavors. No introduction to programming can be considered complete without an understanding of this approach.

We wish to take this opportunity to acknowledge the helpful comments of our reviewers, Keith Carver of Sacramento City College, Richard A. Hatch of San Diego State University, and A. Thomas Mason of Clarkson College. We feel that their many thoughtful suggestions have led to a greatly improved text.

A special thanks goes to Patricia Shea, our typist. Many of her suggestions concerning the text format have been adopted, and her meticulous concern for detail was indispensable. Finally, we are happy to acknowledge the fine cooperation of the staff at Brooks/Cole Publishing Company.

Robert J. Bent
George C. Sethares

CONTENTS

1 COMPUTER PROGRAMMING

An electronic computer system has the ability to store large quantities of data, to process these data at very fast rates, and to present the results of this processing in ways that are meaningful to the task at hand. Thus, if the task is to prepare a payroll, employee data will be stored in the computer, the computer will process these data to calculate relevant wage statistics, and the results will be presented in printed form, possibly including paychecks. This example illustrates the three principal tasks involved in any computer application: data must be presented to the computer (**INPUT**), data must be processed (**PROCESS**), and results must be presented in a meaningful way (**OUTPUT**) (see Figure 1.1).

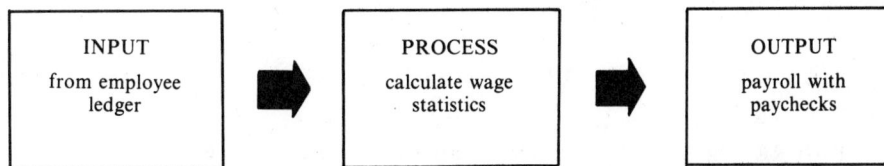

```
┌─────────────────┐      ┌─────────────────┐      ┌─────────────────┐
│      INPUT      │      │     PROCESS     │      │     OUTPUT      │
│  from employee  │ ▶    │ calculate wage  │ ▶    │  payroll with   │
│     ledger      │      │   statistics    │      │   paychecks     │
└─────────────────┘      └─────────────────┘      └─────────────────┘
```

FIGURE 1.1 An INPUT-PROCESS-OUTPUT diagram

The purpose of this chapter is not to convince you that a computer can "do" many things or even to indicate the computer applications you will be able to carry out after completing this text. Rather, the objectives of this chapter are to introduce you to the types of computer equipment you may encounter, to describe what a computer program is, and to introduce you to the process of writing computer programs.

1.1 COMPUTER HARDWARE

Central to every computer system is an **electronic computer** whose principal function is to process data. The computer component that does this is called the **central processing unit (CPU).** The CPU contains an **arithmetic unit,** consisting of circuitry that performs a variety of arithmetic and logical operations; a **control unit,** which controls all electrical signals passing through the computer; and a **memory unit,** which stores data. It is convenient to think of the memory unit as a sequence of locations in which data may be stored and from which it may be retrieved for processing. Fortunately, you need not understand the operation of the CPU to make a computer work for you. The circuitry in a computer is not unlike that in an ordinary pocket calculator, and all who have used calculators know that no knowledge of their circuitry is needed to use them.

Data must be transmitted to the CPU (input), and results of the processing must be returned (output). Devices meeting these two requirements are called **input** and **output devices.** One such device, which does both, is called a teletypewriter (Figures 1.2a and 1.2b). You transmit information to the CPU simply by typing at the teletypewriter keyboard, and the CPU automatically transmits the results back to the teletypewriter, which produces a printed copy for you.

FIGURE 1.2a ASR Model 33 Data Terminal. (Courtesy of Teletype Corporation.)

FIGURE 1.2b DECwriter II Terminal. (Courtesy of Digital Equipment Corporation.)

Most modern computer systems are equipped with additional external storage devices, such as magnetic-tape units (Figure 1.3) and disk-storage units (Figure 1.4). Such units are often used as input

FIGURE 1.3 Magnetic Tape Drive. (Courtesy of Honeywell Information Systems, Inc.)

FIGURE 1.4 IBM 5445 Removable Disk Pack and Drive. (Courtesy of IBM Corporation.)

and output devices, especially when large quantities of data must be processed. All of these mechanical and electrical devices, other than the CPU itself, are referred to as **computer peripherals.** The CPU, together with its peripherals, constitutes what is called the **hardware** of the computer system. Figure 1.5 illustrates the flow of information through a computer system.

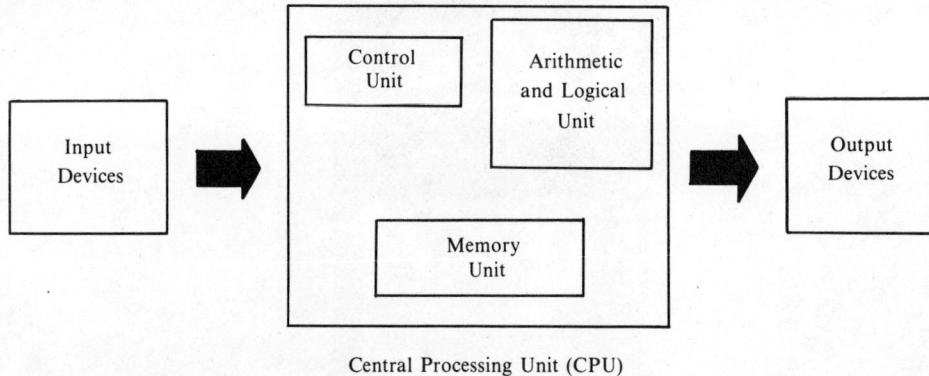

Central Processing Unit (CPU)

FIGURE 1.5 Flow of information through a computer system

1.2   COMPUTER SOFTWARE

The physical components, or hardware, of a computer system are inanimate objects. They cannot prepare a payroll or perform any other task, however simple, without human assistance. This assistance is given in the form of instructions to the computer. A sequence of such instructions is called a **computer program,** and a person who determines what these instructions should be is called a **programmer.**

The precise form that instructions to a computer must take depends on the particular computer system being used. **BASIC** (Beginner's All-purpose Symbolic Instruction Code)* is a carefully constructed English-like language used for writing computer programs. Instructions in the BASIC language are designed to be understood by people as well as by the computer. Even the uninitiated will understand the meaning of this simple BASIC program:

```
1 LET A = 3
2 LET B = A + 5
3 PRINT B
4 END
```

A computer is an electronic device and understands an instruction such as LET A=3 in a very special way. An electronic device can distinguish between two distinct electrical states. Consider, for instance, an ordinary on/off switch for a light fixture. When the switch is in the "on" position, current is allowed to flow and the light bulb glows. If we denote the "on" position by the number 1 and the "off" position by the number 0, we can say that the instruction 1 causes the bulb to glow and the instruction 0 causes it not to glow. In like manner, we could envision a machine with two switches whose positions are denoted by the four codes 00, 01, 10, and 11 and such that each of these four codes causes a different event to occur. It is this ability to distinguish between two distinct electrical states that has led to the development of modern computers. Indeed, modern computers are still based on this principle. Each computer is designed to "understand" a certain set of primitive instructions. On some computers these instructions take the form of sequences of 0s and 1s, but their precise form is not important to the beginner. All such primitive instructions that are meaningful to a particular computer are together called the **machine language** for that computer.

*__BASIC__ was developed at Dartmouth College under the direction of John G. Kemeny and Thomas E. Kurtz.

You will not be required to write programs in machine language. The computer you use will contain an **interpreter** or a **compiler,** which automatically translates your BASIC instructions into equivalent machine-language instructions that are then executed by the computer (Figure 1.6). Thus, when the four-line BASIC program shown above is presented to the computer, the BASIC compiler produces an equivalent machine-language program that instructs the computer to perform the specified task.

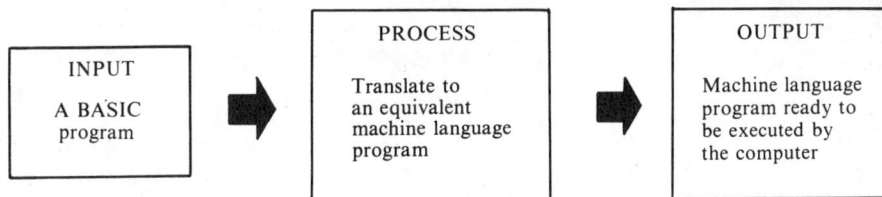

```
┌─────────────┐      ┌─────────────────┐      ┌──────────────────┐
│   INPUT     │      │    PROCESS      │      │    OUTPUT        │
│             │  ▶   │                 │  ▶   │                  │
│  A BASIC    │      │  Translate to   │      │ Machine language │
│  program    │      │  an equivalent  │      │ program ready to │
│             │      │  machine language│     │ be executed by   │
│             │      │  program        │      │ the computer     │
└─────────────┘      └─────────────────┘      └──────────────────┘
```

FIGURE 1.6 INPUT-PROCESS-OUTPUT diagram for a BASIC compiler

BASIC compilers and interpreters are themselves computer programs. They are called **system programs** because they are an integral part of the computer system being used. The BASIC programs appearing in this text, as well as the programs you will write, are called **application programs.** They are not an integral part of the computer system, so they are not called system programs. All computer programs, both system programs and application programs, are called **computer software.** The International Standards Organization (ISO) defines software as "a set of computer programs, procedures and possibly associated documentation concerned with the operation of a data processing system, e.g., compilers, library routines, manuals, circuit diagrams."*

A computer system that accepts BASIC programs will be called a **BASIC system.** Figure 1.7 shows a complete BASIC system that contains a special cassette tape-storage unit. Figure 1.8 depicts a

FIGURE 1.7 Radio Shack TRS-80 Microcomputer System. (Courtesy of Radio Shack, a Division of Tandy Corporation.)

*ADP Glossary, Department of the Navy, December 1970. This glossary may be obtained from the Superintendent of Documents, U.S. Government Printing Office, Washington, D.C. 20402.

FIGURE 1.8 Wang MVP Computer System. (Photo courtesy of Wang Laboratories, Inc., Lowell, Mass.)

more elaborate BASIC system that includes several video displays. Such a system is called a **time-sharing system** because it provides for the simultaneous use of a computer by more than one user.

1.3 PROBLEM SOLVING

A computer program consists of a sequence of instructions to the computer. These instructions describe a step-by-step process for carrying out a specified task. Such a process is called a **procedure,** or an **algorithm.** Algorithms have been with us since antiquity: the familiar division algorithm was known and used in ancient Greece; the activities of bookkeepers have always been guided by algorithms (an algorithm to determine a tax assessment, an algorithm to calculate a depletion allowance, and so on); even the instructions for assembling a child's new toy are often given as an algorithm.

An algorithm is a prescribed set of well-defined rules and processes for solving a problem in a finite number of steps. The process of writing computer programs can be equated to the process of discovering suitable algorithms. For this reason, an understanding of what is—and what is not—an algorithm is indispensable to a programmer. The examples in this section are intended to help you gain an understanding of what an algorithm is and some practice with the process of discovering algorithms.

EXAMPLE 1. An algorithm giving instructions for completing a financial transaction at a drive-in-teller port.

a. Press the call button.
b. Remove the carrier from the tray.
c. Place your transaction inside the carrier.
d. Replace the carrier.
e. When the carrier returns, remove the transaction.
f. Replace the carrier.

To see that these six steps describe an algorithm, we must verify that each step is well defined and that the process stops in a finite number of steps. For example, step (a) requires that there be only one call button, and step (b) requires that there be but one tray containing a single carrier. Having verified that each step is well defined, and noting that the process is obviously finite, we are assured that the process does indeed describe an algorithm. In addition, it should be clear that the algorithm "does" what is claimed.

EXAMPLE 2. Let's find an algorithm to calculate the year-end bonus for all salaried employees in a firm. Employees are to be paid 3% of their annual salary or $400, whichever is larger.

To carry out this task, a payroll clerk might proceed as follows.

a. Open the employee ledger.
b. Turn to the next employee's account.
c. Determine the employee's bonus.
d. Write the employee's name and bonus amount on the bonus sheet.
e. If all bonuses have not been determined, return to step (b).
f. Close the ledger.

It is not difficult to see that these six instructions constitute an algorithm. Each step is well defined, and, since a business can employ only a finite number of people, the algorithm will terminate in a finite number of steps. Moreover, if this algorithm is followed, all employee bonuses will be determined as specified.

Although the algorithm "does" what was asked, the process could be made more specific by including more detail in step (c). Recalling the method specified for calculating bonus amounts, we can substitute the following for step (c).

c1. Multiply the employee's salary by .03 to obtain a tentative bonus.
c2. If the tentative bonus is at least $400, go to step (d).
c3. Set the bonus to $400.

Making this change, or refinement, we obtain the following more detailed algorithm.

a. Open the employee ledger.
b. Turn to the next employee's account.
c. Multiply the employee's salary by .03 to obtain a tentative bonus.
d. If the tentative bonus is at least $400, go to step (f).
e. Set the bonus to $400.
f. Write the employee's name and bonus amount on the bonus sheet.
g. If all bonuses have not been determined, return to step (b).
h. Close the ledger.

Remark 1: The first algorithm is more general than the second. It describes a process one might follow to determine employee bonuses, however they are to be calculated. The second algorithm can be used only if bonuses are calculated as specified in the problem statement.

Remark 2: It is somewhat easier to verify that the first algorithm "does" what was asked. This is because of, and not in spite of, the detail not present in the algorithm. Having verified that the first algorithm is correct, all that is required to verify that the second algorithm is also correct is to check that steps (c1), (c2), and (c3) describe the same task as step (c) of the first algorithm.

EXAMPLE 3. Let's find an algorithm to determine the largest number in a list of 10 numbers.

One way to determine the largest number in a list of numbers is to read them one at a time, remembering only the largest of those already read. To help us give a precise description of this process, let's use two symbols as follows.

L to denote the largest of those numbers already read.

N to denote the number currently being read.

The following algorithm can now be written.

a. Read the first number and denote it by L.

b. Read the next number and denote it by N.

c. If L is at least as large as N, skip the next step.

d. Assign the number N to L.

e. If all 10 numbers have not been read, go to step (b).

f. Print the value of L and stop.

Remark: If the ten numbers are written on a sheet of paper, a person could simply look them over and select the largest. However, this process is *heuristic* and does not constitute an algorithm.* To see that this is so, imagine many hundreds of numbers written on a large sheet of paper. In this case, selecting the largest simply by looking over the numbers can easily result in an error. What is needed is an orderly process that will ensure that the largest number is selected. Examining numbers one at a time, as was done in the algorithm, is such an orderly process.

Algorithms can often be easily and clearly stated if symbols are used to denote certain quantities. Symbols are especially helpful when used to denote quantities that may change during the process of performing the steps in an algorithm. The symbols L and N used in Example 3 are illustrations of this practice. (It would be instructive to write down the algorithm of Example 3 without using symbols.)

A quantity that can change during a process is called a **variable quantity,** or simply a **variable**. A symbol used to denote such a variable quantity is the name of the variable. Thus, L and N, in Example 3, are names of variables. However, it is a common practice to refer to the *symbol* as being the variable itself, rather than just its name. For instance, step (f) of the algorithm for Example 3 says to print the value of L. Certainly, this is less confusing than saying "Print the value of the variable whose name is L."

Each of the preceding three examples concerns an algorithm describing a process to be carried out by people. A computer programmer must be concerned with algorithms describing processes to be carried out by a computer. This means that each step must describe an action that a computer can perform. This constraint is not so restrictive as it may appear. Computer languages, such as BASIC, contain instructions to assign numerical values to variables, to perform arithmetic operations, to compare numerical quantities and transfer to different instructions depending on the result of this comparison, and to print numerical values. Each step in the algorithm of Example 3 represents one of these four types of action, which means that the algorithm does indeed describe a process that can be carried out by a computer.

Even instructions that appear to have nothing at all to do with computers can sometimes describe meaningful computer operations. As you progress through your study of BASIC, you will find that statements such as "Open the employee ledger" can indeed correspond to actions a computer can carry out.

The problems at the end of this chapter are designed to give you practice with the process of discovering algorithms. At this point it is not important that the individual steps in an algorithm correspond to actions that a computer can perform. A knowledge of what constitutes an admissible instruction to a computer will come as you gain experience working with the BASIC language. What is important is that the individual steps are easy to understand and that the process described is an algorithm that, when carried out, does what is asked.

We conclude this chapter with a fourth example concerning the process of discovering algorithms.

EXAMPLE 4. Find an algorithm to prepare a depreciation schedule for a capital investment whose cost is $10,000, whose salvage value is $2000, and whose useful life is five years. Use the straight-line method.

---

*A heuristic process is one involving exploratory methods. Solutions to problems are discovered by a continual evaluation of the progress made toward the final result.

For each year let's agree to write one line showing the year, the depreciation allowance for that year, and the cumulative depreciation. A person carrying out this task might proceed as follows.

a. Look up the cost ($10,000), the salvage value ($2000), and the useful life (five years).
b. Determine the depreciation allowance for one year.
c. Subtract the depreciation allowance from the book value (initially the cost).
d. Add the depreciation amount to the cumulative depreciation (initially zero).
e. Write one line showing the year, the depreciation allowance for that year, and the cumulative depreciation.
f. If the schedule is not complete, go to step (c).
g. Stop.

Let's modify this algorithm to apply to capital items whose cost, salvage value, and useful life are known but are not necessarily equal to those given in the problem statement.

To help describe this more general algorithm, let's first choose variable names to denote the various quantities of interest.

B = book value. (The initial book value is the cost.)
S = salvage value.
Y = useful life in years.
D = depreciation allowance for one year. ($D = (B-S)/Y$.)
C = cumulative depreciation (initially zero).

The following algorithm describes one way to carry out the specified task.

a. Assign values to B, S, and Y.
b. Assign the value $0.00 to C.
c. Calculate $D = (B-S)/Y$.
d. Subtract D from B.
e. Add D to C.
f. Write one line showing the year and the values D and C.
g. If the schedule is not complete, go to step (d).
h. Stop.

Remark: It is not often that a problem statement exactly describes the problem to be resolved. Problem statements are usually written in a natural language, such as English, and thus are subject to the ambiguities inherent in natural languages. Moreover, they are written by people, which means that they are subject to human oversight and error. An algorithm describes a precise, unambiguous process for carrying out a task. Thus the task to be performed must be clearly understood. If it appears ambiguous, the ambiguities must be resolved. If it appears that one thing is being asked where another is actually desired, the difference must be resolved. For example, the problem statement in the present example asks for only a very limited algorithm (a book value of $10,000, a salvage value of $2000, and a useful life of 5 years) when what is really desired is the more general algorithm that has a wider application.

1.4   PROBLEMS

Problems 1–4 refer to the following algorithm, which is intended for completing an invoice.

a. Let AMOUNT = 0.
b. Read QUANTITY and PRICE of an item.
c. Add the product QUANTITY × PRICE to AMOUNT.
d. If there is another item, go to step (b). Otherwise, continue with step (e).
e. If AMOUNT is not greater than $500, go to step (h). Otherwise, continue with step (f).
f. Evaluate the product .05 × AMOUNT.
g. Subtract this product from AMOUNT.
h. Record the value AMOUNT and stop.

1. What interpretation could be given to the product appearing in step (f)?
2. What purpose would you say is served by step (e)?
3. If the values (10, $3.00), (50, $8.00), and (25, $12.00) are read by step (b), what value will be recorded by step (h)?
4. If the values (100, $2.00) and (50, $1.00) are read by step (b), what value will be recorded by step (h)?

Problems 5–8 refer to the following algorithm, which is intended for use by a payroll clerk as a preliminary step in the preparation of a payroll.

   a. Read the next time card.
   b. Let H = number of hours worked.
   c. If H is not greater than 32, let G = B = 0 and go to step (f). Otherwise, continue with the next step.
   d. Evaluate 6 × (H − 32) and assign this value to both G and B.
   e. Let H = 32.
   f. Evaluate 4 × H and add this value to G.
   g. Write the values G and B on the time card.
   h. If there is another time card, go to step (a). Otherwise, stop.

5. What meaning do G, B, and H have?
6. What is the base hourly rate for each employee?
7. What is the overtime rate?
8. Explain step (c).

Write an algorithm to carry out the tasks specified in Problems 9–13.

9. A retail store's monthly sales report shows, for each item, the fixed cost, the sale price, and the number sold. Prepare a three-column report with the column headings ITEM, GROSS SALES, and INCOME.
10. Each of several 3-by-5 cards contains an employee's name, Social Security number, job classification, and date hired. Prepare a report showing the names, job classifications, and complete years of service for employees who have been with the company for more than ten years.
11. A summary sheet of an investor's stock portfolio shows, for each stock, the number of shares owned, the current price, and the earnings as reported for the most recent year. Prepare a six-column report with the column headings CORP. NAME, NO. OF SHARES, PRICE, EARNINGS, EQUITY, and PRICE/EARNINGS. Use the formula Equity = No. of Shares × Price.
12. A local supermarket has installed a check-validation machine. To use this service, a customer must have previously obtained an identification card containing a magnetic strip and also a four-digit code. Instructions showing how to insert the identification card into a special magnetic-strip reader appear on the front panel. To validate a check, a customer must present the identification card to the machine, enter the four-digit code, enter the amount of the check, and place the check, blank side toward the customer, in a special clearly labeled punch unit. To begin this process, the CLEAR key must be depressed, and, after each of the two entries has been made, the ENTER key must be depressed. Prepare an algorithm giving instructions for validating a check.
13. Write an algorithm describing the steps to be taken to cast a ballot in a national election. Assume that a person using this algorithm is a registered voter and has just entered the building in which voting is to take place. While in the voting booth, the voter should simply be instructed to vote. No instructions concerning the actual filling out of a ballot are to be given.

1.5   REVIEW TRUE OR FALSE QUIZ

1. The principal function of a computer is to process data.   T   F
2. The "workhorse" of a computer system is the CPU.   T   F
3. The function of a BASIC compiler is to translate BASIC programs into machine language.   T   F
4. A BASIC compiler is part of the hardware of a computer system.   T   F
5. A BASIC program written to solve a particular problem may accurately be called a system program.   T   F
6. The expressions *computer software* and *computer program* are synonymous.   T   F
7. A computer system must contain at least one teletypewriter.   T   F

8. Input/output devices are called computer peripherals. T F
9. To solve problems using the BASIC language, you must know and understand what a compiler is or what an interpreter is. T F
10. The terms *procedure* and *algorithm* are synonymous. T F
11. The expression *heuristic process* refers to a procedure. T F
12. The term *variable* refers to a quantity that can change during a process. T F

2 A FIRST LOOK AT BASIC

We must communicate with a computer before it will perform any service for us. The vehicle for such communication is the computer program, which, for our purposes, will be a sequence of instructions in the English-like language BASIC. Here is a BASIC program whose purpose is described in the first line.

```
100 REM PROGRAM TO AVERAGE THREE NUMBERS
110 REM    X, Y, AND Z DENOTE THE NUMBERS
120 REM    A DENOTES THE AVERAGE
130 LET X=43
140 LET Y=27
150 LET Z=23
160 LET A=(X+Y+Z)/3
170 PRINT "AVERAGE IS", A
180 END
```

If a computer carries out the instructions appearing in this program, it will produce the following output.

AVERAGE IS   31

The lines in this program are labeled with *line numbers* that determine the order in which the instructions are carried out by the computer. The program uses four words, called *keywords,* from the BASIC language: REM, to include remarks or comments as part of the program; LET, to associate certain numerical values with certain symbols (for example, line 130 associates 43 with the symbol X); PRINT, to print the results; and END, to indicate the last line of the program.

Unlike a natural language, such as English, a programming language must not allow ambiguities. The computer must do precisely what it is instructed to do. For this reason, great care must be taken to write BASIC instructions precisely according to the BASIC **syntax** (BASIC rules of grammar). The following sections describe how the keywords REM, LET, PRINT, and END can be used to form admissible BASIC programs. A complete treatment of these topics is not intended at this time; our immediate goal is to provide you with the minimal information needed to understand and to write some BASIC programs.

12

2.1 NUMERICAL CONSTANTS AND VARIABLES

Three types of numerical constants are allowed in BASIC.

Type	Examples				
Integer	726	99234	−726	+423	−16023	0
Decimal	726.	−133.50	+10.001	−99234.	0.201
Floating-point (exponential)	1E4	−13.6E−2	.12345E03	+2.345E−01

Integers are numbers with no decimal point, and decimals are numbers in which a decimal point appears. The use of commas and dollar signs in numbers is not allowed; using 99,234 to represent 99234 will result in an error. The third type of numerical constant may be new to you. The general form for a floating-point constant, together with its meaning, is

$$nEm = n \times 10^m.$$

Here n may be any integer or decimal but m must be an integer. E stands for "exponent." The values of the four floating-point numbers shown above are:

$$1E4 = 1 \times 10^4 \qquad = 1 \times 10000 \qquad = 10000$$
$$-13.6E-2 = -13.6 \times 10^{-2} = -13.6 \times .01 \quad = -0.136$$
$$.12345E03 = .12345 \times 10^3 = .12345 \times 1000 = 123.45$$
$$+2.345E-01 = 2.345 \times 10^{-1} = 2.345 \times .1 \qquad = 0.2345$$

Note that 1E4 represents 10000, but E4 is meaningless.

Although in some programming languages the programmer must exhibit caution concerning the representation of numbers in these three forms, the BASIC programmer is free to use any form desired.

BASIC allows the following as variable names.

$$A, B, C, \ldots, Z$$
$$A0, A1, A2, \ldots, A9$$
$$B0, B1, B2, \ldots, B9$$

$$\cdot \qquad \cdot$$
$$\cdot \qquad \cdot$$
$$\cdot \qquad \cdot$$

$$Z0, Z1, Z2, \ldots, Z9$$

All other variable names are considered inadmissible at this time.

2.2 ARITHMETIC OPERATIONS AND BASIC EXPRESSIONS

BASIC uses the following symbols to denote arithmetic operations.

BASIC Symbol	Meaning	Priority
↑ or ˆ or **	Exponentiation	1
*	Multiplication	2
/	Division	2
+	Addition	3
−	Subtraction	3

Any meaningful combination of BASIC constants, variable names, and operation symbols is called a BASIC **expression.** In any BASIC expression the order in which the operations are performed is determined first by the indicated priority and then, in any priority class, from left to right. This is in agreement with the usual meaning of arithmetic expressions.

EXAMPLE 1.   In the following expressions the circled numbers indicate the order in which the operations will be performed by the computer.

```
        ①  ②
a.   5 – 4 + 3 =
       1   + 3 =
             4
```

Since + and – have the same priority, they are performed from left to right. Note that performing the + first gives the incorrect value –2.

```
        ③  ①  ②
b.   2 + 6 / 2 * 3 =
     2 +   3  * 3 =
     2 + 9 =
        11
```

Since / and * have the same priority, they are performed from left to right. Note that performing the * first gives the incorrect value 3.

```
        ③  ①  ④  ②
c.   5 * 2 ↑ 2 + 3 ↑ 2
```

Performing these operations one at a time, we obtain

```
     5 * 2 ↑ 2 + 3 ↑ 2 =
     5 *   4   + 3 ↑ 2 =
     5 *   4   + 9   =
        20  + 9 =
             29
```

Expressions such as +5, –1.2, +A, and –B are also allowed in BASIC. Both +A and A have the same meaning, and –B denotes the negative of B. When + and – are used in this manner, they are called *unary operations*. They still have priority 3 but are performed prior to all other + and – operations (not before ↑, *, and /).

EXAMPLE 2.   In the following, A = 3, B = –2, and C = 4.

BASIC Expression	Value of Expression
–2↑4	–16 (not 16)
–A	–3
+B	–2
–B	2
–A+B	–5
–5 * A+4	–11
1–3↑C	–80
4–3+2/4+A	4.5
A↑2+B↑2	13
A/B * C	–6 (not –.375)

Parentheses may be used in BASIC expressions just as in ordinary algebra. They are used to override the normal order in which operations are performed and also to help clarify the meaning of numerical expressions. For example, 5/2*3 and (5/2)*3 have the same meaning in BASIC, but the second form is less likely to be misinterpreted. A third use of parentheses in BASIC is explained following Example 3.

EXAMPLE 3.   In the following, P = 14, Q = –5, and R = 7.

BASIC Expression	Value of Expression
P+(Q–R)	2
P/(4*R)	0.5
(Q+P)/(R–4)	3
Q+P/R–4	–7
(Q+R)↑2+P	18
3↑(R+Q)	9
R*(R*(R+1)+1)	399
(P+Q)*(–2)	–18
(–Q)↑2	25
–Q↑2	–25

Remark: The parentheses surrounding the –2 in (P+Q)*(–2) are necessary in order that two operation symbols do not appear adjacent to each other. Failure to observe this rule will result in an error on most BASIC systems.

Roots of numbers are indicated in BASIC by using the exponentiation operator ↑. Recall from algebra that

$$\sqrt{9} = 9^{1/2} = 3.$$

In BASIC, we write this as

$$9↑(1/2) \quad \text{or} \quad 9↑0.5$$

EXAMPLE 4. In the following, M = 4 and N = 5.

Algebraic Expression	Equivalent BASIC Expression	Value
$\sqrt{M}$	M↑(1/2)	2
$\sqrt{M+N}$	(M+N)↑0.5	3
$\sqrt[3]{2M}$	(2*M)↑(1/3)	2
$\sqrt[3]{7+MN}$	(7+M*N)↑(1/3)	3
$6\sqrt{5+M-N}$	6*(5+M–N)↑0.5	12

Caution: BASIC systems are not designed to take roots of negative numbers. For example, the cube root of –8 is –2, but the BASIC expression (–8)↑(1/3) will not give this value. BASIC expressions such as A↑B will result in an error if the exponent B is not an integer and A is negative.

2.3   PROBLEMS

1. Evaluate the following.
   a. 2+3*5
   b. 5*7–2
   c. –4+2
   d. –(4+2)
   e. –3*5
   f. –3↑2
   g. 1+2↑3*2
   h. 6/2*3
   i. 1/2/2
   j. –2*3/2*3
   k. 2↑2↑3
   l. (2+(3*4–5))↑0.5
2. For A = 2, B = 3, and X = 2, evaluate each of the following.
   a. A+B/X
   b. (A+B)/2*X
   c. B/A/X

    d. B/(A*X)   e. A+X↑3   f. (A+B)↑X

    g. B↑A/X   h. B+A/B−A   i. A↑B+X

    j. B↑(X/A)   k. −A↑B   l. (−A)↑B

3. Some of the following are not admissible BASIC expressions. Explain why.

    a. (Y+Z)X   b. X2*36   c. A*(2.1−7B)

    d. X↑−2   e. A+−B   f. −(A+2B)

    g. 2X↑2   h. X2↑2   i. X−2↑2

    j. A12+B3   k. A+(+B)   l. A2−(−A2)

4. Some of the following are admissible BASIC expressions and some are not. Rewrite those that are not and evaluate all of them.

    a. −3*(4+.1)   b. 2+(2)   c. 4*−3

    d. (5/4)*8   e. −2↑2*3   f. 5E1.0

    g. (−3)↑2   h. −3↑2   i. 7/−14

    j. −3+(−3+1)   k. 4↑1/2   l. −4↑(1/2)

5. Write BASIC expressions for these arithmetic expressions.

    a. $0.06P$ b. $5x + 5y$ c. $a^2 + b^2$

    d. $\frac{6}{5a}$ e. $\frac{a}{b} + \frac{c}{d}$ f. $\frac{a + b}{c + d}$

    g. $ax^2 + bx + c$ h. $\sqrt{b^2 - 4ac}$ i. $(x^2 + 4xy)/(x + 2y)$

2.4   THE **LET** STATEMENT: ASSIGNING VALUES TO VARIABLES

In Section 2.2 you saw how to write arithmetic expressions in a form acceptable to the computer. You will now learn how to instruct the computer to evaluate such expressions.

A BASIC **program statement,** also called a **programming line,** consists of an instruction to the computer preceded by an unsigned integer called the **line number.** The general form is

line number   BASIC instruction

For example,

100 LET A = 2 + 5

is a BASIC statement with line number 100. This statement, called a LET statement, will cause the computer to evaluate the sum 2 + 5 and then assign this value to A.

A BASIC **program** is a collection of BASIC program statements. The instructions are executed by the computer in the order determined by increasing line numbers, unless some instruction overrides this order.

The general form of our first BASIC statement, the LET statement, is

ln LET **a** = **e**

where **ln** stands for line number, **a** denotes a variable name, and **e** denotes a BASIC expression that may simply be a constant. This statement directs the computer to evaluate the expression **e** and then assign this value to the variable **a**.

EXAMPLE 5. In the following, A = 2, B = −2, and C = 3.

BASIC Statement	After Execution
30 LET S = A+B+C	S has the value 3.
55 LET X = A+1	X has the value 3.
90 LET Y = 4	Y has the value 4.
20 LET X = (1+A)↑C*(B+5)	X has the value 81.

EXAMPLE 6. Here is a BASIC program ready to be typed into the computer and run. (The procedure for doing so will be described in the next chapter.) The columns to the right of the program show how the values of the variables are changed during program execution.

After Execution of Each Instruction

The Program	Value of P	Value of Q
100 LET P=12	12	
110 LET Q=P/2+1	12	7
120 LET P=Q/2+1	4.5	7
130 LET Q=P/2+1	4.5	3.25
140 END		

Remark 1: An **END** statement as shown in line 140 should terminate every program. There must be only one END statement, and its line number must be greater than all other line numbers in the program.

Remark 2: Note that no value is shown for Q following execution of line 100. Some, but not all, BASIC systems assign an initial value of zero to all variables.

Remark 3: The practice of incrementing line numbers by something other than 1 is a good one (10 is very popular). It allows the programmer to insert additional instructions, which may have been forgotten, in their proper place.

Remark 4: Newly written programs seldom do what they were meant to do. The programmer must find and correct all errors. (The errors are called **bugs,** and making the corrections is referred to as **debugging** the program.) A very useful debugging technique is to pretend that you are the computer and prepare a table of successive values of program variables, as was done in this example.

The BASIC statement

$$40 \text{ LET N} = \text{N}+1$$

does not mean that N is equal to N+1 (since that is impossible). It means that the expression N+1 is *evaluated* and this value is *assigned* to the variable N. For example, the effect of the two programming lines

$$30 \text{ LET N} = 5$$
$$40 \text{ LET N} = \text{N}+1$$

is that the value 6 is assigned to N. Similarly, the statement

$$70 \text{ LET S} = \text{S}+\text{Y}$$

evaluates S+Y and then assigns this new value to S. Thus, line 40 increases the value of N by 1 and line 70 increases the value of S by Y.

EXAMPLE 7. In the following, S = 3, Y = –2, H = –4, Z = 6, and M = 10.

BASIC Statement	After Execution
35 LET S = S+Y	S has the value 1.
90 LET H = H+2*Z	H has the value 8.
40 LET M = 2*M–Z	M has the value 14.

2.5   THE **PRINT** STATEMENT

Every computer language must be designed so that the results can be made available in a usable form. In BASIC the PRINT statement meets this requirement. The simplest form of this statement is

ln PRINT **a**

where **ln** denotes a line number and **a** denotes any one of the BASIC variables listed in Section 2.1. The effect of this instruction is that the value of **a** is printed and then the teletypewriter carriage moves to the left margin of the next print line. If your system uses a video display screen, the *cursor* is positioned at the left margin of the next display line.

EXAMPLE 8. If the two lines

```
125 PRINT P
135 PRINT Q
```

are added to the program of Example 6,

```
100 LET P=12
110 LET Q=P/2+1
120 LET P=Q/2+1
130 LET Q=P/2+1
140 END
```

and the program is run, the computer will cause the following printout to occur.

```
4.5
3.25
```

It should be noted that the value of a variable, such as P in this program, is not altered after it is printed.

EXAMPLE 9. Here is a program ready to be typed and run. The table shows what will be printed as well as the values of variables during program execution.

The Program	Value of A	Value of B	Output
100 LET A=1	1		
110 LET B=1	1	1	
120 LET A=A+B	2	1	
130 PRINT A	2	1	2
140 LET B=B+A	2	3	
150 PRINT B	2	3	3
160 LET A=A+B	5	3	
170 PRINT A	5	3	5
180 LET B=A+B	5	8	
190 PRINT B	5	8	8
200 END			

BASIC allows you to have messages printed during program execution. These messages can serve as headings or as identifying labels for printed results. The following example illustrates how this can be done.

EXAMPLE 10. A program to calculate the sales tax (5%) on an automobile listing at $5295.00.

```
100 PRINT "TAX COMPUTATION PROGRAM"
110 LET L=5295
120 LET R=0.05
130 LET T=L*R
140 PRINT "SALES TAX IS", T
150 END
```

When this program is executed it will produce the following output.

```
TAX COMPUTATION PROGRAM
SALES TAX IS    264.75
```

In this example, there are two messages, one each in lines 100 and 140, and each message is enclosed (as it must be) in quotation marks.

2.6   THE **REM** STATEMENT: REMARKS AS PART OF A PROGRAM

In the program shown at the outset of this chapter, certain comments are included (lines 100–120) to indicate the purpose of the program and to identify what quantities the variables X, Y, Z, and A represent. The BASIC statement that allows you to insert such comments is the REM (REMARK) statement. The general form is

ln REM **comment**

where **comment** denotes any comment or remark you may wish to include.

EXAMPLE 11.

```
100 REM PROGRAM TO DETERMINE THE RATE OF RETURN
110 REM GIVEN THE CURRENT PRICE AND EARNINGS.
120 REM    P DENOTES THE CURRENT PRICE OF A SECURITY
130 REM    E DENOTES THE RECENT ANNUAL EARNINGS
140 REM    R DENOTES THE RATE OF RETURN
150 LET P=80.00
160 LET E=6.00
170 REM CALCULATE THE RATE OF RETURN AND
180 REM PRINT SUMMARY RESULTS
190 LET R=100*E/P
200 PRINT "PRICE",P
210 PRINT "EARNINGS",E
220 PRINT "RATE OF RETURN",R
230 END
```

If this program is executed, the output will be as follows.

```
PRICE              80
EARNINGS           6
RATE OF RETURN     7.5
```

Remark 1: In this program, REM statements are used for three different purposes: to give a brief description of the program (lines 100 and 110), to describe the quantities represented by the variables used (lines 120, 130, and 140), and to describe the action of certain groups of programming lines (lines 170 and 180). Using REM statements in this manner is an excellent programming practice. Your programs will be easier to read and understand, easier to modify at some later date (should that be required), and easier to debug.

Remark 2: Comments appearing in REM statements need not be enclosed in quotation marks.

Remark 3: Unlike quoted messages appearing in PRINT statements, comments included in REM statements cause nothing to be printed when the program is executed by a computer. Their sole purpose is to document a program.

2.7   PROBLEMS

1. Write LET statements to perform the indicated tasks.
   a. Assign the value 7 to M.
   b. Increase the value assigned to B by 7.
   c. Double the value assigned to H.
   d. Assign the value of the expression $(A-B)/2$ to C2.
   e. Assign the tenth power of 1+R to A.
   f. Decrease the value assigned to X by twice the value assigned to Y.

2. Which of these are incorrect BASIC statements? Explain!
   a. 50 LET X = (A+B)C   b. 60 LET M = A1–A2
   c. 100 LET RJ = M–N   d. 103 LET M3 = A∗A∗A
   e. 15 LET X13 = 2+3∗X   f. 100 LET A+B = S
   g. 20 LET X = 2.3E–05   h. 40 LET Y = 4E0.5
   i. 5 PRINT SUMMING PROGRAM   j. 8 PRINT "5+13=",S

3. What will be printed when each program is run?

   a.
   ```
   100 LET A=5
   110 LET B=A+2
   120 LET C=A+B
   130 PRINT C
   140 END
   ```

   b.
   ```
   10 LET P=100
   20 LET R=8
   30 LET I=R/100
   40 LET A=P+I*P
   50 PRINT "AMOUNT=",A
   60 END
   ```

   c.
   ```
   500 LET X=0
   510 LET X=X-1
   520 LET Y=X↑2+3*X
   530 PRINT Y
   540 END
   ```

   d.
   ```
   10 LET A=2
   20 LET B=6
   30 LET A=2*A
   40 LET B=B/2
   50 LET C=(A↑2+B↑2)↑(1/2)
   60 PRINT C
   70 END
   ```

4. Complete the following tables as was done in Examples 6 and 9.

   a.
   ```
   100 LET A = 1
   110 LET B = 2
   120 LET C = 1
   130 LET C = C+B
   140 LET A = B↑2
   150 LET B = C–B+A
   160 LET C = C–1
   170 LET B = A*B
   180 LET A = A/C
   190 LET C = B/A+1
   200 END
   ```

A	B	C

   b.
   ```
   100 LET N = 1
   110 PRINT N
   120 LET N = N*(N+1)
   130 PRINT N
   140 LET N = N*(N+1)
   150 PRINT N
   160 LET N = N*(N+1)
   170 PRINT N
   180 END
   ```

N	Output

   c.
   ```
   100 LET X = 0
   110 LET Y = X + 7
   120 LET Z = Y+X↑2
   130 PRINT Z
   ```

X	Y	Z	Output

	X	Y	Z	Output
140 LET X = Z				
150 LET Y = X*Y*Z				
160 PRINT Y				
170 END				

5. Prepare tables showing the successive values of all variables and what will be printed.

a.
```
100 LET S=0
110 LET A=25
120 LET S=S+A
130 PRINT S
140 LET S=S+A
150 PRINT S
160 LET S=S/2
170 PRINT S
180 END
```

b.
```
100 LET X=1.5
110 LET Y=3/(2*X+2)
120 PRINT Y
130 LET X=-X
140 PRINT X
150 PRINT Y
160 END
```

c.
```
100 LET N=130
110 LET C=3.00
120 REM N=COUNT
130 REM C=COST
140 REM S=PRICE
150 LET S=1.2*C
160 LET G=N*S
170 LET P=G-N*C
180 PRINT "SALES",G
190 PRINT "PROFIT",P
200 END
```

d.
```
100 PRINT "NTH POWERS OF 7"
110 LET A=7
120 LET P=7
130 LET P=A*P
140 PRINT "FOR N=2",P
150 LET P=A*P
160 PRINT "FOR N=3",P
170 LET P=A*P
180 PRINT "FOR N=4",P
190 REM "END OF TABLE"
200 END
```

2.8   REVIEW TRUE OR FALSE QUIZ

1. The order of operations in BASIC is different from that used in arithmetic.   T   F
2. Parentheses may be used only to override the normal order in which operations are performed by the computer.   T   F
3. A BASIC program is a collection of BASIC programming lines.   T   F
4. The terms *program statement* and *programming line* are used synonymously.   T   F
5. $(A+B)\uparrow.5$ and $(A+B)\uparrow 1/2$ have the same meaning.   T   F
6. 2/3 is a numerical constant in BASIC.   T   F
7. If A = 3, the statement   43 LET 1+A$\uparrow$2 = B1   assigns the value 10 to the variable B1.   T   F
8. 150 LET A3 = A3*A3 is a valid BASIC statement.   T   F
9. 1.0E1 = 10   T   F
10. There may be more than one END statement in some BASIC programs.   T   F
11. REM statements are often used to explain the purpose of groups of programming lines.   T   F
12. REM statements can be used to print messages during program execution.   T   F
13. Comments appearing in REM statements must be enclosed in quotation marks.   T   F
14. The sole purpose of REM statements is to document computer programs.   T   F
15. The BASIC instruction LET X = X+1 is a valid BASIC instruction but will result in an error because there is no value X for which X = X+1.   T   F

3 LOADING AND RUNNING A PROGRAM

Chapter 2 presented examples of BASIC programs ready to be transmitted to the computer. There are several devices used for this purpose, but the most common is the **teletypewriter** (Figures 1.2a and 1.2b). Such a device, which serves as the principal link between you and the computer, is called the **computer terminal,** the **remote terminal,** or simply the **terminal.** The use of the word *remote* indicates that the terminal need not be situated next to the computer; it may in fact be located many miles away. In this case, communication between terminal and computer is established by telephone.

Every teletypewriter has a keyboard, which is much like an ordinary typewriter keyboard (Figure 3.1). It consists of keys for the 26 uppercase letters of the English alphabet, the digits 0 through 9,

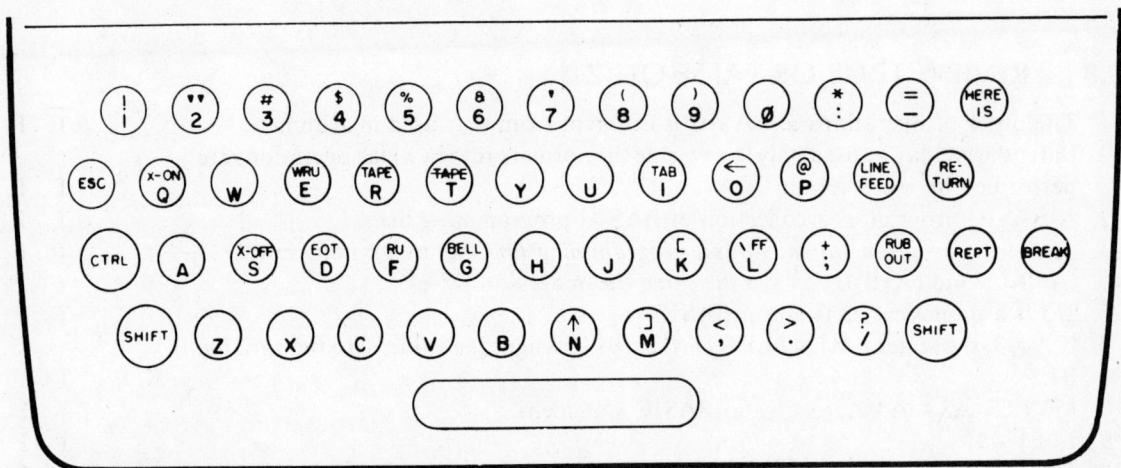

FIGURE 3.1 Data Terminal Keyboard. (Courtesy of Teletype Corporation.)

and certain other familiar characters, such as $#,.;:=()-/ . In addition, there is a space bar, a carriage-return key, and several other keys whose functions will be explained as the need arises.

Communication must be established between you and the computer before you can begin typing in a program. When this has been accomplished, you are *on line*. Going *on line* can be as simple as pushing a button or turning a knob, or it may require a slightly more complicated *log-in procedure*. A typical log-in procedure is described in Appendix A. In what follows, we will assume that you are *on line*.

3.1 ENTERING A PROGRAMMING LINE: THE **RETURN** KEY

Here is a program ready to be entered at the terminal.

```
100 REM SUM AND DIFFERENCE PROGRAM
110 LET P=5
120 LET Q=8
130 LET S=P+Q
140 LET D=Q-P
150 END
```

To enter this program, you first type

```
100 REM SUM AND DIFFERENCE PROGRAM ®
```

where ® denotes the RETURN key on your keyboard. (On some systems this key is labeled ENTER.) Depressing the return key ® causes two things to happen:

1. The line just typed is entered as part of the program.
2. The teletypewriter carriage moves to the beginning of the next line.

You would then continue typing:

```
110 LET P=5
120 LET Q=8
130 LET S=P+Q
140 LET D=Q-P
150 END
```

At the end of each line, you must type ® to enter the line. This program contains no PRINT statement, so, if it is executed, there will be no output—that is, the computer will give no results. To rectify this situation, you could add PRINT lines simply by typing the following:

```
135 PRINT "SUM IS", S
145 PRINT "DIFFERENCE IS", D
```

BASIC allows you to enter these lines out of their natural numerical order; the program will still be executed according to the sequence of line numbers from smallest to largest. Thus, if a line is omitted in the initial typing of a program, it can be inserted at any time before execution simply by typing it in.

3.2 THE SYSTEM COMMANDS **LIST** AND **RUN**

A printed list of all program statements already transmitted to the computer can be obtained by typing LIST. This is the first of several commands referred to as **system commands.** A system command has no line number and is not part of a BASIC program. It is an instruction to the computer to do a specific task at the time the command is issued. We illustrate for the program entered in Section 3.1.

LIST ®   (You type this.)

```
100 REM SUM AND DIFFERENCE PROGRAM       (This is printed by the computer.)
110 LET P=5
120 LET Q=8
130 LET S=P+Q
135 PRINT "SUM IS", S
140 LET D=Q-P
```

```
145 PRINT "DIFFERENCE IS", D
150 END
READY
```

Note that lines 135 and 145 have been inserted in their proper places even though they were actually typed after line 150. READY is the computer's signal that it is ready for you to make another entry (your system may use something other than READY).

When you are reasonably certain that the program has been typed correctly, you can cause it to be executed (run) with the system command RUN. This command will cause the program instructions to be processed according to the sequence of their line numbers. We illustrate for the program just entered.

```
RUN ®                              (You type this.)


SUM IS           13               (This is printed by the computer.)
DIFFERENCE IS    3
READY
```

3.3   MAKING CORRECTIONS

During a session at the terminal it is almost inevitable that typing errors will occur. Two methods for correcting such errors will now be described.

The simpler way to correct an error is to retype the entire line. This method must be used if the error is not noticed until after the line has been entered. Retyping the line will replace the incorrect line with the latest version entered.

EXAMPLE 1.

```
210 LET X=5                        (You type this.)
220 PRENT X
230 END
220 PRINT X
LIST ®

210 LET X=5                        (This is printed by the computer.)
220 PRINT X
230 END
READY
```

Some systems will not allow a typing error such as

220 PRENT S

to go undetected. If such a line is entered, the computer will immediately print a message indicating that this is an illegal statement.

An entire line may be deleted from a program simply by typing its line number followed by the RETURN key.

EXAMPLE 2.

```
30 LET Z=5                         (You type this.)
40 PRINT X
50 LET Z-7=X
60 PRINT X
70 END
```

```
40
50 LET X=Z-7
LIST Ⓡ

30 LET Z=5                          (This is printed by the computer.)
50 LET X=Z-7
60 PRINT X
70 END
READY
```

The second method of correcting typing errors can be used if an error is noticed before the line being typed has been entered—that is, before the return key Ⓡ has been depressed. For example, while typing in the line

55 LET S=35.2

you notice that you have typed

55 LRT

At this point you should depress the RUBOUT key two times to erase the characters T and R.* You then type the correct characters E and T and continue typing to the end of the line. Using this method, you can erase as many characters as is required. For example, depressing the RUBOUT key four times will erase the last four characters typed.

What is actually printed at your terminal when you erase characters in this manner depends on the system you are using. (Experiment!)

3.4   ERROR MESSAGES

You may not always be fortunate enough to detect *syntax errors* (violations of BASIC rules of grammar) before attempting to "run" your program. Should you issue the RUN command for such an incorrect program, appropriate *error messages* will be printed. These messages will indicate the type of error and, on many systems, the line number on which the error occurs. The exact form of such messages depends on the BASIC system being used. The following example illustrates how such error messages can be of help in correcting a program.

EXAMPLE 3.

```
10 LET X=7                          (You type this.)
20 LET X+9=Z
30 PRINT "ANSWER IS,Z
40 END
99 END
RUN Ⓡ

ILLEGAL STATEMENT AT 20             (This is printed by the computer.)
ILLEGAL STATEMENT AT 30
END NOT LAST AT 40
READY
```

---

*The RUBOUT key is not standard; your system may instead require you to depress the BACKSPACE key or to type some other combination of keys, such as SHIFT/0 or CTRL/H.

```
20 LET Z=X+9                              (You type this.)
30 PRINT "ANSWER IS",Z
40
RUN Ⓡ

ANSWER IS        16                       (This is printed by the computer.)
READY
```

As illustrated in the following example, error messages are sometimes printed even though a program contains no syntax errors.

EXAMPLE 4. A program to compute the ratio

$$\frac{COST + MARKUP}{COST - MARKUP}.$$

```
10 REM C DENOTES THE COST
20 LET C=100
30 REM M DENOTES THE MARKUP
40 LET M=100
50 LET R=(C+M)/(C-M)
60 PRINT "RATIO =",R
70 END
RUN Ⓡ

DIVISION BY ZERO AT 50
READY
```

Each line in this program is an admissible BASIC program statement; hence the program is syntactically correct. When run, the computer assigns 100 to C (line 20), assigns 100 to M (line 40), and then attempts to evaluate the expression in line 50. The error message tells you that the computer does not "know" how to divide by zero.

Normally, error messages will not be printed if syntax errors are not present—even if the program is incorrect. The following example illustrates such a situation.

EXAMPLE 5.

```
10 REM COMPUTE THE AVERAGE OF X AND Y.
20 REM THIS PROGRAM IS SYNTACTICALLY CORRECT
30 REM BUT PRODUCES INCORRECT RESULTS.
40 LET X=10
50 LET Y=5
60 LET A=X+Y/2
70 PRINT "AVERAGE IS",A
80 END
RUN

AVERAGE IS        12.5
READY
```

The computer does precisely what you instruct it to do; it does not do what you meant it to do. The programming error in line 60 is an error in the logic of the program and is not a syntax error. Such errors are often very difficult to find.

If a system command (rather than a programming line) is typed incorrectly, the system will respond with a message indicating that the command is unrecognizable. Thus, you needn't worry about harming the system with novice mistakes.

3.5   SPACING

Spaces may be used to improve the appearance and legibility of BASIC programs. During program execution, the computer will ignore all spaces other than those appearing in quoted messages. (Other exceptions to this rule will be described as the need arises.) Thus, the three programming lines

        210 LETY=4
        210 LET Y = 4
        2 1 0 LE T Y= 4

are equivalent BASIC statements.

Good programming practice dictates that this freedom of spacing be used to advantage; a program listing should be easily readable. Two good rules to follow are:

1. Insert a space between every line number and the BASIC instruction on the line.
2. Keep variable names separate from other words in an instruction.

Easily readable forms for the programming line given above would be

        210 LET Y = 4

        or

        210 LET Y=4

3.6   WRITING YOUR FIRST PROGRAM

You are now ready to write your first program. Even for very simple problems, certain steps should be followed. First, be sure you thoroughly understand the problem statement. Having done this, proceed as follows.

1. Find and describe a procedure that, if followed, will result in a correct solution.
2. Write the programming lines to carry out the procedure you have described. This step is called **coding** the program.

EXAMPLE 6. Write a program to compute and print the simple interest and the amount due for a loan of P dollars, at an annual interest rate R, for a time of T years. Use the program to find the interest and the amount due when P = $600, R = 0.0875, and T = 2.

We should all recognize the familiar formulas that govern this situation.

        Simple interest: I = PRT
        Amount due: A = P+I

Knowing these formulas, we can write the following procedure.

a. Assign values to P, R, and T.
b. Compute the interest and the amount due.
c. Print the results (I and A) and stop.

The Program

```
100 REM SIMPLE INTEREST PROGRAM
110 REM    P DENOTES AMOUNT OF LOAN
120 REM    R DENOTES ANNUAL INTEREST RATE
130 REM    T DENOTES TERM OF LOAN IN YEARS
140 REM ASSIGN VALUES TO P,R, AND T
150 LET P=600
160 LET R=0.0875
170 LET T=2
180 REM COMPUTE THE INTEREST I AND AMOUNT DUE A
190 LET I=P*R*T
200 LET A=P+I
210 REM PRINT THE RESULTS
220 PRINT "INTEREST",I
230 PRINT "AMOUNT DUE",A
240 END
RUNⓇ

INTEREST        105
AMOUNT DUE      705
READY
```

Remark 1: To find the interest and amount due for other loans, it is necessary only to retype the given conditions at lines 150, 160, and 170. (In Chapter 4 you will see how different values can be assigned to P, R, and T without having to retype programming lines.)

Remark 2: Notice that the REM statements in lines 140, 180, and 210 correspond to the three steps in the procedure written for this example. Not only does this emphasize how the coding process follows from the procedure, but also it suggests that each step in a procedure should contain enough detail so that it can be easily coded. Writing your procedures according to this principle and using the individual steps as REM statements are excellent programming practices.

The development of programming habits, both good and bad, begins with your first program. At the end of this chapter you will be asked to write some programs. To learn good habits from the start, you should follow the steps suggested in this section. *Coding should almost never be your first step.*

3.7   PROBLEMS

In Problems 1–3, assume that the lines shown are typed immediately after communication with your BASIC system has been established. What will be printed if the LIST command is entered? The RUN command?

1.
```
100 LET A=14
110 LET B=20
120 LET S=A+B
130 PRINT "SUM IS S"
140 END
110 LET B=30
130 PRINT "SUM IS",S
```

2.
```
100 LET X=5
110 LET X=10
120 LET Y=20
130 PRINT "X+Y"=S
110
125 LET S=X+Y
130 PRINT "X+Y=",S
140 END
150 RUN
150
```

```
3.    100 PRINT "DISCOUNT CALCULATION"
      100 REM DISCOUNT PROGRAM
      100
      110 LET P=120
      120 LET D=0.1*P
      130 LET P=P-D
      140 PRINT "DISCOUNT",D
      150 PRINT "COST",C
      130 LET C=P-D
      160 END
```

The programs in Problems 4–9 contain one or more bugs—either syntax errors (violations in the BASIC rules of grammar) or programming errors (errors in the logic of a program). Find each bug, tell which type of error it is, correct the programs, and show what will be printed if the corrected programs are run.

```
4.    10 REM PROGRAM TO COMPUTE          5.    10 REM PROGRAM TO AVERAGE
      20 REM SIX PERCENT OF $23,000           20 REM TWO NUMBERS
      30 LET D=23,000                         30 LET N1=24
      40 LET R=6                              40 LET N2=15
      50 LET R*D=A                            50 LET A=N1+N2/2
      60 PRINT "ANSWER IS",A                  60 PRINT AVERAGE IS,A
      70 END                                  70 END
```

```
6.    10 REM SALES TAX PROGRAM          7.    10 REM PROGRAM TO FIND A SOLUTION X
      20 REM     T=TAX RATE                   20 REM TO THE FOLLOWING EQUATION
      30 REM     P=PRICE                       30 REM     35X+220=0
      40 LET 5=T                               40 LET A=35
      50 LET P=120.00                          50 LET B=220
      60 LET S=P+T*P                           60 LET A*X+B=0
      70 PRINT "TOTAL COST"=S                  70 PRINT "SOLUTION IS",X
      80 END                                   80 END
```

```
8.    100 REM PROGRAM TO SWAP THE       9.    100 REM "PROGRAM TO COMPUTE THE"
      110 REM VALUES OF A AND B                110 REM "EXCISE TAX T ON TWO CARS'
      120 LET A=5                              120 REM "VALUED AT V DOLLARS,IF THE"
      130 LET B=8                              130 REM "RATE IS 66 DOLLARS PER 1000."
      140 PRINT "A=",A                         140 LET V=4500
      150 PRINT "B=,B                          150 LET R=66/1000
      160 REM INTERCHANGE A AND B              160 LET T=V*R
      170 LET A=B                              170 PRINT TAX ON FIRST CAR IS T
      180 LET B=A                              180 LET V=5700
      190 PRINT "A=",A                         190 PRINT TAX ON SECOND CAR IS T
      200 PRINT "B=",B                         200 END
      210 END
```

Listed below are a number of tasks to be performed. Write a BASIC program for each. Use PRINT statements to label your output, and also include REM statements as suggested in Section 3.6.

10. Compute the selling price S for an article whose list price is L if the rate of discount is D%.
11. Compute the original price if an article is now selling at S dollars after a discount of D%.
12. Compute the state gasoline tax S in dollars paid by a driver who travels M miles per year if the car averages G miles per gallon and the tax is T cents per gallon.

13. Find the commission C on sales of S dollars if the rate of commission is R%.

14. Find the principal P that, if invested at a rate of interest R for time T years, yields the simple interest I. (Recall that I = PRT.)

15. Compute the weekly salary, both gross G and net N, for a person who works H hours a week for D dollars an hour (no overtime). Deductions are S% for state taxes and F% for federal taxes.

16. Compute the batting average A of a baseball player who has S singles, D doubles, T triples, and H home runs in B times at bat. (A = number of hits/B.)

17. Compute the slugging percentage P of the baseball player described in Problem 16. (P = total bases/B.)

18. Find the total cost C of four tires if the list price of each is L dollars, the federal excise tax is E dollars per tire, and the sales tax is S%.

19. Compute the total cost C of a table listed at L dollars selling at a discount of D% if the sales tax is S%.

20. Find the total taxes T on the McCormick property assessed at D dollars if the rate is R dollars/1000. In addition, if the community uses X% of all taxes for schools, find how much of the McCormick tax is spent for schools.

21. The market value of a home is M dollars, the assessment rate is A% of the market value, and the tax rate is R dollars per 1000. Compute the property tax.

3.8 REVIEW TRUE OR FALSE QUIZ

1. System commands are carried out as soon as they are entered. T F

2. To correct an error committed while typing a program, you must retype the entire line. T F

3. A line may be deleted from a program simply by typing its line number and then depressing the RETURN key. T F

4. The program statement 20 PRINT "13(2+3) = 500" contains a syntax error. T F

5. A program containing syntax errors will cause error messages to be printed when it is run. T F

6. A program containing no syntax errors can cause error messages to be printed. T F

7. Each step in a procedure for a computer program should correspond to a single program statement. T F

8. A good programming practice is to choose REM statements to correspond to the individual steps of a procedure. T F

9. Coding a BASIC program involves determining the programming lines to carry out a known procedure. T F

4 INTERACTING WITH THE COMPUTER

In this chapter we discuss two BASIC statements. The first is the INPUT statement, which allows you to type in values for variables during program execution and thus interact with the computer while your program is running. To help you make this two-way communication more meaningful, we will describe a more general form of the PRINT statement. The second BASIC statement that we will discuss is the GO TO statement, which allows you to override the normal sequential order in which programming lines are executed.

4.1 THE INPUT STATEMENT

This new BASIC instruction is best illustrated by example.

EXAMPLE 1.

```
10 INPUT T
20 LET A=T↑2
30 PRINT A
40 END
```

When line 10 is executed, a "?" will be printed and nothing further will take place until you type a BASIC constant and enter it by depressing Ⓡ. This value will be assigned to T, and only then will program execution continue. Let's run this program.

RUN Ⓡ

? 13 Ⓡ   (Underlined characters are printed by the computer.)
169
READY

More than one value may be assigned by an INPUT statement. The program statement

90 INPUT X,Y

causes "?" to be printed, and two values, separated by a comma, should be typed. Thus, if you type 5,3 after this "?" and then depress Ⓡ, the value 5 will be assigned to X and 3 to Y. The general form of the INPUT statement is

In INPUT list of variables separated by commas

EXAMPLE 2. A program to compute the cost C of renting a car for D days and driving it M miles. The rental rate is 12 dollars per day and 11 cents per mile.

```
10 INPUT D,M
20 LET C=12*D+0.11*M
30 PRINT "TOTAL COST IS",C
40 END
RUN Ⓡ

? 3,253 Ⓡ                        (Underlined characters are printed by the computer.)
TOTAL COST IS      63.83
READY
```

PRINT statements can be used in conjunction with INPUT statements to instruct a user about how INPUT values should be entered. We illustrate by modifying the car-rental program of Example 2.

EXAMPLE 3.

```
10 PRINT "ENTER NUMBER OF DAYS AND NUMBER"
20 PRINT "OF MILES, SEPARATED BY A COMMA."
30 INPUT D,M
40 LET C=12*D+0.11*M
50 PRINT "TOTAL COST IS",C
60 END
RUN Ⓡ

ENTER NUMBER OF DAYS AND NUMBER      (Underlined characters are printed by the computer.)
OF MILES SEPARATED BY A COMMA
?
```

At this point you simply follow the instructions and type two numbers separated by a comma. Let's complete this run as follows.

```
? 3,253 Ⓡ
TOTAL COST IS      63.83
READY
```

The readability of an output document can often be enhanced by having an input value appear on the same line as the message identifying this value. This can be accomplished by placing a semicolon after the quoted message in a PRINT statement. If this is done, the carriage return normally occurring after execution of the PRINT statement is suppressed. Thus, if you type 345 in response to the following INPUT statement,

```
200 PRINT "NUMBER OF MILES";
210 INPUT M
```

the printed output will be

NUMBER OF MILES ? 345   (Underlined characters are printed by the computer.)

EXAMPLE 4. Determine the yearly income and savings of a person whose weekly income and average monthly expenses are given.

Two values must be specified (weekly income and monthly expenses), and two values must be determined (yearly income and savings). Let's agree to use the following variable names.

I = weekly income.
E = monthly expenses.
Y = yearly income (note that Y = 52I).
S = yearly savings (note that S = Y – 12E).

A procedure for solving this problem can now be written.

a. Assign values to I and E.
b. Determine yearly income and savings.
c. Print results.

Before this procedure can be coded, you must decide how to assign values to I and E. Available are the LET and INPUT statements. Since we may use this program for different weekly incomes and monthly expenses, the decision is easy: use an INPUT statement.

The Program

```
100 REM PROGRAM TO FIND YEARLY INCOME AND SAVINGS
110 REM GIVEN THE WEEKLY INCOME AND MONTHLY EXPENSES
120 REM
130 PRINT "WEEKLY INCOME";
140 INPUT I
150 PRINT "MONTHLY EXPENSES";
160 INPUT E
170 REM COMPUTE YEARLY INCOME AND SAVINGS
180 LET Y=52*I
190 LET S=Y-12*E
200 PRINT "YEARLY INCOME",Y
210 PRINT "YEARLY SAVINGS",S
220 END
RUN

WEEKLY INCOME? 250                 (Underlined characters are printed by the computer.)
MONTHLY EXPENSES? 840
YEARLY INCOME   13000
YEARLY SAVINGS   2920
READY
```

Remark 1: The short discussion appearing just before the procedure description is called a **problem analysis.** It may simply contain a description of variables and how they are interrelated, as is the case here, or it may include a thorough analysis of alternative approaches to a solution. In any case, a problem analysis is the process of discovering a suitable procedure.

Remark 2: Some BASIC systems allow you to include messages to be printed as part of an INPUT statement. For example, your system may allow you to replace the two lines

130 PRINT "WEEKLY INCOME";
140 INPUT I

with the single equivalent line

130 INPUT "WEEKLY INCOME"; I

4.2 PROBLEMS

Complete the following partial program so that it will perform the tasks specified in Problems 1–9. Be sure that messages printed by line numbers 100 and 130 are appropriate to the particular problem being solved. No references to the variable names X and A should be made in these messages.

```
100 PRINT "        "
110 INPUT X
120 LET A=
130 PRINT "        ",A
140 END
```

1. Determine how much $100 earning 6% interest compounded annually will be worth in X years (value after X years is $100(1 + .06)^x$).
2. Determine the commission earned by a salesperson who sells a $625 television set if the rate of commission is X%.
3. Determine the total cost of an article whose selling price is X dollars if the sales tax is 4.5%.
4. Determine the weekly salary of a part-time employee working X hours at $2.47 per hour (no overtime).
5. Determine the cost per driving mile for a car that averages 19.2 miles per gallon if gasoline costs X cents per gallon.
6. Determine the average of the four grades for a student who has received grades of 73, 91, 62, and X on four exams.
7. Determine the equivalent hourly salary, assuming a 40-hour week, for a worker whose annual salary is X dollars.
8. Determine the area of a circle given its diameter.
9. Determine the diameter of a circle given its area.

Write a program to perform each task specified in Problems 10–16. Use PRINT statements to label results and to instruct a user concerning what values are to be entered.

10. For any three numbers A, B, and C, determine the three sums A + B, A + C, and B + C, and find the average of these sums.
11. For any three numbers P, Q, and R, determine the mean M, the differences P – M, Q – M, and R – M, and the sum of these differences.
12. Semester grades are based on three one-hour tests and a two-hour final examination. The one-hour tests are weighted equally, but the final counts as two one-hour tests. (All exams are graded from 0 to 100.) Determine the semester average for a student whose grades are G1, G2, G3, and F (F for final).
13. Janet and Jim are bricklayers. In one hour Janet can lay J1 bricks and Jim can lay J2. Determine how long it will take both of them to complete a job if the number of bricks required is known.
14. A baseball player is to be paid P dollars the first year of a three-year contract. Find the total dollar value of the contract over three years if the contract calls for an increase of I% the second year and J% the third year.
15. Determine the yearly gross pay, net pay, combined tax deductions, and retirement deductions for a person whose monthly salary is given. The combined tax rate is R%, and 6% of the gross salary is withheld for retirement.
16. A manufacturer produces three items that sell for $550, $620, and $1750. A profit of 10% is realized on items selling below $1000, and 15% is realized on all other items. Determine the profit before and after taxes for a particular year, given the quantity of each item sold. The current tax rate on profits is R%.

4.3 THE **GO TO** STATEMENT: A FIRST LOOK AT LOOPS

As we mentioned at the outset of this chapter, the GO TO statement allows you to override the normal sequential order in which programming lines are executed. This means that you can direct the computer to execute sections of your program repeatedly and thus to perform many hundreds of calculations with only a few programming lines. Using only the LET, INPUT, GO TO, and PRINT statements, the computer is transformed into a very fast and useful calculator.

The general form of the GO TO statement is as follows.

$$\textbf{ln}_1 \text{ GO TO } \textbf{ln}_2$$

When executed, the statement transfers control to line number ln_2; that is, the next instruction to be executed is the one whose line number is ln_2

EXAMPLE 5. The program

```
100 LET I=0
110 PRINT I
120 LET I=I+1
130 GO TO 110
140 END
```

will cause the numbers 0, 1, 2, 3, . . . to be printed one number per line. Each time the GO TO instruction at line 130 is executed, control is transferred back to line 110. This is what is meant by a loop. The loop consists of the three program statements 110, 120, and 130.

If the program in Example 5 is run, it will not halt of its own accord. You must stop it manually. How you do this depends on your system. You may be required to depress the S, I, ESC, or BREAK key, or some combination of keys such as CTRL/C. In this text we will indicate that a program run has been terminated manually by including the following in the printout.

TERMINATED
READY

Thus, a run of the program of Example 5 would be shown as follows.

```
RUN
 0
 1
 2
 3
  *TERMINATED*
READY
```

EXAMPLE 6. The program

```
100 LET X=0
110 LET X=X+1
120 GO TO 110
130 END
```

will cause the variable X to take on the successive values 0, 1, 2, 3, . . . but will not print or do anything else. Again, the program must be stopped manually.

EXAMPLE 7. A program to do multiplication.

```
100 PRINT "AFTER EACH '?' ENTER TWO NUMBERS"
110 INPUT A,B
120 LET P=A*B
130 PRINT "PRODUCT IS",P
140 PRINT
150 GO TO 110
160 END
RUN
```

```
AFTER EACH '?' ENTER TWO NUMBERS
? 5,3
PRODUCT IS        15

? 14,11
PRODUCT IS        154

? 9,13.69
PRODUCT IS        123.21

? *TERMINATED*
READY
```

Remark 1: The PRINT statement at line 140 causes nothing to be printed but does advance the print mechanism one line, as seen in the output.

Remark 2: The program run was halted manually while the computer was waiting for a response to the INPUT statement at line 110.

Programming tasks often call for output documents in tabular form. Normally, these will consist of one or more columns of data, each with a descriptive column heading. The following form of the PRINT statement can be used to print both column headings and the values appearing in the body of the table.

ln PRINT a,b,c,...

Here, **a, b,** and **c** denote messages or variable names. This form of the PRINT statement can be used to print up to five messages or numerical values on a single line (four on some systems).

EXAMPLE 8. Prepare a table showing the weekly and annual salaries for persons working 40 hours a week if their hourly rates are $2.50, $2.60, $2.70, . . . , $3.50.

Problem Analysis: The weekly pay W for a person working 40 hours a week at H dollars an hour is W = 40H dollars; the annual salary A for this person is A = 52W dollars.

We will evaluate W and A for each value of H, beginning with H = 2.50 and increasing to 3.50 in increments of 0.10. The following is one way to do this.

a. Print column headings.
b. Let H = 2.50.
c. Evaluate W = 40H and then A = 52W.
d. Print H, W, and A on one line.
e. Add 0.10 to H and go to step (c).

The Program

```
100 REM SALARY TABLE PROGRAM
110 REM    H DENOTES HOURLY RATE
120 REM    W DENOTES EQUIVALENT 40 HOUR WEEK SALARY
130 REM    A DENOTES EQUIVALENT YEARLY SALARY
140 PRINT "HOURLY RATE","WEEKLY SALARY","ANNUAL SALARY"
150 LET H=2.50
160 LET W=40*H
170 LET A=52*W
```

```
180 PRINT H,W,A
190 LET H=H+0.10
200 GO TO 160
210 END
RUN
```

HOURLY RATE	WEEKLY SALARY	ANNUAL SALARY
2.5	100	5200
2.6	104.	5408.
2.7	108.	5616.
2.8	112.	5824.
2.9	116.	6032.
3.	120.	6240.
3.1	124.	6448.
3.2	128.	6656.
3.3	132.	6864.
3.4	136.	7072.
3.5	140.	7280.
3.6	144	

```
  *TERMINATED*
READY
```

Remark 1: Lines 160–200 constitute the loop used to print the table values. Since the column headings must be printed first, and only once, the statement that does this (line 140) must appear before the loop is entered.

Remark 2: Again, the program run must be terminated manually. Not only does this clutter the output, but it means that you must be present to stop the program when the desired output has been printed. This awkward situation can be avoided. In the next chapter you will learn how to program an automatic exit from a loop when the desired output has been printed.

We conclude this section with two examples illustrating the following programming practices stressed to this point.

1. To discover a correct procedure, carefully analyze the problem statement and record this analysis in writing.
2. Use PRINT statements to identify what numbers are to be entered during program execution and also to label results clearly. The precise form of such PRINT statements is normally not determined until the procedure has been described.
3. Use REM statements to make your program more readable and to clarify what is being done at any particular point.

EXAMPLE 9. A man has a large house with many rooms. He wants to paint the walls and ceiling of each room, but, before buying the paint, he naturally needs to know how much paint is necessary. On the average, each window and door covers 20 sq ft. According to the label, each quart of paint covers 110 sq ft. Write a program that will allow the man to enter the dimensions of each room and the number of doors and windows in each room and then determine how many quarts of wall paint and how many quarts of ceiling paint are needed for that room.

Problem Analysis: A good way to begin an analysis of a somewhat lengthy problem is to read it carefully and try to decide what variables will be needed and, where possible, how they are related to each other. For the current problem, let's agree on the following variables.

L,W,H = the length, width, and height of a room.
   T = the total number of windows and doors in a room.

S = the area of all walls in a room (S = 2(L + W)H).
B = the area of the T doors and windows (B = 20T).
C = the area of a ceiling (C = LW).
S1 = the number of quarts of wall paint (S1 = (S – B)/110).
C1 = the number of quarts of ceiling paint (C1 = C/110).
N = the number of the room in question (this was not asked for, but a good programmer will often provide the user with helpful results not specifically requested).

Using these variable names, you can write the following procedure. Note that the order in which the steps are to be taken is just how you might do this task with tape measure, pencil, and paper.

a. Enter values for L, W, H, and T.
b. Determine the areas S, B, and C.
c. Determine the number of quarts of paint needed (S1 and C1).
d. Print the room number N and the values of S1 and C1.
e. Go to step (a) and repeat.

This procedure is incomplete; it does not specify how the room number N is to be increased as we pass from room to room. Of the many ways to accomplish this, perhaps the simplest is to precede step (a) with the statement "Let N = 0" and then modify step (d) to read

d. Add 1 to N and then print the room number N and the values of S1 and C1.

The Program

```
100 REM PAINT CALCULATOR PROBLEM
110 LET N=0
120 PRINT "LENGTH, WIDTH, HEIGHT";
130 INPUT L,W,H
140 PRINT "TOTAL NUMBER OF WINDOWS AND DOORS";
150 INPUT T
160 REM CALCULATE AREAS
170 REM
180 LET S=2*(L+W)*H
190 LET B=20*T
200 LET C=L*W
210 REM QUARTS OF WALL AND CEILING PAINT
220 REM
230 LET S1=(S-B)/110
240 LET C1=C/110
250 REM PRINT RESULTS
260 REM
270 LET N=N+1
280 PRINT "ROOM NUMBER",N
290 PRINT "QUARTS OF WALL PAINT",S1
300 PRINT "QUARTS OF CEILING PAINT",C1
310 PRINT
320 GO TO 120
330 END
RUN

LENGTH, WIDTH, HEIGHT? 13,13,9
TOTAL NUMBER OF WINDOWS AND DOORS? 5
ROOM NUMBER       1
QUARTS OF WALL PAINT         3.34545
QUARTS OF CEILING PAINT      1.53636
```

```
LENGTH, WIDTH, HEIGHT? 12,9,9
TOTAL NUMBER OF WINDOWS AND DOORS? 4
ROOM NUMBER      2
QUARTS OF WALL PAINT          2.70909
QUARTS OF CEILING PAINT       .981818

LENGTH, WIDTH, HEIGHT?
  *TERMINATED*
READY
```

EXAMPLE 10. A manufacturer uses the following method to determine the selling price for an item. First, the cost of materials is doubled to cover labor expenses. Then, this figure is increased by 20% to cover overhead. Finally, this last figure is increased by X% or Y% depending on whether or not it is over $500. (The programmer is not told the values of X and Y.) This last increase is to cover research-and-development (R & D) costs as well as profits. Write a program to assist in this task.

Problem Analysis: Let's begin by choosing variable names.

C = cost of materials.
E = expenses, including cost of materials and labor (E = 2C).
T = total expenses, including overhead (T = E + 0.2E).
P = percentage to be added for R & D and for profit.
S = selling price (S = T + (P/100)T).

According to the problem statement, the manufacturer must enter two values: the cost C of materials and the percentage P for R & D and for profit. So that the correct choice (X or Y) can be made for P, the value of T must be shown to the manufacturer. That is, C must be entered and T printed before a value for P can be typed.

a. Input C (cost of materials).
b. Compute E.
c. Compute and print T (cost of materials, labor, overhead).
d. Input P (percentage for profit and for R & D).
e. Compute and print S (selling price).
f. Go to step (a) for next item.

The Program

```
100 REM PROGRAM TO DETERMINE SELLING PRICE
110 REM
120 PRINT "COST OF MATERIALS";
130 INPUT C
140 LET E=2*C
150 LET T=E+0.2*E
160 PRINT "COST OF MATERIALS, LABOR, OVERHEAD",T
170 PRINT "R & D - PROFIT PERCENTAGE";
180 INPUT P
190 LET S=T+P/100*T
200 PRINT "SELLING PRICE",S
210 PRINT
220 GO TO 120
230 END
RUN

COST OF MATERIALS ? 248
COST OF MATERIALS,LABOR,OVERHEAD          595.2
```

```
R & D - PROFIT PERCENTAGE ? 30
SELLING PRICE    773.76

COST OF MATERIALS ? 163.50
COST OF MATERIALS,LABOR,OVERHEAD              392.4
R & D - PROFIT PERCENTAGE ? 20
SELLING PRICE    470.88

COST OF MATERIALS ?
 *TERMINATED*
READY
```

4.4   PROBLEMS

1. For each program shown, make a table showing the values of the variables after execution of each line. Include a separate column to show what will be printed.

a.
```
100 LET A=1
110 PRINT A
120 LET B=1
130 PRINT B
140 LET C=A+B
150 PRINT C
160 LET A=B
170 LET B=C
180 GO TO 140
190 END
```

b.
```
100 LET A=1
110 LET B=2
120 LET C=3
130 PRINT A,B,C
140 LET T=B
150 LET B=C
160 LET C=T
170 PRINT A,B,C
180 LET T=C
190 LET C=A
200 LET A=T
210 GO TO 130
220 END
```

c.
```
10 LET X=1
20 LET P=1
30 LET P=P*X
40 PRINT X,P
50 LET X=X+1
60 GO TO 30
70 END
```

d.
```
10 LET S=0
20 LET A=5
30 LET S=S+A
40 PRINT S
50 LET A=-(A+1)
60 GO TO 30
70 END
```

2. Correct the following programs.

a.
```
10 REM PROGRAM TO PRINT THE
20 REM ODD WHOLE NUMBERS
30 LET N=1
40 PRINT N
50 LET N=N+2
60 GO TO 30
70 END
```

b.
```
10 REM PROGRAM TO DO SUBTRACTION
20 PRINT "TYPE TWO NUMBERS";
30 INPUT A,B
40 LET D=A-B
50 GO TO 20
60 PRINT "SECOND - FIRST =",D
70 END
```

c.
```
10 REM PROGRAM TO PRINT AN
20 REM 8 PERCENT TAX TABLE
30 LET X=100
40 LET T=8*X
50 PRINT "PRICE","TAX"
```

d.
```
10 REM PROGRAM TO PRINT A
20 REM TABLE OF SQUARE ROOTS
30 LET N=2
40 PRINT "NUMBER","SQUARE ROOT"
50 LET R=N↑1/2
```

```
60 PRINT X,T          60 PRINT N,R
70 LET X=X+1          70 LET N=N+1
80 GO TO 40           80 GO TO 60
90 END                90 END
```

Write a program to print each table described in Problems 3–12. Begin each program with a PRINT statement describing the table. If a table has more than one column, column headings should be printed.

3. The first column contains the number of miles (1, 2, 3, . . .), and the second column gives the corresponding number of kilometers (1 mile = 1.6093 kilometers).

4. The first column contains the temperature in degrees Celsius from –20 to 40 in increments of 2, and the second column gives the corresponding temperature in degrees Fahrenheit (F = 9/5C + 32).

5. A one-column table (list) containing the terms of the arithmetic progression $a, a + d, a + 2d, a + 3d, ...$ Values for a and d are to be assigned by the user.

6. A one-column table (list) of the terms of the geometric progression $a, ar, ar^2, ar^3, ...$ Values for a and r are to be assigned by the user.

7. The first column gives the amount of sales (500, 1000, 1500, . . .), and the second gives the commission at a rate of R%.

8. The first column contains the principal (50, 100, 150, . . .), and the second column gives the corresponding simple interest for 6 months at an annual interest rate of R%.

9. The first column contains the annual interest rate (7.0%, 7.25%, 7.5%, . . .), and the second column gives the simple interest on a principal of $1000 for 9 months.

10. The first column gives the list price of an article ($25, $50, $75, . . .), the second gives the amount of discount at 25%, and the third gives the corresponding selling price.

11. Ucall Taxi charges 45 cents for a ride plus 13 cents for each tenth of a mile. The first column gives the number of miles (0.1, 0.2, 0.3, . . .), and the second gives the total charges.

12. The first column contains the number of years (n = 1, 2, 3, . . .), the second the amount in the account, and the third the interest earned at the end of n years on a principal of $1000 at 6.5% compounded annually $(a = p(1 + r)^n)$.

Write a program to perform each task specified in Problems 13–16.

13. A list of numbers is to be typed at the terminal. After each number is typed, the program should cause two values to be printed: a count of how many numbers have been typed and the average of all numbers entered to that time.

14. A program should continually request two numbers of the user. After each pair of numbers is entered, the program should cause two values to be printed: the product of the two numbers just typed and the average of all products printed to that point.

15. A person wishes to determine the dollar amount of any collection of U.S. coins simply by specifying how many of each type of coin is included.

16. A philanthropist, having decided to donate to a cause, uses the following method to determine an amount to give. The figure asked for is decreased by 20%, and this value is compared with the average of last year's actual donation and this year's request. If it is less than this average, it is reduced by P%; otherwise it is reduced by Q%. (Only the philanthropist knows P and Q.) Your program is to assist with these calculations. (You may wish to refer to the problem analysis in Example 10.)

4.5 REVIEW TRUE OR FALSE QUIZ

1. The PRINT and INPUT statements provide the means for two-way communication between a user and a running program. T F

2. Using a PRINT statement immediately following an INPUT statement is a very useful method of identifying what values should be typed at the terminal. T F

3. A single PRINT statement may be used to print headings for more than one column. T F

4. If the statements

```
149 PRINT "FIRST", "SECOND", "THIRD"
150 PRINT A, B, C
```

appear in a loop, all A, B, and C values will be printed in columns with the headings FIRST, SECOND, and THIRD.   T   F

5. If the statement 50 PRINT X,Y appears in a loop, the column of X values and the column of Y values that are printed will "line up" according to decimal points.   T   F

6. If a program contains the line 100 GO TO 130, the lines 110 and 120 will never be executed.   T   F

7. A program is written using only LET, PRINT, and GO TO statements. If, during execution, any one line of this program is executed twice, the program will not stop of its own accord. (The program does include a proper END statement.)   T   F

8. A *problem analysis* is the process of discovering a correct procedure.   T   F

5 THE COMPUTER AS A DECISION MAKER

In this chapter we introduce the IF statement, whose purpose is to override the normal sequential execution of a program—but only if a certain condition is satisfied. Every programming language has at least one such **conditional transfer statement.** It is with this ability to "make decisions" that the full potential of the computer is realized.

5.1 THE **IF** STATEMENT

The simplicity and usefulness of the IF statement are best illustrated by example.

EXAMPLE 1. A program to print the message FIVE if a 5 is typed or otherwise NOT FIVE.

```
100 INPUT X
110 IF X=5 THEN 140
120 PRINT "NOT FIVE"
130 GO TO 150
140 PRINT "FIVE"
150 END
```

After a value is INPUT, the condition X = 5 in line 110 is tested. If it is true, control passes to line 140 and the message FIVE is printed. If the condition is false, the normal sequential execution of the program is not interrupted and control passes to line 120, which prints the message NOT FIVE.

EXAMPLE 2. A program to add the integers from 1 to 10.

```
100 LET N=0
110 LET S=0
120 LET N=N+1
130 LET S=S+N
140 IF N<10 THEN 120
150 PRINT "SUM IS",S
160 END
RUN

SUM IS          55
READY
```

43

N denotes the integer being added, and S denotes the sum. In line 140 the condition $N < 10$ is tested. If it is true, control is transferred back to line 120, which increases N by 1; line 130 adds this next integer to S, and then the condition in line 140 is tested again. However, if the condition is false, control passes to line 150, the line immediately following the IF statement.

These two examples illustrate the two very different uses of IF statements: *to construct loops* (Example 2) and *to make decisions* (Example 1). When used to construct loops, certain difficulties encountered with the GO TO statement are easily avoided.

Loops Using the IF Statement	*Loops Using Only the GO TO Statement*
1. An exit from a loop can be made under program control.	1. The only way out of a loop is to stop the program manually.
2. Results can be printed after completing a loop.	2. Results obtained in a loop can be printed only by using PRINT statements within the loop. This often results in the printing of unwanted intermediate results.
3. More than one loop can be included in a program.	3. A program can contain only one loop.

As a *decision maker* the IF statement has many applications. As illustrated in Example 1, it can be used to "recognize" a value typed at the terminal and then take a course of action that depends on this value.

The general form of the IF statement is

$$ln_1 \text{ IF condition THEN } ln_2$$

If the condition is satisfied (that is, is true), transfer is made to ln_2; if the condition is not satisfied, program execution continues with the next sequential line number following ln_1. The precise form that the condition in an IF statement can take is the subject of the next section.

5.2 RELATIONAL EXPRESSIONS

The condition in an IF statement involves the comparison of two BASIC expressions. The BASIC symbols used to make such comparisons, together with their arithmetic counterparts, are shown in Table 5.1.

TABLE 5.1 Relational symbols used in IF statements

BASIC Symbol	*Arithmetic Symbol*	*Meaning*
$=$	$=$	Equal
$<$	$<$	Less than
$>$	$>$	Greater than
$<>$	$\neq$	Not equal to
$<=$	$\leq$	Less than or equal to
$>=$	$\geq$	Greater than or equal to

Any two BASIC expressions can be compared using these BASIC symbols. Some examples of correctly written conditions are as follows.

$$X > 200 \qquad 13 = B - C$$
$$M <> N \qquad (A + B)/2 < A$$
$$17 <= 13 \qquad Y1 - Z1 >= 45$$

Expressions such as these are called **relational expressions** and may be used as the condition in an IF statement. Their use in such statements is illustrated in the following examples.

EXAMPLE 3. In each part of this example we are given values for certain variables and an IF statement. We are to tell whether or not transfer is made to the given line number.

  a. With X = 5000, consider

$$40 \text{ IF } .07*X > 300 \text{ THEN } 70$$

Since .07*X has the value 350, the condition .07*X>300 is satisfied. Transfer is made to line 70.
  b. With A = 2, B = 3, and C = 1, consider

$$50 \text{ IF } A-B <= C \text{ THEN } 27$$

Since A−B has the value −1 and C has the value 1, the relational expression $A - B <= C$ is true. Transfer is made to line 27.
  c. With M = 2 and N = 4, consider

$$120 \text{ IF } N <> 2*M \text{ THEN } 200$$

Both N and 2*M have the value 4; hence, the condition N<>2*M is false. No transfer is made to line 200, and control passes to the statement immediately following the IF statement.

EXAMPLE 4. A program to compare the average of any two numbers with their difference.

```
10 INPUT X,Y
20 IF (X+Y)/2>X-Y THEN 50
30 PRINT "DIFFERENCE"
40 GO TO 60
50 PRINT "AVERAGE"
60 END
RUN

? 10,4
AVERAGE
READY
```

Since the average of 10 and 4 is 7 and the difference 10 – 4 is 6, the condition is satisfied, causing transfer to line 50 and the output AVERAGE.

Remark 1: A common beginning programming error is to omit line 40. When this is done, the program will produce the correct printout if the condition in line 20 is satisfied; if the condition is not satisfied, both messages will be printed.

Remark 2: The GO TO at line 40 simply serves to terminate this program. The BASIC statement

$$40 \text{ STOP}$$

does the same thing. You may include a STOP statement anywhere in your program and use as many as you wish.

EXAMPLE 5. Let's write a program to input two numbers A and B and print the message BOTH if both are negative and the message NOT BOTH otherwise.

Problem Analysis: The logic of this problem is slightly complicated. First, the number A must be tested to determine if it is negative. If it is, then B must be tested. But, as soon as a number being tested is not negative, the message NOT BOTH should be printed. A procedure for doing this is as follows.

a. Input values for A and B.
b. If A is not negative, print NOT BOTH and stop.
c. If B is not negative, print NOT BOTH and stop.
d. Print BOTH and stop.

The Program

```
10 INPUT A,B
20 IF A>=0 THEN 60
30 IF B>=0 THEN 60
40 PRINT "BOTH"
50 STOP
60 PRINT "NOT BOTH"
70 END
RUN

? -5,-4
BOTH
READY
```

Remark: Beginning programmers are often tempted to begin coding a program without first describing the procedure to be followed. If this practice were followed for the problem at hand, we could easily be led into making the tests $A<0$ and $B<0$ rather than the tests $A>=0$ and $B>=0$ as was done in lines 20 and 30. The result would be a program similar to the following.

```
10 INPUT A,B
20 IF A<0 THEN 40
30 GO TO 50
40 IF B<0 THEN 70
50 PRINT "NOT BOTH"
60 STOP
70 PRINT "BOTH"
80 END
```

This is a correct but rather poor program. It contains a GO TO statement that makes its logic more difficult to follow than that of the first program. There are no hard and fast rules for choosing between the two tests $<$ and $>=$. The "best" choice will be dictated by a carefully prepared procedure.

5.3 PROBLEMS

1. If $A = 1$, $B = 2$, and $C = 3$, which of the following relational expressions are true?
   a. A+B<=C
   b. A+B>=C
   c. 3<>C
   d. 7.0>=7
   e. A/C*B<=.5
   f. 3−(C/B)=3−C/B
   g. A/B/C>A
   h. −A−B−C<=−(A+B+C)*B
2. Each of the following contains an error (not necessarily a syntax error). Find it, and explain what will happen if a program containing the given line is run.
   a. 57 IF (A−B)*(A+B) THEN 47
   b. 60 IF M−N<27, THEN 13
   c. 90 IF 2<Y<4 THEN 27
   d. 70 IF A<B THEN 70
   e. 50 IF X<X−B THEN 51
   f. 40 IF A1>A2 PRINT A1
3. Correct this program.

```
110 REM TELL WHETHER ANY NON-ZERO
120 REM NUMBER IS POSITIVE OR NEGATIVE
130 INPUT A
```

```
140 IF A=0 THEN 130
150 IF A>0 THEN 160
160 PRINT "A IS POSITIVE."
170 STOP
180 IF A<0 THEN 190
190 PRINT "A IS NEGATIVE."
200 END
```

4. What will be printed when each of the following is run?

a.
```
10 LET A=3
20 LET B=3
30 LET C=(A+B)/B
40 LET D=B/A-C
50 IF D<0 THEN 70
60 LET D=13
70 PRINT D
80 END
```

b.
```
10 LET A=5
20 LET B=-A
30 IF A+B<>0 THEN 70
40 LET A=-B
50 PRINT A
60 GO TO 80
70 PRINT B
80 END
```

c.
```
1 LET S=0
2 LET S=S+2
3 IF S<13 THEN 2
4 LET S=S/2
5 IF S>3.3 THEN 4
6 PRINT S
7 END
```

d.
```
10 LET X=5
20 LET X=X+5
30 LET Y=X↑2
40 IF Y<=200 THEN 20
50 IF X>20 THEN 80
60 REM PRINT Y
70 PRINT Y
80 PRINT
90 PRINT X
99 END
```

5. Pretending that you are the computer, prepare a table showing the values of A, B, and I during execution of the following programs.

a.
```
100 LET B=0
110 LET I=0
120 LET A=11
130 LET B=B+I+2
140 IF A<B THEN 180
150 LET I=I+1
160 LET A=A-1
170 IF B<A THEN 130
180 PRINT I
190 END
```

b.
```
100 LET B=0
110 LET A=1
120 LET B=B+A
130 IF A>0 THEN 170
140 LET I=5
150 LET A=A-1
160 GO TO 180
170 LET A=A+1
180 LET A=-A
190 IF A<5 THEN 120
200 LET I=6
210 PRINT B,I,A
220 END
```

6. Write programs that are equivalent to the following but contain no GO TO statements.

a.
```
10 INPUT N
20 IF N>=50 THEN 40
30 GO TO 50
40 LET N=N/2
50 IF N>=25 THEN 70
```

b.
```
10 LET S=10
20 INPUT A
30 IF A>0 THEN 50
40 GO TO 60
50 LET S=20
```

```
      60 LET N=N/2              60 PRINT S
      70 PRINT N                70 END
      80 END
```

```
   c. 10 INPUT X,Y          d. 10 INPUT A,B
      20 IF X>0 THEN 40         20 IF A>B THEN 60
      30 GO TO 10               30 PRINT "SMALLEST IS",A
      40 IF Y>0 THEN 60         40 PRINT "LARGEST IS",B
      50 GO TO 10               50 STOP
      60 LET S=X+Y              60 LET T=A
      70 PRINT S                70 LET A=B
      80 END                    80 LET B=T
                                90 GO TO 30
                                99 END
```

Write a program to perform each task specified in Problems 7–17. Appropriate messages should be printed (keep them short) that give instructions to the user concerning values to be entered.

7. Two numbers A and B are to be typed. If the first is larger, print A IS LARGER. Otherwise, print A IS NOT LARGER.
8. Two numbers M and N are to be typed. If the sum is equal to 5, print 5. Otherwise, print NOT 5.
9. Two numbers X and Y are to be typed. If the product is less than or equal to the quotient, print PRODUCT. Otherwise, print QUOTIENT.
10. Three numbers are to be typed. If the second is less than the sum of the first and third, print LESS. Otherwise, print NOT LESS.
11. A person earns R dollars an hour with time-and-a-half for all hours over 32. Determine the gross pay for a T-hour week. (R and T are to be entered during program execution.)
12. The cost of sending a telegram is $1.35 for the first ten words and 9¢ for each additional word. Find the cost if the number of words is input at the terminal.
13. If the wholesale cost of an item is under $100, the markup is 20%. Otherwise, the markup is 30%. Determine the retail price for an item whose wholesale cost is entered during program execution.
14. Two numbers X and Y are to be typed. If the sum of X and Y is greater than 42, print 42. If not, increase X by 10 and Y by 3, print the new X and Y, and again check to see if the sum is greater than 42. Continue until the sum is greater than 42.
15. One number is to be typed. If it is between 7 and 35, inclusive, print BETWEEN and stop. If it is less than 7, increase it by 5; if it is greater than 35, decrease it by 5. In either case, print the value obtained. The program should continue with this new value until it is between 7 and 35.
16. For any two numbers M and N, print POSITIVE if both are positive and NEGATIVE if both are negative. Otherwise, print NEITHER.
17. For any three numbers typed at the terminal, print ALL if all three are negative; otherwise, print NOT ALL.

5.4 FLOWCHARTS

While attempting the problems in the previous section, you must have become aware of the increasing difficulty in the construction of a procedure that leads to a working program. This difficulty arises from the more complicated logic necessitated by the conditional nature of the problems. As the logic becomes more involved, it will often be helpful to display this logic pictorially. One way to do this for the program of Example 5 in Section 5.2 is shown on page 49.

Such a pictorial representation of the sequence of instructions in a program is called a **programming flowchart** or simply a **flowchart**. Carefully constructed flowcharts, together with carefully written procedures, can serve as excellent documentation for your programs. It should be noted that these flowcharts describe the logic of your program—that is, "how" the computer carries out a process. Documentation describing "what" task is being performed must also be included. For the reasonably short tasks encountered by a beginning programmer, thoughtfully chosen REM statements and a carefully written problem statement should be adequate.

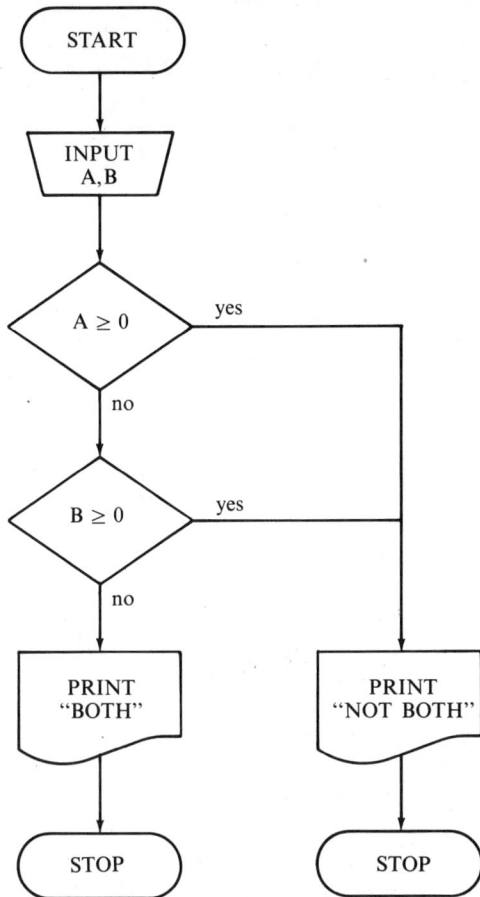

The following three examples illustrate some of the symbols used to construct flowcharts.

EXAMPLE 6. A flowchart for a program to calculate 6% of any number typed at the terminal.

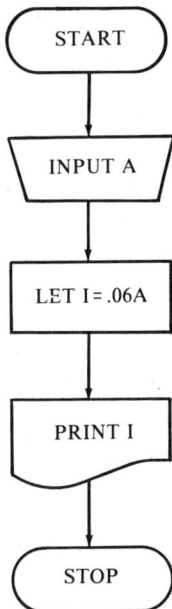

EXAMPLE 7. A flowchart for a program to recognize whether or not a 5 is input.

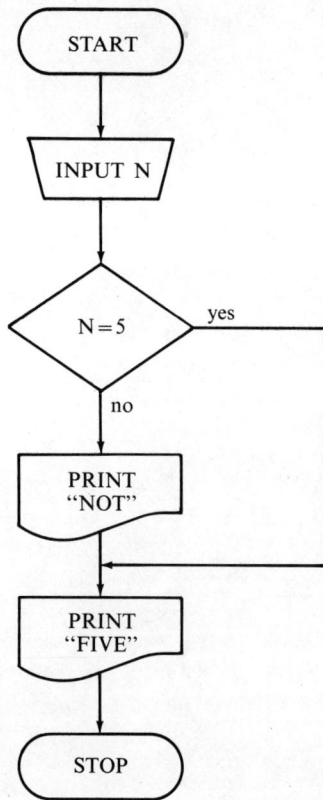

```
        ( START )
            │
            ▼
       [ INPUT N ]
            │
            ▼
          ╱   ╲        yes
         ╱ N=5 ╲──────────┐
         ╲     ╱          │
          ╲   ╱           │
            │ no          │
            ▼             │
       [ PRINT           │
         "NOT" ]          │
            │             │
            ◄─────────────┘
            ▼
       [ PRINT
         "FIVE" ]
            │
            ▼
        ( STOP )
```

EXAMPLE 8. Two equivalent flowcharts for a program to print the integers from 1 to 10, inclusive.

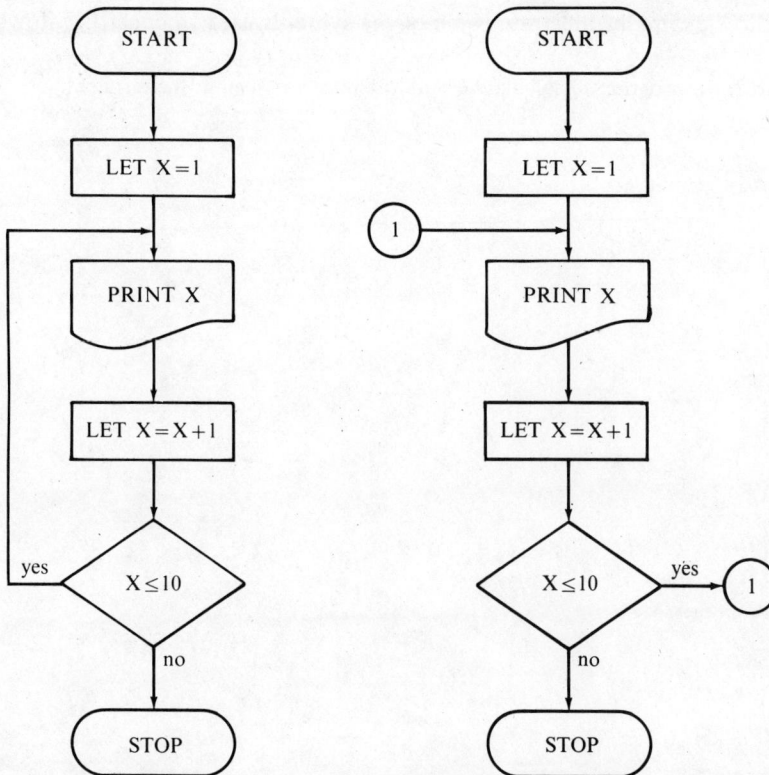

```
        ( START )                        ( START )
            │                                │
            ▼                                ▼
       [ LET X=1 ]                      [ LET X=1 ]
            │                        (1)─────►│
        ┌──►│                                 │
        │   ▼                                 ▼
        │ [ PRINT X ]                    [ PRINT X ]
        │   │                                 │
        │   ▼                                 ▼
        │ [ LET X=X+1 ]                  [ LET X=X+1 ]
        │   │                                 │
        │   ▼                                 ▼
   yes  │  ╱   ╲                            ╱   ╲    yes
        └──╱ X≤10╲                         ╱ X≤10╲──────►(1)
           ╲     ╱                         ╲     ╱
            ╲   ╱                           ╲   ╱
             │ no                            │ no
             ▼                               ▼
         ( STOP )                        ( STOP )
```

In these examples arrows connecting six different types of symbols are used to display the sequence of instructions. Although there are many such flowchart symbols* in use, the six used here are adequate for displaying the flow of instructions for many BASIC programs. A brief description of how these symbols are used is given in Table 5.2.

TABLE 5.2 Flowchart symbols

The Symbol	Its Use
(rounded rectangle)	To designate the start and end of a program.
(trapezoid)	To describe data to be INPUT during program execution.
(output shape)	To describe the output.
(rectangle)	To describe any processing of data.
(diamond)	To designate a decision that is to be made.
(circle)	A connector—used so that flow from one segment of a flowchart to another can be displayed and also to avoid drawing long lines.

When possible, the flow should be directed from left to right or from top to bottom, as was done in the preceding three examples.

It is often easier to prepare a pictorial description of a process to be followed than to attempt a detailed description in words. The flowchart is an excellent way to do this. The process of preparing a flowchart is called **flowcharting.** There are no fixed rules on how one should proceed toward the preparation of a flowchart; flowcharting must be practiced. We conclude this chapter with three examples illustrating this process. Once a flowchart has been prepared, the task of writing the program is reasonably routine; it consists only of coding the instructions appearing in the flowchart.

EXAMPLE 9. Construct a flowchart for a program to determine the number of years required for an investment of $1000 earning 7.5% compounded annually to double in value.

Problem Analysis: The compound interest formula is

$$A = P(1 + R)^N,$$

in which

P denotes the principal (P = 1000);
R denotes the rate per period (R = 0.075);
N denotes the number of periods; and
A denotes the value after N periods.

For N = 1, 2, 3, and so on, we must calculate the amount A and then test the condition

$$A \geq 2P \text{ (double the initial investment)}.$$

The first value of N for which this condition is satisfied must be printed, and the process should then stop. Following is one procedure for doing this.

---

*Flowchart symbols as proposed by the American National Standards Institute (ANSI) are described in "Flowcharting with the ANSI Standard: A Tutorial," by Ned Chapin, *Computing Surveys*, Vol. 2, No. 2, June 1970.

a. Initialize: $P = 1000$, $R = 0.075$, $N = 0$.
b. Add 1 to N.
c. If $P(1 + R)^N \geq 2P$, print N and stop.
d. Go to step (b).

The Flowchart

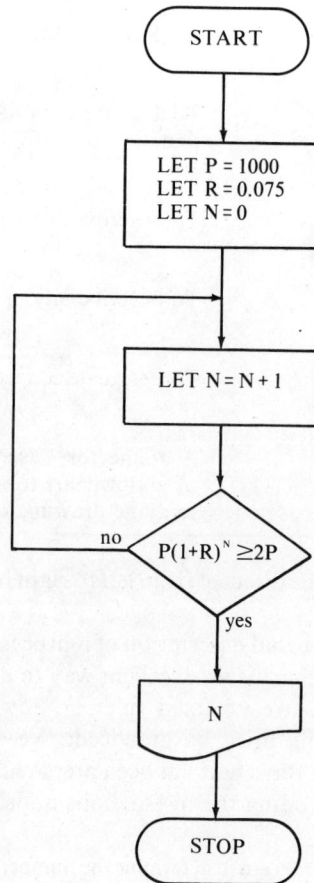

Remark: The flowchart symbols used to display output and input are used only for this purpose. Hence, to include the words PRINT or INPUT would be redundant.

If this flowchart is coded, a GO TO statement will be needed following the IF statement. This can be avoided by using $<$ rather than $\geq$ in the decision box. The flowchart will have exactly the same structure, but the program will be easier to read.

The Program

```
100 LET P=1000
110 LET R=0.075
120 LET N=0
130 LET N=N+1
140 IF P*(1+R)↑N<2*P THEN 130
150 PRINT "NUMBER OF YEARS TO DOUBLE",N
160 END
RUN
```

NUMBER OF YEARS TO DOUBLE   8
READY

EXAMPLE 10. Construct a flowchart for a program to determine a salesperson's commission if the schedule is 4% on the first $2000 in sales and 6% on everything over $2000. The total sales are to be input at the terminal.

Problem Analysis: Let's denote the total sales by S and the commission by C. The following formulas govern this situation.

If S ≤ 2000, C = .04S
If S > 2000, C = .04(2000) + .06(S−2000)

The following procedure allows many commissions to be determined during a single program run. The process will stop when the user types zero or a negative amount.

Algorithm

a. Input a value for S.
b. If S ≤ 0, stop.
c. If S ≤ 2000, let C = .04S. Otherwise, let C = .04(2000) + .06(S−2000).
d. Print C and go to step (a).

The Flowchart

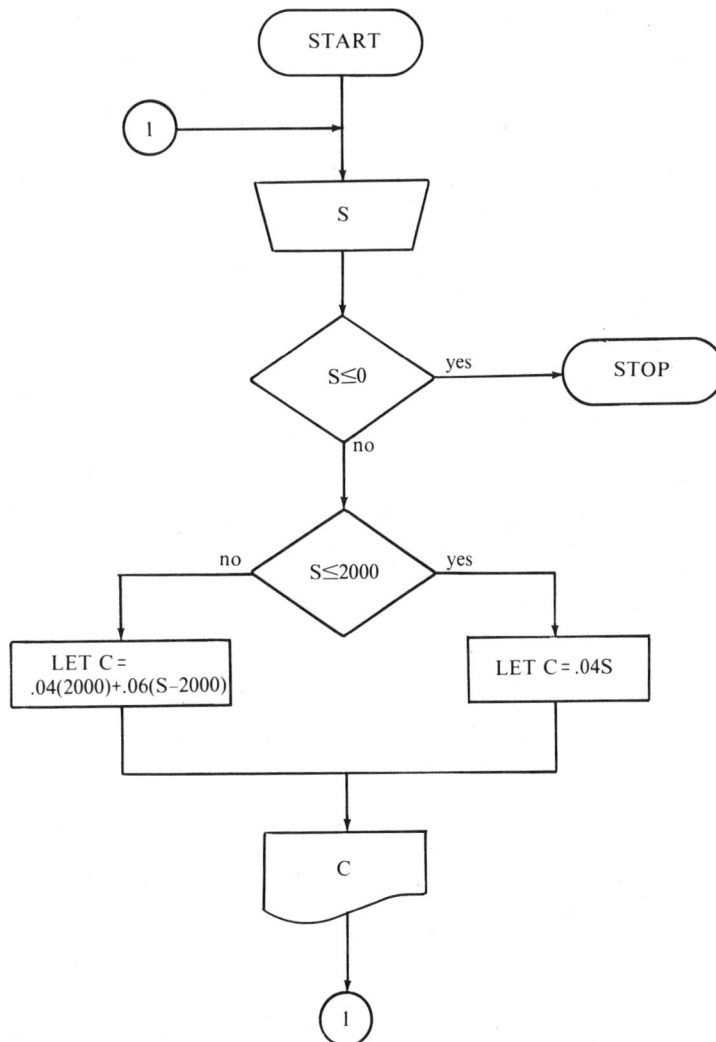

Remark: If a flowchart containing the flowchart construct

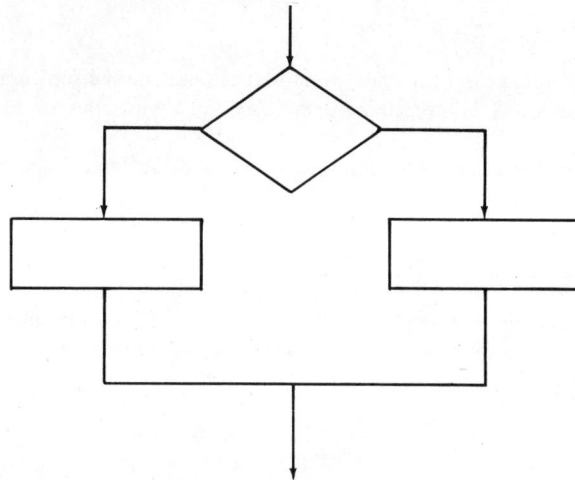

is coded, a GO TO statement will be required. It is often possible to avoid this—for instance, for the present example, by replacing the indicated flowchart segment with the following.

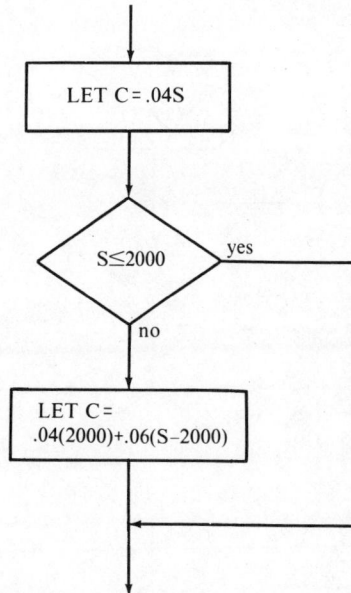

Some BASIC systems include an extended form of the IF statement that simplifies coding such constructs. For example, your system may allow you to write

```
IF S=2000 THEN LET C=.04*S
ELSE LET C=.04*2000+.06*(S-2000).
```

This statement is called the IF-THEN-ELSE statement, and it can be used in the following general form.

```
IF (condition) THEN (a BASIC instruction)
ELSE    .
          .
          .
          .
        (a sequence of BASIC instructions)
          .
          .
          .
```

If your system includes the IF-THEN-ELSE statement, you should use it. You will be less likely to make errors during the coding process, and your programs will be easier to read and understand.

EXAMPLE 11. Construct a flowchart for a program to find the averages of several sets of numbers typed in at the terminal. The value 9999, when typed, means that all entries for that particular set of numbers have been made.

Problem Analysis: Let's assign the variable names as follows.

N = the value being typed at the terminal.
S = the sum at any time (initially zero).
K = the number of values entered (initially zero).
A = the average (A = S/K).

When a number N is typed, we must determine if N is 9999. If it is not, the sum S is increased by N, the counter K is increased by 1, and a new value is entered for N. If N is 9999, all numbers in the set have been entered, so the average A = S/K is printed. Before entering the next set of numbers, we must reset S and K to zero.

Algorithm

a. Initialize S = 0 and K = 0.
b. Input a number N.
c. If N = 9999, go to step (e).
d. Let S = S + N and K = K + 1, and go to step (b).
e. Let A = S/K.
f. Print A and go to step (a).

The Flowchart

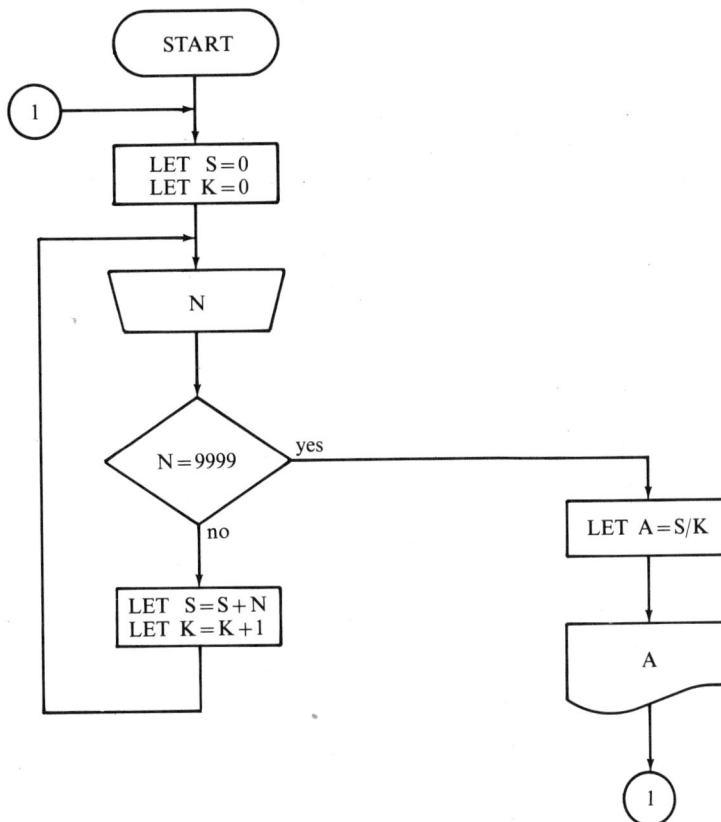

5.5   PROBLEMS

1. Write equivalent BASIC programs that contain no GO TO statements.

a.
```
10 INPUT A
20 IF A<=1000 THEN 50
30 LET S=200+.05(A-1000)
40 GO TO 60
50 LET S=200
60 PRINT S
70 END
```

b.
```
100 INPUT X
110 IF X<100 THEN 150
120 IF X<200 THEN 170
130 LET S=3
140 GO TO 180
150 LET S=1
160 GO TO 180
170 LET S=2
180 PRINT S
190 END
```

Prepare a flowchart and then a program to accomplish each task specified in Problems 2–20. Try to avoid GO TO statements in your programs.

2. Input one number. If it is between 3 and 21, print BETWEEN. Otherwise, print NOT BETWEEN.
3. Input two numbers. If either one is positive, print EITHER. Otherwise, print NEITHER.
4. Input three numbers. If the first is the largest, print LARGEST. Otherwise, print NOT LARGEST.
5. Input three numbers. If the second is the largest, print LARGEST. If it is the smallest, print SMALLEST. Otherwise, print NEITHER.
6. Input two values A and B. Print the value 1 if A = B = 0 or A = B = 1. Print the value 0 in all other cases.
7. Calculate the sum $1 + 2 + 3 + \ldots + N$. N is to be input.
8. Calculate the sum $5 + 7 + 9 + \ldots + 91$.
9. Calculate the sum $3 + 8 + 13 + 18 + \ldots + 93$.
10. Input a list of numbers whose last value is 9999. Calculate the sum and the average of all numbers in the list excluding the 9999.
11. Input a list of N numbers and print the largest value in the list. N is to be input. (*Hint:* see Example 3, Section 1.3.)
12. Input a list of numbers whose last value is 9999. Print the smallest and largest values in the list excluding the 9999.
13. A company payroll clerk needs a computer program to assist in preparing the weekly payroll. For each employee the clerk is to enter the hours worked H, the hourly pay rate R, the federal tax rate F, the state tax rate S, and the Social Security rate T. The clerk needs to know the gross pay, the net pay, and the amount of each deduction. Employees receive time-and-a-half for each hour worked over 40 hours. (The algorithm should not be too detailed. For example, after H, R, F, S, and T have been called for, a single line might read "Determine the gross pay, the three deductions, and the net pay." The details for doing this would then be worked out during the flowchart construction.)
14. A salesperson's monthly commission is determined according to the following schedule.

Net Sales	Commission Rate
Up to $10,000	6%
Next $4000	7%
Next $6000	8%
Additional amounts	10%

Determine the monthly commission given the total monthly sales.
15. Andrew's parents deposit $500 in a savings account on the day of his birth. The bank pays 6.5% compounded annually. Construct a table showing how this deposit grows in value from the date of deposit to his 21st birthday.
16. Sally receives a graduation present of $1000 and invests it in a long-term certificate that pays 8% compounded annually. Construct a table showing how this investment grows to a value of $1500.
17. A young man agrees to begin working for a company at the very modest salary of a penny per week, with the stipulation that his salary will double each week. At the end of six months, what is his weekly salary and how much has he earned?

18. A list of numbers, terminated with the special value 9999, is to be typed. Each successive pair is to be added and the average of these sums determined.
19. Find the total amount credited to an account after four years if $25 is deposited each month at an annual interest rate of 5.5% compounded monthly.
20. On the first of each month other than January, a person deposits $100 into an account earning 6% interest compounded monthly. The account is opened on February 1st. How much will the account be worth in five years just prior to the February deposit?

5.6 REVIEW TRUE OR FALSE QUIZ

1. Conditional transfer statements are to be avoided, because they result in programs whose logic is difficult to follow. T F
2. The value of a relational expression may be assigned to a variable by using a LET statement. T F
3. The question that is asked in a decision box of a flowchart is the basis for the relational expression in an IF statement. T F
4. If the relational expression in an IF statement is false, the normal sequential execution of the program is interrupted. T F
5. Although successive programming lines may contain IF statements, it is best to avoid this practice. T F
6. In BASIC the IF statement is used for two fundamentally different purposes. T F
7. The IF statement makes it possible to write all BASIC programs so that they need not be terminated manually. T F
8. If a program is to print results and terminate when P < Q, it is always best to use an IF statement with the condition P < Q. T F
9. If the END statement is at line 999, it is never necessary to include the instruction GO TO 999 in your program. T F
10. At most, one STOP statement may be used in a BASIC program. T F
11. A flowchart is an excellent way to display the logic of a program, but flowcharting is of little value while writing the program. T F
12. Once a flowchart has been constructed, the program is easily written. T F

6 MORE ON THE PRINT STATEMENT

Up to now we have been working with the restriction that at most five values can be printed on any one line and, that, moreover, the spacing of these results is determined by the computer, not by us. In this chapter we will show how more than five values can be printed on a line and how, using the TAB function, you can prescribe the precise position on a line for each value being printed. These forms of the PRINT statement are acceptable to essentially all BASIC systems. In addition, we will describe the PRINT USING statement, an extended form of the PRINT statement that has been implemented on many BASIC systems.

6.1 PRINTING MORE NUMBERS ON A LINE

A teletypewriter will normally print up to 72 characters per line. It is common practice to number these print positions 0 through 71.* When programming in BASIC, we consider a line to be divided into five zones. One way of doing this is as follows:

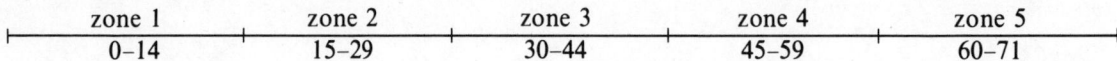

zone 1	zone 2	zone 3	zone 4	zone 5
0–14	15–29	30–44	45–59	60–71

The instruction PRINT A,B,C,D,E will cause the values of the five variables to be printed, one number per zone. If more than five variables appear in a PRINT statement, the sixth value is printed on the next line in zone 1, the seventh in zone 2, and so on. When the value of a variable is printed, the first position of the zone in which it is printed is reserved for the sign of the number. However, if the number is positive or zero, the sign is omitted and the first position is left blank.

EXAMPLE 1.

```
100 LET A=20
110 LET B=-3
120 LET C=3.123
130 PRINT A,B,C,A,B,C
```

---

*The proposed American National Standard for Minimal BASIC (Dec. 1, 1976) specifies that print positions be numbered beginning with 1 and not 0. With some hesitation, we adhere to the old practice of numbering these positions beginning with 0. To the best of our knowledge, this is still the situation on most BASIC systems. Copies of the Standard may be obtained by writing to CBEMA, 1828 L St. N.W., Washington, D.C. 20036.

```
140 END
RUN
```

zone 1	zone 2	zone 3	zone 4	zone 5
20	-3	3.123	20	-3 (printed for us)
3.123				

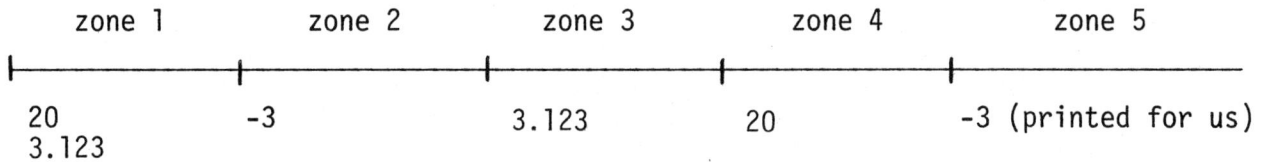

In the same way, up to five messages (also called **strings**) can be printed on one line, provided that each string fits in its zone. Strings are printed beginning in the first position of a zone.

EXAMPLE 2.

```
100 PRINT "FIRST COLUMN","THE SECOND COLUMN","THIRD COLUMN"
110 END
RUN
```

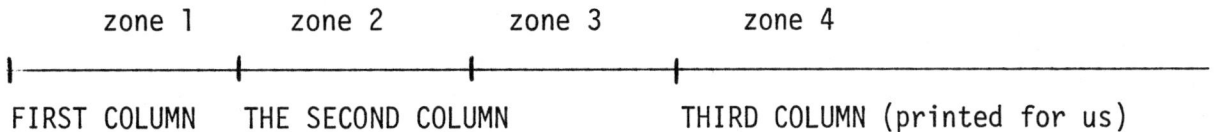

zone 1	zone 2	zone 3	zone 4
FIRST COLUMN	THE SECOND COLUMN		THIRD COLUMN (printed for us)

The second string uses all 15 positions in zone 2 and 2 positions from zone 3. This means that the third string must start in zone 4.

More than five values can be printed per line if we use semicolons instead of commas to delimit (separate) the variables in a PRINT statement. If this is done, zones will be ignored and the numbers will be packed more closely. Normally, one space will separate numbers, with a possible second space if a number is not negative (the sign position). As many numbers will be printed on a line as will fit. If line 130 of Example 1 were changed to

130 PRINT A;B;C;A;B;C

the output would be

20 –3   3.123   20 –3   3.123

Using a semicolon as a delimiter preserves the identity of numerical values; that is, numbers being printed will be separated by at least one space and will not be merged together. However, strings separated by semicolons in a PRINT statement will be merged.

```
100 PRINT "TO";"GET";"HER!!!"
110 END
RUN

TOGETHER!!!
READY
```

If spaces are desired, they must be included as part of a string.

PRINT statements using semicolons as delimiters may contain both strings and variables.

```
10 LET X=5                        10 LET X=5
20 LET Y=-3                       20 LET Y=-3
30 PRINT X;"IS POSITIVE"          30 PRINT "X=";X;"AND Y=";Y
40 PRINT Y;"IS NEGATIVE"          40 END
50 END                            RUN
RUN
                                  X= 5 AND Y=-3
 5 IS POSITIVE                    READY
-3 IS NEGATIVE
READY
```

6.2 SUPPRESSING THE CARRIAGE RETURN

It often happens that a program contains a loop in which a new value to be printed is determined each time the loop is executed. If the print instruction is of the form

PRINT T

successive values of T will be printed on separate lines (to the delight of paper manufacturers). However, if you terminate this print line with a comma or a semicolon, more than one value will be printed on each line: up to five if a comma is used and as many as will fit on the line if a semicolon is used.

EXAMPLE 3.

```
100 LET N=1
110 LET T=2*N-1
120 PRINT T;
130 LET N=N+1
140 IF N<15 THEN 110
150 PRINT
160 PRINT "THAT'S ALL FOLKS!"
170 END
RUN

 1  3  5  7  9  11  13  15  17  19  21  23  25  27
THAT'S ALL FOLKS!
READY
```

Remark: When the last number (27) is printed by line 120, the semicolon prevents the print mechanism from being positioned at the beginning of the next line. The PRINT instruction in line 150 causes a carriage return so that the subsequent printout will appear on a new line.

EXAMPLE 4.

```
10 REM PROGRAM TO PRINT A ROW OF 50 DASHES
20 LET N=0
30 PRINT "-";
40 LET N=N+1
50 IF N<50 THEN 30
60 END
RUN

--------------------------------------------------
READY
```

6.3   PRINTING VALUES OF NUMERICAL EXPRESSIONS

BASIC allows us to include any arithmetic expression, not just variables, in a PRINT statement. For instance, if A has the value 4, the instruction PRINT 3.1, 2*A+1 will cause the two numbers 3.1 and 9 to be printed in zones 1 and 2 of the same line. The instruction PRINT 3.1;2*A+1 will cause these same two numbers to be printed closer together.

EXAMPLE 5.

```
10 PRINT "2+3*5 =";2+3*5
20 END
RUN

2+3*5 = 17
READY
```

EXAMPLE 6.

```
10 INPUT A
20 LET R=5
30 PRINT R;"PERCENT OF";A;"IS";A*R/100
40 LET R=R+1
50 IF R<9 THEN 30
60 END
RUN

? 500

 5 PERCENT OF 500 IS 25.
 6 PERCENT OF 500 IS 30.
 7 PERCENT OF 500 IS 35.
 8 PERCENT OF 500 IS 40.
READY
```

Remark: Variable names should be used in programs only if there is a good reason for doing so. For example, to print the value of R% of A, the single instruction

PRINT A*R/100

should be used rather than the following two instructions.

LET T=A*R/100
PRINT T

Similarly, if the average of three numbers A, B, and C is required, write

PRINT (A+B+C)/3

and not

LET S=A+B+C
PRINT S/3

Variables such as T and S in these two illustrations are called **temporary variables,** since they are used to store values only temporarily. There are times when temporary variables are needed; there are also times when their use will lead to a "better" program even though they are not actually needed. However, it is generally a good programming practice to avoid them when possible. The resulting programs will be easier to understand.

6.4 PROBLEMS

1. Exactly what will be printed when each program is run?

a.
```
10 PRINT "BASEBALL'S HALL OF FAME",
20 PRINT "COOPERSTOWN,N.Y.","U.S.A."
30 END
```

b.
```
100 LET N=0
110 PRINT N,
120 LET N=N+5
130 IF N<38 THEN 110
140 PRINT "FINI"
150 END
```

c.
```
10 LET X=5
20 LET Y=X+3
30 PRINT X;"TIMES";Y;"=";X*Y
40 END
```

d.
```
10 PRINT "HAPPY"
20 PRINT "          HAPPY"
30 PRINT " ","HOLIDAY"
40 END
```

e.
```
10 LET N=1
20 PRINT N;
30 LET N=N+1
40 IF N>=30 THEN 90
50 IF N<8 THEN 20
60 LET N=N-7
70 PRINT
80 GO TO 20
90 END
```

f.
```
10 LET X=5
20 PRINT "IF A=";
30 PRINT X;"THEN ";
40 PRINT "A+2=";
50 PRINT X+2,
60 LET X=X+5
70 PRINT
80 IF X<=15 THEN 20
90 END
```

2. Assuming that X = 1 and Y = 2, write PRINT statements to print the following. No numbers are to appear in the PRINT statements. (The spacing need not be exactly as shown; BASIC systems do differ.)

a. 1/2 = .5   b. X + Y = 3   c. X – 2 = –1
d. SCORE: 2 TO 1   e. DEPT. NO. 5   f. BLDG 4.25

3. The following programs do not do what is claimed. Correct them.

a.
```
100 REM A PROGRAM TO PRINT
101 REM    1  2  3
102 REM    4  5  6
110 LET X=1
120 PRINT X;
130 LET X=X+1
140 IF X<=3 THEN 120
150 LET X=X+1
160 PRINT X
170 IF X<=6 THEN 150
180 END
```

b.
```
100 REM A PROGRAM TO PRINT
101 REM    777777
110 LET X=1
120 PRINT 7;
130 LET X=X+1
140 IF X<=6 THEN 120
150 END
```

c.
```
100 REM A PROGRAM TO PRINT
101 REM    TEA FOR TWO
110 PRINT "TEA","FOR","TWO"
120 END
```

Write a program to perform each task specified in Problems 4–14.

4. Fifteen years ago the population of Easton was 3571; it is currently 7827. Find the average increase in population per year. The output should be

FIFTEEN YEAR POPULATION INCREASE IS _____ .
THIS REPRESENTS AN AVERAGE INCREASE OF _____ PER YEAR.

5. An item has a list price of L dollars but is on sale at a discount of D%. Find the selling price. The output should be

LIST PRICE $_____
DISCOUNT OF _____ PERCENT IS $_____
SELLING PRICE $_____

6. If the wholesale price of a car is under $4300, the markup is 22%; otherwise the markup is 27%. Determine the retail price if the wholesale price is input at the terminal. The output should be

WHOLESALE PRICE IS _____ DOLLARS.
MARKUP IS _____ PERCENT.
RETAIL PRICE IS _____ DOLLARS.

7. A manufacturer produces an item at a cost of C dollars per unit and sells each unit for S dollars. In addition, a fixed yearly cost of F dollars must be absorbed in the manufacture of this item. The number of units that must be sold in one year to break even (breakeven volume) is given by the formula

$$\text{Breakeven volume} = \frac{F}{S - C} \text{ units.}$$

For any values of C, S, and F input, the printed output is to be

FIXED COST PER YEAR? _____
PRICE PER UNIT? _____
COST PER UNIT? _____
_____ UNITS MUST BE SOLD TO BREAK EVEN.
THIS REPRESENTS _____ DOLLARS IN SALES.

8. Print a row containing M dashes followed by the string THE END. M is to be input.
9. Print THE END beginning in column position N. N is to be input. (Use the statement   PRINT " "; to print a space.)
10. Print a square array of asterisks with M rows and M columns. M is to be input.
11. Print a square array of # symbols with N rows and N columns. Printing is to begin in column position P. N and P are to be input.
12. Print a square array of asterisks with 12 rows and 12 columns. The design is to be centered on the page.
13. Print a rectangular array of + signs with R rows and C columns. The design is to be centered on the page. R and C are to be input.
14. Determine the largest and smallest of a collection of numbers. The results are to be printed as follows.
_____ IS THE SMALLEST AND _____ IS THE LARGEST.

6.5   THE TAB FUNCTION

By using the semicolon in PRINT statements, you can specify the exact form of your output. However, as you probably found while writing the programs for the preceding problem set, this process can be cumbersome. To relieve you of this burden, BASIC includes the TAB function, which may be included in a PRINT statement to specify the column position at which printing is to commence.

EXAMPLE 7.

```
10 PRINT TAB(7);"WET"
20 PRINT TAB(6);"PAINT"
30 END
RUN
```

01234567890123456789 0   (For reference only)

```
       WET
      PAINT
READY
```

EXAMPLE 8.

```
10 LET I=1
20 PRINT TAB(I);3*I
30 LET I=I+1
40 IF I<6 THEN 20
50 END
RUN
```

```
01234567890123456789        (For reference only)

   3
    6
     9
      12
       15
```
READY

Each time line 20 is executed, the instruction PRINT TAB(I) will cause the value of 3∗I to be printed beginning in column position I, as shown in the printout. The apparent discrepancy is due to the suppressed plus sign, which, if printed, would occupy column position I.

EXAMPLE 9.

```
100 LET K=8
110 PRINT TAB(K);"*";TAB(22-K);"*"
120 LET K=K+1
130 IF K<=10 THEN 110
140 PRINT TAB(11);"*"
150 END
RUN
```

```
012345678901234567890012        (For reference only)

        *      *
         *    *
          *  *
           *
```
READY

Each time line 110 is executed, the expression TAB(K) will cause the string ∗ to be printed in column position K and TAB (22-K) will cause the second asterisk to be printed in column position 22-K. Line 140 prints the final asterisk.

We conclude this section by giving the general form of the PRINT statement that includes the TAB function.

ln PRINT TAB(a); e; TAB(b); f; . . .

where

    a, b, . . . are expressions whose values are rounded to integers (truncated, on some systems) to determine the print positions for the values to be printed;

    e, f, . . . are BASIC expressions (arithmetic expressions or strings) whose values are to be printed.

A semicolon or comma may terminate such a PRINT statement, in which case the carriage return will be suppressed.

6.6 PROBLEMS

1. Exactly what will be printed when each program is run?

a.
```
10 LET I=0
20 PRINT TAB(2*I+1);-I
30 LET I=I+1
40 IF I<=4 THEN 20
50 PRINT "THAT'S ENOUGH";
60 END
```

b.
```
10 PRINT " 7777777"
20 LET N=1
30 LET S=6
40 PRINT TAB(S-1);S+N
50 LET N=N+1
60 LET S=S-1
70 IF S>=1 THEN 40
80 END
```

c.
```
10 LET X=0
20 PRINT TAB(X↑2);"*"
30 LET X=X+1
40 IF X<=5 THEN 20
50 END
```

d.
```
10 LET X=0
20 PRINT TAB(5);"X";TAB(15);"X↑2"
30 PRINT
40 LET X=X+1
50 PRINT TAB(4);X;TAB(14);X↑2;
60 GO TO 30
70 END
```

2. Write PRINT statements to do the following.
   a. Print the letter B in print position 6 and the digit 3 in print position 10.
   b. Print the values of X, .04X, .06X, and .08X on one line about equally spaced. Do not use commas.
   c. Print six zeros on one line equally spaced along the entire print line.
   d. Print your name centered on the page.

Write a program to perform each task specified in Problems 3–8. Use the TAB function.

3. Print your name on one line, street and number on the next line, and city or town and state on the third line. Your name should begin at the center of the paper, and successive lines should be indented.
4. Print a row of 15 As beginning in print position 21 and a row of 13 Bs centered under the As.
5. Print a rectangular array of asterisks with five rows and eight columns, centered on the page.
6. Print a square array of # symbols with M rows and M columns, centered on the page. M is to be input.
7. Produce a six-column tax table showing 5%, 6%, 7%, 8%, 9%, and 10% for the amounts $100 to $300 in increments of $25. The table should have a title centered on the page, and each column should be labeled appropriately.
8. A person earning H dollars an hour, with time-and-a-half for hours over 32, has the following deductions: F% for federal taxes, S% for state taxes, and R% for retirement. Prepare a table with an appropriate title and with each column appropriately labeled showing the hours worked T, the gross pay, the net pay, and the amounts of the three deductions. The values T = 20, 21, 22, ..., 50 are to appear in the first column.
9. Produce the following designs.

a.
```
      1
       2
        3
         4
          5
           6
            7
```

b.
```
******
 *    *
 *    *
 *    *
 *    *
******
```

c.
```
          *
        *   *
       *     *
      *       *
     *         *
    **********
        *  *
        *  *
        ***
```

d.
```
          *
         ***
        *****
       *******
      *********
     **********
         ***
         ***
         ***
```

6.7 THE **PRINT USING** AND **IMAGE** STATEMENTS

Consider the following simple program with output.

```
10 PRINT TAB(4);"N";TAB(14);"1/N↑2"
20 PRINT
30 LET N=1
40 PRINT TAB(3);N;TAB(12);1/N↑2
50 LET N=N+1
60 IF N<=10 THEN 40
70 END
RUN

    N         1/N↑2

    1         1
    2         .25
    3         .111111
    4         .0625
    5         .04
    6         2.77778E-2
    7         2.04082E-2
    8         .015625
    9         1.23457E-2
    10        .01
READY
```

Even though the TAB function is used to control the output format, the second column appears rather cluttered. The PRINT USING and IMAGE statements provide a simple way to rectify this situation. BASIC systems differ in how these statements must be written. We present one of these forms to show how this extended version of the PRINT statement can be used to help you prepare improved output documents.

The IMAGE statement specifies the exact output format to be followed, and the PRINT USING statement specifies the values to be printed and also the line number of the IMAGE statement to be used in printing these values. For example, the programming line

100 PRINT USING 250,A

instructs the computer to print the value of A according to the format appearing in the IMAGE statement at line 250. Assuming that A has the value 23.487 and line 250 is

250 :ASSETS INCREASED BY ##.# PERCENT.

the computer will print

ASSETS INCREASED BY 23.5 PERCENT.

The control over the output format that can be achieved using these two statements is further illustrated in Example 10, which modifies the preceding program to print a table of values.

EXAMPLE 10.

```
10 PRINT TAB(4);"N";TAB(14);"1/N↑2"
20 PRINT
30 LET N=1
40 PRINT USING 70,N,1/N↑2
50 LET N=N+1
60 IF N<=10 THEN 40
70 :   ##          #.####
80 END
RUN
```

N	1/N↑2
1	1.0000
2	.2500
3	.1111
4	.0625
5	.0400
6	.0278
7	.0204
8	.0156
9	.0123
10	.0100

READY

Notice that the second column now lines up according to the decimal points and that the exponential forms of numbers are not printed. The format specification #.#### in line 70 controls this.

Here are three correctly written PRINT USING statements.

```
50 PRINT USING 75,A,B+5,47.3
90 PRINT USING 30,X,"LIABILITIES",M−N
45 PRINT USING 80,M+X,N−Q
```

Notice that, in each, a line number referencing an IMAGE statement and a comma follow the keywords PRINT USING. Next comes a list made up of BASIC expressions and quoted messages separated by commas. When executed, the values of the expressions and the messages will be printed in the order shown and according to the format specifications contained in the indicated IMAGE statement.

Here are three correctly written IMAGE statements.

```
120 :LIABILITIES   ###.##      ASSETS   ###.##

200 : WEIGHT IN POUNDS      #####

280 :VALUATION      TAX RATE      TAX
```

The keyword for the IMAGE statement is the colon (:). It is followed by strings and format specifications. Each format specification consists of pound (#) characters and possibly a decimal point. Strings are not in quotation marks unless they contain the pound character. A pound symbol is used to specify a position for a possible digit or character to be printed.

EXAMPLE 11. If X = 453, the two lines

```
100 PRINT USING 110,X
110 :ITEM NUMBER #####
```

will cause the printout

ITEM NUMBER   453

The format specification ##### is used to specify how 453 is to appear in the output. Since 453 uses only three of the possible five positions, it is printed right justified; that is, it appears in the rightmost three positions reserved by the specification. (Notice that only one space precedes ##### in the IMAGE statement, whereas three spaces precede 453 in the output.)

EXAMPLE 12. If A = 42.237 and B = 25, the two lines

```
100 PRINT USING 110,A,B
110 :####.## ####.##
```

will cause the printout

42.24   25.00

This example illustrates two points: numbers are rounded (not truncated) to fit a format specification (42.237 is rounded to 42.24), and all decimal positions included in a specification will be printed (25 is printed as 25.00).

EXAMPLE 13. If N = 16, the two lines

```
80 PRINT USING 90, "BLDG.",N
90 :######## ##
```

will cause the printout

BLDG.   16

Since the string "BLDG." uses only five of the eight positions reserved by the specification ########, it is printed left justified; that is, it appears in the leftmost five positions reserved by the format specification. Thus, numerical values are printed right justified (see Example 11) and strings are printed left justified.

The PRINT USING statement is especially useful when reports are to be printed in which the columns must line up according to the decimal points. The program in the following example illustrates such an application.

EXAMPLE 14.

```
100 REM----PROGRAM TO PRINT PROPERTY TAX TABLES-------
110 REM ASSESSED VALUE IS P PERCENT OF MARKET VALUE.
120 REM LOWEST AND HIGHEST MARKET VALUES IN TABLE ARE TO BE INPUT.
130 REM TAXES ARE SHOWN FROM LOWEST TO HIGHEST IN INCREMENTS OF $100.
140 REM
150 PRINT "LOWEST AND HIGHEST MARKET VALUES";
160 INPUT L,H
170 PRINT "ASSESSMENT PERCENT";
```

```
180 INPUT P
190 PRINT "TAX RATE PER THOUSAND";
200 INPUT R
210 PRINT
220 PRINT
230 PRINT USING 330
240 PRINT USING 340
250 PRINT
260 REM CALCULATE THE ASSESSMENT (A) AND TAX (T)
270 REM FOR THE MARKET VALUE L.
280 LET A=L*P/100
290 LET T=A*R/1000
300 PRINT USING 350,L,A,T,T/2,T/12
310 LET L=L+100
320 IF L<=H THEN 280
330 :   MARKET     ASSESSED     TOTAL    SEMIANNUAL  MONTHLY
340 :   VALUE       VALUE        TAX        BILL       BILL
350 : #####.##   #####.##    #####.##   #####.##   #####.##
360 END
RUN

LOWEST AND HIGHEST MARKET VALUES? 12500,13400
ASSESSMENT PERCENT? 87
TAX RATE PER THOUSAND? 56.45
```

MARKET VALUE	ASSESSED VALUE	TOTAL TAX	SEMIANNUAL BILL	MONTHLY BILL
12500.00	10875.00	613.89	306.95	51.16
12600.00	10962.00	618.80	309.40	51.57
12700.00	11049.00	623.72	311.86	51.98
12800.00	11136.00	628.63	314.31	52.39
12900.00	11223.00	633.54	316.77	52.79
13000.00	11310.00	638.45	319.22	53.20
13100.00	11397.00	643.36	321.68	53.61
13200.00	11484.00	648.27	324.14	54.02
13300.00	11571.00	653.18	326.59	54.43
13400.00	11658.00	658.09	329.05	54.84

```
READY
```

Remark 1: The PRINT USING statements in lines 230 and 240 use the IMAGE statements in lines 330 and 340 to print column headings. Note that lines 230 and 240 contain no values to be printed.

Remark 2: It is often convenient to group all IMAGE statements near the end of a program, as was done in this example.

6.8 PROBLEMS

1. What will be printed when each program is run?

a.
```
10 REM STOCK FRACTION VALUES
20 LET D=8
```

b.
```
10 LET J=1
20 LET A=0.004*J
```

```
30 LET N=1                          30 PRINT USING 60,J,A
40 PRINT USING 70,N,D,N/D*100       40 LET J=J+1
50 LET N=N+2                        50 IF J<=3 THEN 20
60 IF N<=7 THEN 40                  60 :TIME## A= #.##
70 :  #/#=##.# CENTS                70 END
80 END
```

c.
```
10 LET A=23.60                  d.  10 PRINT USING 30,"BOAT"
20 PRINT USING 50                   20 PRINT USING 40,"BOAT"
30 PRINT USING 60,A                 30 :RIVER######
40 PRINT TAB(2);A                   40 :       ####SWAIN
50 :01234567890                     50 END
60 :  ##.##
70 END
```

Write a program to perform each task specified in Problems 2–5.

2. Print the numbers 1, 10, 100, 1000, 10000, 100000, and 1000000 in a column in the middle of the page so that they are "lined up" on the right.

3. Print the numbers .33333, 3.3333, 33.333, 333.33, and 3333.3 in a column so that the decimal points line up.

4. Produce a table showing 1%, 2%, 3%, ... 8% of the values from ten cents to two dollars in increments of ten cents. Your table should have nine columns, each with a column heading, and all columns are to line up according to the decimal points.

5. An employer is considering giving all employees a flat across-the-board raise R in addition to a percentage increase P. P and R are to be input at the terminal. A three-column table, with the column headings

PRESENT SALARY, AMOUNT OF RAISE, NEW SALARY,

is to be printed. The first column is to list the possible salaries from $10,000 to $15,000 in increments of $500. Columns must line up according to the decimal points.

6.9   REVIEW TRUE OR FALSE QUIZ

1. The use of a semicolon in a PRINT statement always causes a separation of at least one space between the items being printed.   T F

2. PRINT statements containing messages that are separated by commas may cause these messages to be merged in the output.   T F

3. If you want to suppress the carriage return following execution of a PRINT statement, a semicolon must be used to terminate the PRINT line.   T F

4. If commas are used to separate values to be printed, columns will "line up." However, this will generally not be the case when semicolons are used.   T F

5. Although temporary variables are sometimes convenient to use in a program, they are never actually needed.   T F

6. If a message is to be centered in the printout, the TAB function must be used.   T F

7. The IMAGE statement allows us to include in a program an "image" of how we wish an output line to be formatted.   T F

8. A PRINT USING statement must reference one and only one IMAGE statement.   T F

9. There must be exactly the same number of IMAGE statements as PRINT USING statements in any program.   T F

10. Blank spaces following the colon in an IMAGE statement are not ignored during program execution. They are treated either as strings or as parts of strings and, as such, appear as blank spaces in the output.   T F

11. A PRINT USING statement containing no values to be printed will cause a carriage return to occur, but nothing will be printed.   T F

7 ENTERING LARGE QUANTITIES OF DATA

Many applications call for programs to process long lists of data values. BASIC includes two statements, the READ and DATA statements, that together allow you to include such lists as part of a program. The inconvenience of typing large quantities of data during program execution can thus be avoided. These two statements, along with the RESTORE statement, which is often used with them, are described in this chapter.

7.1 THE **READ** AND **DATA** STATEMENTS

These two statements are best illustrated by example.

EXAMPLE 1. A program to "read" two values and print their sum.

```
100 READ A
110 READ B
120 PRINT A+B
130 DATA 17,8
140 END
RUN

 25
READY
```

Line 130 contains the data to be added. Line 100 assigns the first of these values (17) to A, and line 110 assigns the next (8) to B. When line 130, the DATA line, is encountered, it is ignored and control passes to the next line, which in this program terminates the run.

The two READ statements in this program can be replaced by the single statement

READ A,B

as shown in the following equivalent program.

```
100 READ A,B
110 PRINT A+B
120 DATA 17,8
130 END
```

71

EXAMPLE 2. A program to "read" and type a list of numbers.

```
100 READ X
110 PRINT X
120 GO TO 100
130 DATA 7,-123,40
140 END
RUN

 7
-123
 40

OUT OF DATA AT 100
READY
```

Line 130 contains the list of numbers. When line 100 is first executed, the first data value (7) is assigned to X and control passes to line 110, which prints this value. The GO TO statement transfers control back to line 100, which then assigns the next value (–123) to X. This process is repeated until the data list is exhausted. This will happen when the READ statement is executed for the fourth time. Since only three values are supplied in the DATA line, this attempt to read a fourth value causes the OUT OF DATA message to be printed, and program execution terminates.

EXAMPLE 3. A program to average N sets of scores with each set containing three numbers.

```
100 REM      N DENOTES THE NUMBER OF SETS OF SCORES
110 REM      I COUNTS HOW MANY SETS HAVE BEEN READ
120 REM      A,B,C DENOTE THE THREE SCORES IN ONE SET
130 PRINT "SCORE 1","SCORE 2","SCORE 3","AVERAGE"
140 READ N
150 LET I=1
160 READ A,B,C
170 PRINT A,B,C,(A+B+C)/3
180 LET I=I+1
190 IF I<=N THEN 160
200 DATA 4
210 DATA 71,78,79,80,71,83
220 DATA 65,75,85,90,95,97
230 END
RUN
```

SCORE 1	SCORE 2	SCORE 3	AVERAGE
71	78	79	76
80	71	83	78
65	75	85	75
90	95	97	94
READY			

The first READ statement (line 140) assigns the first data value (4) to the variable N. This N is then used to ensure that exactly four sets of scores are read and processed. By using one of the data values in this manner, you can ensure that a READ statement will not be executed after the data list is exhausted.

The general forms of the READ and DATA statements are as follows.

    ln READ (list of variables separated by commas)
    ln DATA (list of BASIC constants separated by commas)

The following rules govern the use of these two statements.

1. As many DATA lines as desired may be included in a program, and as many values as will fit may appear on each line.
2. All values appearing in the DATA lines constitute a single list, called the **data list.** The order in which data values appear in this list is precisely the order in which they appear in the DATA lines. When a READ statement is executed, the variable or variables appearing are assigned successive values from the data list.
3. It is not necessary that all data values be read. However, if a READ statement is executed after the data values have all been used, an OUT OF DATA message will be printed and program execution will terminate.
4. If a DATA statement is encountered during program execution, the statement is ignored and control passes to the next line. For this reason, DATA lines may appear anywhere in the program prior to the END statement. However, they should be positioned to enhance the readability of your programs. Placing them just before the END statement is a common practice.

The statements READ N and READ A, B, C in the previous example would appear in a flowchart as follows.

READ N   READ A,B,C

A different symbol is needed for the READ statement, because the symbol for the INPUT statement is used to signify that data are to be input *manually* during program execution. The READ statement requires no such action on the part of the user.

The first data value in Example 3 (the 4 in line 200) is used to indicate that four sets of numbers are to be processed. This same program can be used to process more than four sets of numbers. A user would simply retype the data lines, making sure that the first data value tells how many sets are included. However, a user should not be required to make this count without good reason. For long lists, the task is boring and errors are likely. To avoid these problems, you can use a special value to terminate the list rather than a count to start it. Such a value is called an **End of Data (EOD) tag.** Each time a READ statement is executed, the value or values read are checked for this EOD tag. This technique is illustrated in the following example.

EXAMPLE 4. Write a program to find the largest number in a data list and also to determine how many numbers are included in the list.

Problem Analysis: Let's assign variable names as follows.

X = the most recent number read from the data list.
N = a count of how many numbers have been read.
L = the largest of the numbers read.

An algorithm for finding the largest number in a list is shown in Example 3 of Section 1.3. The following flowchart describes a slight modification of this algorithm that can be used in the present situation.

The Flowchart

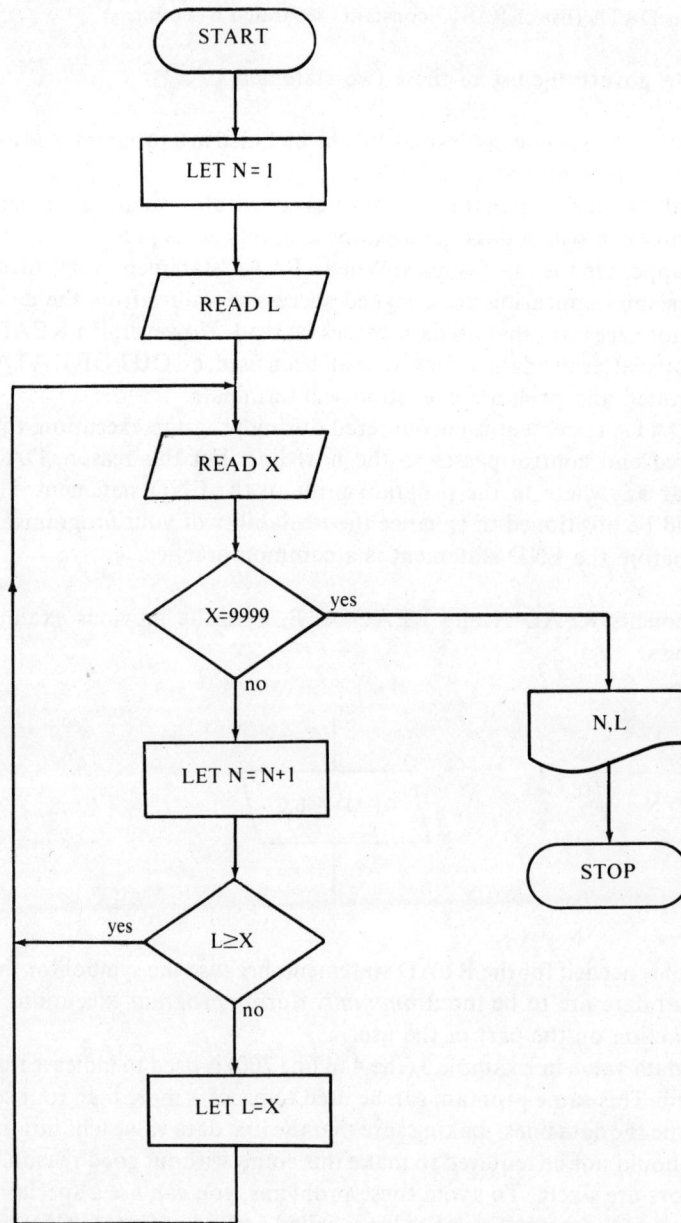

The Program

```
100 REM FIND THE LARGEST DATA VALUE
110 REM
120 REM    X=VALUE LAST READ
130 REM    N=NUMBER OF VALUES READ
140 REM    L=LARGEST OF ALL VALUES READ
150 LET N=1
160 READ L
170 READ X
180 IF X=9999 THEN 230
```

```
190 LET N=N+1
200 IF L>=X THEN 170
210 LET L=X
220 GO TO 170
230 PRINT "NUMBER OF DATA VALUES";N
240 PRINT "LARGEST DATA VALUE";L
250 DATA 88,72,64,89,93,72,65
260 DATA 84,92,69,73,91
998 DATA 9999
999 END
RUN

NUMBER OF DATA VALUES 12
LARGEST DATA VALUE 93
READY
```

Remark 1: The EOD tag is 9999. Each time a value is read for X (line 170), a comparison is made (line 180) to see if the list has been exhausted.

Remark 2: Note that there is no flowchart symbol for DATA statements. DATA statements simply provide a means of presenting data to the computer for processing. They cause nothing to happen during the actual execution of the program; hence, they have no place in a flowchart whose purpose is to describe the flow of activity in a program.

7.2   PROBLEMS

1. What will be printed when each program is run?

a.
```
10 LET I=1
20 READ A,B,C
30 IF A=7 THEN 50
40 PRINT C
50 LET I=I+1
60 IF I<=4 THEN 20
70 DATA 2,7,4,3,4,7,7
80 DATA 6,9,12,7,1,6
90 END
```

b.
```
10 READ N
20 LET J=1
30 READ X
40 LET Y=X+1
50 PRINT Y
60 LET J=J+1
70 IF J<=N THEN 30
80 DATA 2,5,3,7,8,-4
90 END
```

c.
```
100 LET I=1
110 READ X
120 IF X=9999 THEN 180
130 PRINT X
140 LET I=I+1
150 IF I<=3 THEN 110
160 PRINT I
170 DATA 7,3,18,21,42,9999
180 END
```

d.
```
10 LET I=1
20 READ I
30 IF I=9999 THEN 90
40 LET J=I-1
50 PRINT J
60 LET I=I+1
70 IF I<=8 THEN 20
80 DATA 4,12,33,27,9999
90 END
```

2. The following programs do not do what they claim. Find and correct all errors.

a.
```
100 REM SUM 5 VALUES
110 REM IN A DATA LINE
120 LET S=0
```

b.
```
100 REM PRINT SQUARES OF
110 REM 12,37,21,96
120 LET N=1
```

```
130 LET I=1                    130 READ A↑2
140 READ I                     140 PRINT A↑2
150 LET S=S+I                  150 LET N=N+1
160 LET I=I÷1                  160 IF N<4 THEN 130
170 IF I<=5 THEN 140           170 DATA 12,37,21,96
180 PRINT S                    180 END
190 DATA 7,12,14,-3,6,4
200 END
```

c.
```
100 REM AVERAGE N DATA VALUES    d.  100 REM SUM MANY SETS OF NUMBERS.
110 READ X                           110 REM 999 ENDS EACH SET.
120 IF X=1E-30 THEN 160              120 REM 9999 ENDS THE RUN.
130 LET S=0                          130 LET S=0
140 LET S=S+X                        140 READ X
150 GO TO 120                        150 IF X=9999 THEN 999
160 PRINT "AVERAGE IS",S/N           160 LET S=S+X
170 DATA 18,23,17,22                 170 IF X=999 THEN 190
180 DATA 1E-30                       180 GO TO 140
190 END                              190 PRINT S
                                     200 GO TO 140
                                     500 DATA 5,9,4,2,6,999
                                     510 DATA 41,16,18,2,999
                                     998 DATA 9999
                                     999 END
```

Write a program to perform each task specified in Problems 3–8. In each case supply your own DATA statements to test your program.

3. Read values from DATA lines two at a time. Print each pair of values, their product, and their quotient on one line.

4. Read values three at a time from DATA lines, and print the third number if it is greater than the product of the first two.

5. Find the sum of all numbers lying between 6 and 12 that appear in DATA statements.

6. Determine the largest and smallest values in a DATA set.

7. A list of numbers is to be examined to determine how many times a number is strictly larger than the one just before it. For example, if the list is 17, 3, 19, 27, 23, 25, the answer will be 3, since 19 > 3, 27 > 19, and 25 > 23. The list is to be presented in DATA lines.

8. A list of scores in the range 0 to 100 is to be examined to determine the following counts.

   C1 = number of scores less than 20.
   C2 = number of scores less than 40 but at least 20.
   C3 = number of scores less than 60 but at least 40.
   C4 = number of scores less than 80 but at least 60.
   C5 = number of scores not less than 80.

Determine these counts for any list appearing in DATA lines.

Write a program to produce a printed report as specified in Problems 9–14. Make sure that each report has a title, centered on the page, and that each column has an appropriate heading. All data are to be presented in DATA lines unless otherwise specified.

9. Given the employee number and monthly sales, print a three-column report showing the employee number, monthly sales, and commission if the commission rate for each person is 6%.

Employee Number	Monthly Sales
34	$4,050
51	6,500
21	3,750
18	3,640
49	7,150

10. Given the employee number, monthly sales, and commission rate for each person, print a four-column report showing the employee number, the monthly sales, the commission rate, and the total commission.

Employee Number	Monthly Sales	Commission Rate
401	$28,400	2%
513	34,550	2.5%
193	19,600	3%
184	14,500	2%
237	22,300	3.25%
207	31,350	1.5%

11. Given the employee number, base salary, monthly sales, and commission rate, print a four-column report showing the employee number, base salary, commission, and total monthly earnings.

Employee Number	Base Salary	Monthly Sales	Commission Rate
18	$400	$6,900	3%
25	445	8,400	2.5%
31	430	9,250	3%
12	465	8,920	4%
27	425	9,725	3.5%

12. Given the employee number, base salary, quota, commission rate, and monthly sales, print a four-column report showing the employee number, the base salary, the commission, and the total earnings. A salesperson receives a commission only on those sales that exceed the quota.

Employee Number	Base Salary	Quota	Commission Rate	Sales
47	$350	$7,000	5%	$10,900
16	400	9,000	5.5%	7,600
37	390	6,500	6%	9,700
25	425	3,500	5%	10,200
29	450	7,500	4.7%	7,100

13. Given the item number, the quantity, and the unit value of each item, print a four-column report showing the item number, the quantity, the unit value, and the total value of each item. The total value of the entire inventory should be printed below the report.

Item Number	Quantity	Unit Value
3047	198	$ 2.43
3055	457	3.97
3068	237	1.96
3093	1047	5.47
3247	593	10.93
3346	1159	12.41
3469	243	.83
3947	2042	8.37

14. (Electric Bill Problem) Given the customer number, the previous month's reading, and the current reading in kilowatt hours (KWH), print a report showing the customer number, the total number of KWHs used, and the total monthly bill. The charges are computed according to the following schedule: $1.41 for the first 14 KWH,

the next 85 KWH at \$.0389/KWH, the next 200 at \$.0214/KWH, the next 300 at \$.0134/KWH, and the excess at \$.0099/KWH. In addition, there is a fuel-adjustment charge of \$.0322/KWH for all KWHs used.

Customer Number	Previous Month's Reading	Current Reading
2516	25,346	25,973
2634	47,947	48,851
2917	21,342	21,652
2853	893,462	894,258
3576	347,643	348,748
3943	41,241	41,783
3465	887,531	888,165

7.3   THE **RESTORE** STATEMENT

We have described a *data list* as the list of all data values appearing in all DATA lines in a program. Associated with a data list is a conceptual *pointer* indicating the value to be read by the next READ statement. The pointer is initially set to the first value in the list, and, each time a value is read, the pointer moves to the next value. The BASIC statement

ln RESTORE

positions this pointer back to the beginning of the data list so that the values can be read again.

EXAMPLE 5. A program to illustrate the RESTORE statement.

```
10  READ A,B
20  RESTORE
30  READ C
40  RESTORE
50  READ D,E,F
60  PRINT A;B;C;D;E;F
70  DATA 1,2,3,4,5,6
80  END
RUN

  1  2  1  1  2  3
READY
```

Line 10 assigns the first two data values (1 and 2) to A and B, respectively. The RESTORE statement at line 20 positions the pointer back to the beginning of the data list; hence, when line 30 is executed, the first data value is again assigned, this time to the variable C. Line 40 once again restores the pointer so that, when line 50 is executed, the values 1, 2, and 3 are assigned to D, E, and F.

Many applications require that the values given in DATA lines be used more than once. For example, suppose the O'Halloran Shoe Company wants to know the average monthly income for its retail store and also the number of months in which the income exceeds this average. To determine this information, we must first find the average, a task that requires reading each number once, and then compare each number with this average, which requires a second look at each data value. In the following example this task is accomplished with the RESTORE statement.

EXAMPLE 6. Determine the average monthly income over a full year and the number of months in which the income exceeds this average.

Problem Analysis: To count the number of months in which the income exceeds the average, we must first find the average. This suggests the following algorithm.

a. Calculate the average monthly income for one year.
b. Count the number of months in which the income exceeds the average.
c. Print the results.

Before attempting to write the program segments that correspond to these three steps, we must choose variable names. Since exactly 12 values (the 12 income figures) must be read in each of steps (a) and (b), we must keep a count of how many of these have been read. Let's use M to denote this count and I for the monthly income figure last read. Also, let's use S for the sum of the monthly income figures, A for their average, and C for the count to be found in step (b). (This choice of variable names is summarized in lines 100–140 of the program.)

Using these variable names, we can rewrite the algorithm as follows. Steps (a1) through (a5) describe step (a), and steps (b1) through (b5) describe step (b).

Algorithm (Refined)

a1. Initialize the counters: S = 0, M = 0.
a2. Read I.
a3. Add I to S and 1 to M.
a4. If M < 12, go to step (a2).
a5. Let A = S/12.
b1. Restore the data pointer.
b2. Initialize the counters: C = 0, M = 0.
b3. Read I and add 1 to M.
b4. Add 1 to C if I > A.
b5. Go to step (b3) if M < 12.
 c. Print the results.

Remark: In this problem analysis, we took considerable care to proceed in an orderly way toward an algorithm that would be easy to understand and whose correctness would be fairly obvious. We started by subdividing the task described in the problem statement into three simpler subtasks. Detailed algorithms for the first two of these subtasks were then written and inserted into the three-step algorithm to give us the final refined algorithm. This approach is called the **method of step-wise refinement** or **top-down programming** and will be discussed and further described in the next section.

The Program

```
100 REM     M DENOTES THE MONTH (M=1,2,3,...,12)
110 REM     I DENOTES INCOME FOR A SINGLE MONTH
120 REM     S DENOTES THE CUMULATIVE INCOME
130 REM     A DENOTES THE AVERAGE MONTHLY INCOME
140 REM     C COUNTS THE NUMBER OF TIMES I EXCEEDS A
150 REM     CALCULATE THE AVERAGE MONTHLY INCOME FOR ONE YEAR
160 LET S=0
170 LET M=0
180 READ I
190 LET S=S+I
200 LET M=M+1
210 IF M<12 THEN 180
220 LET A=S/12
230 REM COUNT THE NUMBER OF MONTHS IN WHICH THE INCOME EXCEEDS THE AVERAGE
240 RESTORE
250 LET C=0
260 LET M=0
270 READ I
280 LET M=M+1
```

```
290 IF I<=A THEN 310
300 LET C=C+1
310 IF M<12 THEN 270
320 REM PRINT THE RESULTS
330 PRINT "AVERAGE MONTHLY INCOME";A
340 PRINT "NUMBER OF MONTHS INCOME EXCEEDS AVERAGE";C
500 DATA 13200.57,11402.48,9248.23,9200.94
510 DATA 11825.50,12158.07,11028.40,22804.22
520 DATA 18009.40,12607.25,19423.36,24922.50
999 END
RUN

AVERAGE MONTHLY INCOME 14652.6
NUMBER OF MONTHS INCOME EXCEEDS AVERAGE 4
READY
```

Remark: Note that the REM statements in lines 150, 230, and 320 correspond exactly to the three steps of the original algorithm. Thus, the program is *segmented* into three parts just as the original problem was *segmented* into three subtasks.

7.4 TOP-DOWN PROGRAMMING

Programming is essentially a three-step process.

1. Carefully read the problem statement so that it is completely understood. If necessary, rewrite the problem statement to clarify what is being asked.
2. Discover and describe a procedure (algorithm) that, when followed, will lead to a solution to the problem.
3. Using the procedure described in step (2), write and debug the program.

For lengthy problem statements or for tasks that are intrinsically difficult, step (2) can be troublesome. When you are confronted with such a situation, it is natural to segment the problem into simpler, more manageable tasks.

> We understand complex things by systematically breaking them down into successively simpler parts and understanding how these parts fit together locally.*

As natural as the idea of problem segmentation may appear, choosing subtasks that actually simplify matters may not be easy. Unfortunately, a formula for identifying appropriate subtasks is not known. What is known is a method that will help in your attempts to find such subtasks. This method was illustrated in Example 6 of Section 7.3. The task to be performed in that example was as follows.

Problem Statement: Determine the average monthly income over a full year and the number of months in which the income exceeds this average.

The approach taken was to begin with an algorithm containing as little detail as possible. The objective was to describe a procedure that would be easy to understand. The algorithm chosen was as follows.

a. Calculate the average monthly income for one year.
b. Count the number of months in which the income exceeds the average.
c. Print the results.

*“Structured Programming with **go to** Statements,” by Donald E. Knuth, *Computing Surveys,* Vol. 6, No. 4, December 1974.

That this algorithm describes a process for carrying out the stated task should be evident—in spite of the detail *not present*. For example, the algorithm contains no variable names (they were chosen later), and it does not tell "how" to find the average or "how" to determine the required count. Details of any kind should be introduced only as needed; each time a detail is introduced, the complexity of the procedure increases. The algorithm was kept simple by considering "what" must be done, not "how" it should be done.

The next step was to introduce variable names and show "how" the steps in the algorithm could be carried out. The variable names chosen were as follows.

M = the month (M = 1, 2, 3, ..., 12).
I = the income for a single month.
S = the cumulative income.
A = the average monthly income.
C = a count of the number of times I exceeds A.

Step (a) was then broken down into steps (a1) through (a5), and step (b) was rewritten as steps (b1) through (b5). Replacing steps (a) and (b) with these refinements, we obtained the following more detailed algorithm.

a1. Initialize the counters: S = 0, M = 0.
a2. Read I.
a3. Add I to S and 1 to M.
a4. If $M < 12$, go to step (a2).
a5. Let $A = S/12$.
b1. Restore the data pointer.
b2. Initialize the counters: C = 0, M = 0.
b3. Read I and add 1 to M.
b4. Add 1 to C if $I > A$.
b5. Go to step (b3) if $M < 12$.
 c. Print the results.

This algorithm was then translated into a BASIC program. Knowing that the original three-step algorithm was correct, and also that the refinements of steps (a) and (b) correctly carry out these two tasks, we can be sure that this final 11-step algorithm is also correct.

We illustrate this process of step-wise refinement with another example.

EXAMPLE 7. At the end of each month, a wholesale firm makes an inventory that shows, for each item in stock, the item code, the quantity on hand, and the average cost per unit. Following is a portion of the most recent inventory.

Item Code	Units on Hand	Average Cost/Unit
1015	844	1.63
1230	182	5.93
.	.	.
.	.	.
.	.	.

We are asked to prepare an inventory report that contains the given information and also the total cost of the inventory by item. In addition, a second short report is to be printed identifying the item (or items) whose inventory represents the greatest cost to the company.

Total Cost = (Units on hand) × (Average cost per unit)

Problem Analysis: Let's begin with the following simple algorithm.

a. Prepare the inventory report.

b. Determine the item (or items) whose inventory represents the greatest cost.

Writing a program segment to produce a printed report such as the one required in step (a) is not new to us. After printing a report title and appropriate column headings for the values to be printed, we will process the data, item by item, to determine and print these values.

To carry out step (b), we must first find the greatest total cost of all items in stock and then compare the total cost for each item with this largest value. Thus, step (b) can be broken down into the two simpler tasks (b1) and (b2) shown in the following refined algorithm.

a. Prepare the inventory report.

b1. Determine the greatest total cost of all items in stock.

b2. Print a report identifying each item whose inventory represents this greatest cost figure.

The task of finding the largest number in a set of numbers is likewise not new to us (see Example 4 of Section 7.1). We simply calculate the total cost of the items in stock, one at a time, always keeping track of the largest of the amounts encountered. To carry out step (b2), we must again calculate the total cost amounts, item by item, and then compare each with the largest amount found in step (b1).

Having identified *what* tasks must be performed, we must consider *how* to carry them out using the BASIC language. Let's agree to include the inventory data in DATA lines. Each DATA line will contain the three values associated with a single stock item. Three 0s are placed in line 998 to denote the end of the data.

```
500 DATA 1015, 844, 1.63
510 DATA 1230, 182, 5.93
           .
           .
           .
998 DATA 0,0,0
```

The next task is to choose variable names. To carry out step (a), we will need variables for the three values in a DATA line and a fourth to calculate the cost amounts required in the inventory report. In addition, we need a variable for the largest amount to be found in step (b1). These variable names are shown in lines 110–150 of the program.

The Program

```
100 REM-----INVENTORY PROGRAM---------
110 REM     N = ITEM CODE NUMBER
120 REM     Q = QUANTITY (IN UNITS) ON HAND
130 REM     C = AVERAGE COST PER UNIT
140 REM     T = TOTAL COST REPRESENTED BY ITEM N
150 REM     L = LARGEST OF ALL COST FIGURES
160 REM PREPARE AND PRINT THE INVENTORY REPORT
170 PRINT "            WAREHOUSE INVENTORY REPORT"
180 PRINT
190 PRINT "ITEM CODE","UNITS ON HAND","AV. COST/UNIT","TOTAL COST"
200 PRINT
210 READ N,Q,C
220 IF N=0 THEN 260
230 LET T=Q*C
240 PRINT N,Q,C,T
250 GO TO 210
260 PRINT
```

```
270 PRINT
280 REM DETERMINE THE LARGEST SALES FIGURE
290 RESTORE
300 READ N,Q,C
310 LET L=Q*C
320 READ N,Q,C
330 IF N=0 THEN 370
340 IF L>=Q*C THEN 320
350 LET L=Q*C
360 GO TO 320
370 REM PRINT REPORT OF ITEM (ITEMS) WHOSE INVENTORY
380 REM REPRESENTS THE GREATEST COST
390 RESTORE
400 READ N,Q,C
410 IF N=0 THEN 999
420 IF L<>Q*C THEN 400
430 PRINT "ITEM";N;"REPRESENTS THE MAXIMUM COST";L
440 GO TO 400
998 DATA 0,0,0
999 END
```

If this program is run with these DATA lines

```
500 DATA 1015, 844, 1.63
510 DATA 1230, 182, 5.93
520 DATA 2561, 467, 4.37
530 DATA 9856, 764, 5.62
540 DATA 3756, 875, 4.73
550 DATA 3321, 636, 2.64
560 DATA 1437, 292, 9.63
570 DATA 5738,1067, 3.78
580 DATA 2364, 532, 7.41
590 DATA 7576, 103,11.53
```

it will produce the following report.

```
                WAREHOUSE INVENTORY REPORT

ITEM CODE      UNITS ON HAND  AV. COST/UNIT  TOTAL COST

  1015             844            1.63         1375.72
  1230             182            5.93         1079.26
  2561             467            4.37         2040.79
  9856             764            5.62         4293.68
  3756             877            4.73         4148.21
  3321             636            2.64         1679.04
  1437             292            9.63         2811.96
  5738            1067            3.78         4033.26
  2364             532            7.41         3942.12
  7576             103           11.53         1187.59

ITEM 9856 REPRESENTS MAXIMUM COST 4293.68
```

Remark: The job of finding the greatest cost L (lines 280-360) could have been accomplished by modifying the first program segment (lines 160-270). The resulting program would have been slightly shorter, but not necessarily better. Indeed, combining tasks during the coding process can easily lead to serious programming errors. The problem analysis we carried out led us to consider three separate tasks. The program is segmented into three parts corresponding to these tasks. They are identified in the REM statements in lines 160, 280, and 370. As a result, the program is easy to read and understand, even though it may be longer than necessary. In addition, because of the systematic way in which tasks were broken down into simpler tasks, we can be confident that the program is absolutely correct (barring syntax or typing errors).

The problem analysis carried out in the preceding example can be displayed in a diagram as follows. At the "top" is the problem statement. It contains a complete description of what is to be done. The two tasks at the next "lower" level show how the problem was broken down into two slightly simpler tasks. The second of these, step (b), was broken down again, and it was then found that each of the terminal tasks, steps (a), (b1), and (b2), could easily be translated into a BASIC program. Hence, no further subdivision was carried out.

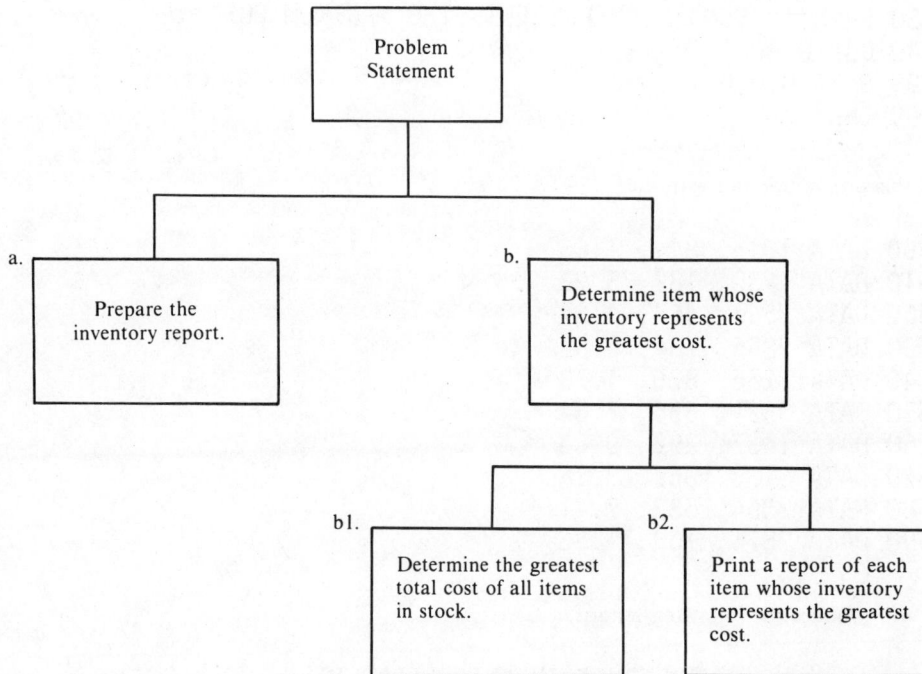

The **method of step-wise refinement,** illustrated in Examples 6 and 7, is also called **top-down programming.** You start at the top (the problem statement), break this task down into simpler tasks, then break these tasks into even simpler ones, and continue this process, all the while knowing how the tasks at each level combine, until the tasks at the lowest level contain whatever detail is desired.

Let's summarize some of the more relevant aspects of the method of top-down programming.

1. Each procedure (algorithm) is obtained from the preceding one by subdividing one or more of the individual tasks into simpler ones. At each step, or level of refinement, more details emerge to bring you closer to a solution—that is, to the desired program.
2. At the upper levels of refinement, dependence on the particular computer being used is avoided; procedures are expressed without regard to the computer language being employed. The objective is to determine "what" tasks must be performed, not "how" to carry them out.

3. At the lower levels of refinement, dependence on the computer language being used is unavoidable; the individual tasks in the final refinement correspond to actual program segments.
4. At each level, the procedure obtained must be *debugged*. If the procedure at one level is correct, it should be a simple matter to *debug* the procedure at the next lower level. You need only check to ensure that each task broken down into simpler tasks is broken down correctly. It is this aspect of the top-down approach that increases the likelihood that the final program will be correct.

We don't mean to imply that the method of top-down programming will always lead directly to a "good" program. It may be that a level of refinement is reached that, for some reason, is undesirable. When this happens, you may either start over at the top or *back up* one or more levels and continue from that point with a different refinement. Difficult problems may require backing up in this manner several times before a satisfactory procedure emerges.

The step-by-step process of segmenting complex tasks into simpler ones is not new; good programmers have always used such an approach. However, giving a name to the process has had two significant consequences. It has introduced the method of step-wise refinement to many people who previously programmed in a more or less haphazard fashion. As a result, better programs—that is, programs that are easier to read and more likely to be correct—are being written. The second consequence is that the method of problem segmentation has been carefully studied and formulated into an orderly process, as illustrated in the two worked-out examples. Since the way in which tasks are broken down into subtasks depends on who is carrying out this process, top-down programming is not a *procedure* that will always lead to the same program. Rather, it is a *process* that brings order to an otherwise disorderly human activity—namely, programming. We might say that some "structure" has been introduced into the process of designing programs.

As noted, one of the benefits of using a top-down approach is that the resulting programs are more likely to be correct. But *to know* that a program is correct is another matter. Any serious consideration of this topic must necessarily concern the structure of the program itself, not just the structure of the process that leads to the program. It is in this context that the expression **structured programming** has emerged. Top-down programming is one aspect of structured programming. Although it would be a simple matter to indicate what constitutes a structured program, as currently conceived, there is great danger of oversimplification. The topic should be broached only if it can be treated seriously, and such a treatment does not belong in an introductory text such as this. Suffice it to say that the goal of structured programming is to produce programs that are easy to understand, easy to modify, and absolutely correct the first time they are written.

We conclude this section by quoting Edsger W. Dijkstra, who gave structured programming its name* and who remains a central figure in the effort to discover the true nature of programs and the programming process.

> We understand walls in terms of bricks, bricks in terms of crystals, crystals in terms of molecules, etc.

> The only effective way to raise the confidence level of a program significantly is to give a convincing proof of its correctness. But one should not first make the program and then prove its correctness, because then the requirement of providing the proof would only increase the poor programmer's burden. On the contrary: the programmer should let the correctness proof and program grow hand in hand.†

Structured Programming, Software Engineering Techniques, by E. W. Dijkstra (J. N. Buxton and B. Randell, Eds.), NATO Scientific Affairs Division, Brussels, Belgium, 1970, pp. 84–88.
†"The Humble Programmer" (1972 ACM Turing Award Lecture), by E. W. Dijkstra, *Communications of the ACM,* Vol. 15, No. 10, October 1972, pp. 859–866.

7.5 PROBLEMS

1. What will be printed when each program is run?

a.
```
10 LET I=2
20 READ Y
30 PRINT Y
40 LET I=I+2
50 IF I<=6 THEN 20
60 RESTORE
70 DATA 9,3,5,8,12
80 END
```

b.
```
100 LET I=1
110 READ X
120 IF X=5 THEN 150
130 PRINT X
140 GO TO 160
150 RESTORE
160 LET I=I+1
170 IF I<=4 THEN 110
180 DATA 3,5,8,9,6
190 END
```

2. The following programs do not do what they claim. Find and correct all errors.

a.
```
100 REM PROGRAM TO PRINT
110 REM 10 20 30
120 REM 30 20 10
130 READ A1,A2,A3
140 PRINT A1,A2,A3
150 RESTORE
160 READ A3,A2,A1
170 PRINT A3,A2,A1
180 DATA 10,20,30
190 END
```

b.
```
100 REM PROGRAM REQUESTS NUMBERS
110     UNTIL THE NUMBER TYPED
120     IS IN THE DATA LIST
130 LET I=0
140 INPUT N
150 LET I=I+1
160 IF I>4 THEN 140
170 READ A
180 IF A<>N THEN 150
190 PRINT "OK"
200 DATA 1,5,9,8
210 END
```

3. Write a program to allow a user to input several values to determine if they appear in the DATA lines. For each number input, the message IS IN THE LIST or IS NOT IN THE LIST, whichever is appropriate, is to be printed. The user should be able to terminate the run by typing 0. Try your program using the following DATA statements.

```
500 DATA 40, 83, 80, 65, 32, 91, 90, 41, 92, 86, 80, 70, 55
998 DATA 9999
```

(9999 is an EOD tag.)

4. Several pairs of numbers are included in DATA lines. The first of each pair represents an item code number, and the second represents the current selling price. Write a program to allow a user to type several code numbers to obtain the current selling prices. If an incorrect code is typed, an appropriate message should be printed. The user should be allowed to terminate the run by typing 0. Use the following data lines.

```
500 DATA 1235, 12.39, 2865, 17.99, 4020, 23.00, 3640, 20.50
510 DATA 4930, 43.50, 5641, 88.20, 6600, 94.55, 5020, 16.79
998 DATA 0,0
```

5. I.M. Good, a candidate for political office, conducted a preelection poll. Each voter polled was assigned a number from 1 to 5 as follows.

(1) Will vote for Good.
(2) Leaning toward Good but still undecided.
(3) Will vote for Shepherd, Good's only opponent.
(4) Leaning toward Shepherd but still undecided.
(5) All other cases.

The results of the poll are included in DATA lines as follows.

500 DATA 1, 1, 2, 5, 3, 3, 5, 1, 2
510 DATA 5, 5, 2, . . .

.
.
.

998 DATA 9999

Write a program to print two tables as follows.

TABLE 1

	FOR	LEANING
GOOD	-	-
SHEPHERD	-	-

TABLE 2

	FOR OR LEANING	PERCENTAGE OF TOTAL NUMBER OF PEOPLE POLLED
GOOD	-	-
SHEPHERD	-	-
OTHERS	-	-

Write a program to perform each task described in Problems 6–9. In each case, be sure to begin by segmenting the given task into subtasks.

6. Print all numbers appearing in a data list, in the order in which they appear, up to but not including the largest value in the list. Nothing else is to be printed. Test your program using the data shown in Problem 3.
7. Print all numbers appearing in a data list that differ from the average of all numbers in the list by no more than D. (A value for D is to be input.) Test your program using the data shown in Problem 3.
8. A wholesale firm has two warehouses, numbered 19 and 35. During a recent inventory, the following data were compiled.

Item	Warehouse	Quantity on Hand	Average Cost per Unit
6625	19	52000	1.954
6204	19	40000	3.126
3300	35	8500	19.532
5925	19	22000	6.884
2202	35	6200	88.724
2100	35	4350	43.612
4800	19	21500	2.741
7923	19	15000	1.605
1752	35	200	193.800

Prepare a separate inventory report for each warehouse. Each report is to contain the given information and also is to show the total cost represented by the inventory of each item.

9. Using the inventory data shown in Problem 8, prepare an inventory report for the warehouse whose entire stock represents the greatest cost to the company.

7.6   REVIEW TRUE OR FALSE QUIZ

1. The READ and DATA statements provide the means to present large quantities of data to the computer without having to type them in during program execution.   T   F
2. DATA statements must follow the READ statements that "read" the data values.   T   F

3. The line   90 DATA 5,-3E2,7+3,12   is a valid BASIC statement. T F
4. A pointer is a special value appearing in a DATA list. T F
5. More than five variables may appear in a READ statement. T F
6. It is not necessary to read an entire DATA list before the first value can be read for a second time. T F
7. At most, one RESTORE statement may be used in a BASIC program. T F
8. When large quantities of data are included in DATA lines, the first value must be a count of the number of values included. T F
9. The READ and DATA statements are often useful when no interaction between the computer and the user is required. T F
10. The method of top-down programming is an advanced and difficult programming technique. T F
11. When you are using the top-down approach, a good first step is to read the problem statement carefully and to determine variable names to be used. T F
12. In the top-down approach, debugging is simply the process of checking to see that individual tasks are correctly broken down into simpler tasks. T F

8 LOOPS MADE EASIER

Loops occur in all but the most elementary computer programs. However, it is not always easy to construct loops using only the IF and GO TO statements, and programs written in this manner are often difficult to understand. Because of this, BASIC contains the FOR statement and the NEXT statement, which greatly simplify writing loops and which also result in more readable programs. In this chapter the FOR and NEXT statements are described and a special symbol for displaying them in flowcharts is introduced.

8.1 FOR/NEXT LOOPS

Following are two ways to print the integers from 1 to 5.

Program 1

```
100 LET I=1
110 PRINT I;
120 LET I=I+1
130 IF I<=5 THEN 110
140 END
RUN

 1  2  3  4  5
READY
```

Program 2

```
100 LET I=1
110 IF I>5 THEN 150
120 PRINT I;
130 LET I=I+1
140 GO TO 110
150 END
RUN

 1  2  3  4  5
READY
```

The same thing can be accomplished by the following program.

Program 3

```
100 FOR I=1 TO 5
110 PRINT I;
120 NEXT I
130 END
RUN

 1  2  3  4  5
READY
```

89

This program simply instructs the computer to execute line 110 five times, once for each integer I from 1 to 5. Just how the computer will accomplish this depends on the particular implementation of BASIC on your system. Our assumption in this text is that Program 3 is equivalent to Program 2. This assumption conforms to the ANSI standard for minimal BASIC. Thus, the action of Program 3 can be described as follows.

a. When line 100 (the FOR statement) is encountered, I is assigned the initial value 1.
b. I is compared with the terminal value 5.

If I > 5, control passes to the line following the NEXT statement.
The loop has been satisfied.
If I ≤ 5, control passes to the line following the FOR statement.

c. Line 110 prints the current value of I.
d. When the NEXT statement, line 120, is encountered, I is incremented by 1 and the comparison in step (b) is repeated.

Following are three examples further illustrating the use of the FOR and NEXT statements to construct loops. To clarify the meaning of the FOR/NEXT loop, we have written each program in two ways, without and with the FOR and NEXT statements.

EXAMPLE 1. A loop to read and print five values appearing in DATA lines.

```
100 LET I=1                    100 FOR I=1 TO 5
110 IF I>5 THEN 170            110 READ X
120 READ X                     120 PRINT X;
130 PRINT X;                   130 NEXT I
140 LET I=I+1                  140 DATA 8,5,2,7,6
150 GO TO 110                  150 END
160 DATA 8,5,2,7,6             RUN
170 END
RUN                             8  5  2  7  6
                              READY
 8  5  2  7  6
READY
```

The FOR/NEXT loop instructs the computer to execute lines 110 and 120 five times, once for each integer I from 1 to 5. (Compare with the program to print the integers from 1 to 5.)

EXAMPLE 2. A loop to print the numbers –4, 2, 0, 2, 4, 6.

```
100 LET J=-4                   100 FOR J=-4 TO 6 STEP 2
110 IF J>6 THEN 150            110 PRINT J;
120 PRINT J;                   120 NEXT J
130 LET J=J+2                  130 END
140 GO TO 110                  RUN
150 END
RUN                            -4 -2  0  2  4  6
                              READY
-4 -2  0  2  4  6
READY
```

The first program describes the action of the second as follows:

a. The FOR statement, line 100, assigns the initial value –4 to J.
b. J is compared with the terminal value 6.

If J > 6, control passes to line 130, the line following the NEXT statement.
If J ≤ 6, control passes to line 110, the line following the FOR statement.

c. Line 110 prints the current value of J.
d. When the NEXT statement, line 120, is encountered, J is incremented by 2 (STEP 2) and the comparison in step (b) is repeated.

EXAMPLE 3. A loop to print 5, 4, 3, 2, 1.

```
100 LET N=5
110 IF N<1 THEN 150
120 PRINT N;
130 LET N=N+1
140 GO TO 110
150 END
RUN

  5  4  3  2  1
READY
```

```
100 FOR N=5 TO 1 STEP -1
110 PRINT N;
120 NEXT N
130 END
RUN

  5  4  3  2  1
READY
```

This example illustrates that negative increments are acceptable. The initial value of N is 5, and, after each pass through the loop, N is decreased by 1 (STEP –1). As soon as N attains a value less than 1 (as specified in the FOR statement), control passes out of the loop to the statement following the NEXT statement.

The general form of a FOR/NEXT loop is

$$\text{FOR } \mathbf{v} = \mathbf{a} \text{ TO } \mathbf{b} \text{ STEP } \mathbf{c}$$

.
.
.

$$\text{NEXT } \mathbf{v}$$

where **v** denotes a simple variable name and **a**, **b**, and **c** denote arithmetic expressions. (If STEP **c** is omitted, **c** is assumed to have the value 1.) To describe the action, we denote the value of the variable **v** by V and the values of the expressions **a**, **b**, **c** by A, B, C, respectively. A is called the *initial value,* B the *limit* or *terminal value,* and C the *increment.* The variable **v** is called the *control variable.*

a. The initial value of **v** is A.
b. V is compared with the terminal value B.

Case 1: C ≥ 0

If V > B, control passes to the line following the NEXT statement.
If V ≤ B, control passes to the line following the FOR statement.

Case 2: C < 0

If V < B, control passes to the line following the NEXT statement.
If V ≥ B, control passes to the line following the FOR statement.

c. The program segment consisting of the lines between the FOR and NEXT statements is called the *body of the loop.* It is executed once on each pass through the loop.

d. When the NEXT statement is encountered, C is added to V and the comparison in step (b) is repeated.

To make programs with loops easier to read, we can indent the statements that make up the body of the loop. This policy will be adhered to throughout.

EXAMPLE 4. A program to print a table showing the 5.5%, 6%, 6.5%, ..., 10% discount on any amount A typed at the terminal. However, if for some percentage rate the discount exceeds $50, the printing is to terminate.

```
100 PRINT "AMOUNT";
110 INPUT A
120 PRINT
130 PRINT "PERCENT RATE","DISCOUNT"
140 FOR R=5.5 TO 10 STEP 0.5
150     LET D=(R/100)*A
160     IF D>50 THEN 200
170     PRINT R,D
180 NEXT R
190 STOP
200 PRINT "DISCOUNT FOR RATE";R;"PERCENT IS";D
210 END
RUN

AMOUNT? 700

PERCENT RATE    DISCOUNT
 5.5             38.5
 6.              42.
 6.5             45.5
 7.              49.
DISCOUNT FOR RATE 7.5 PERCENT IS 52.5
READY
```

This program illustrates the following points.

1. The body of a loop may contain any admissible BASIC statements and as many of these as you wish.
2. Exit from a loop may be caused by a statement within the loop. In this example, the discount D is 52.5 for the rate R = 7.5; hence, the IF statement at line 160 will transfer control to line 200 when R has this value.
3. The initial, terminal, and step values in a loop need not be integers. Here, the initial value is 5.5 and the step value is 0.5.

EXAMPLE 5. A program to examine six numbers appearing in a DATA line and print only those that exceed 40.

```
100 FOR N=1 TO 6
110     READ X
120     IF X>40 THEN 150
130 NEXT N
140 STOP
150 PRINT X;"EXCEEDS 40"
160 GO TO 130
170 DATA 52,37,49,41,25,40
180 END
RUN
```

```
52 EXCEEDS 40
49 EXCEEDS 40
41 EXCEEDS 40
READY
```

Line 120 causes a *temporary exit* from the loop whenever the value just read for X exceeds 40; line 160 gets us back in. Although making a temporary exit from a loop is allowed, this practice is not encouraged. Such programs can and should be improved by rewriting them. The preceding program can be rewritten as follows.

```
100 FOR N=1 TO 6
110    READ X
120    IF X<=40 THEN 140
130    PRINT X;"EXCEEDS 40"
140 NEXT N
150 DATA 52,37,49,41,25,40
160 END
```

Now the loop is written between the FOR and the NEXT statements, fewer lines are needed, and the program is easier to read.

EXAMPLE 6. A loop to print a row of N dashes.

```
200 FOR I=1 TO N
210    PRINT "-";
220 NEXT I
```

Of course, N must be assigned a value prior to execution of line 200. If N is 15, a row of 15 dashes will be printed.

If the terminal value N in Example 6 is 0, then the entire loop will be skipped, since the initial value, I = 1, will be greater than the terminal value, N = 0. However, as noted previously, the precise action caused by a FOR/NEXT loop may differ on your system. Many BASIC systems are designed so that execution of the FOR statement results in at least one pass through the loop (the comparison is made at the end of the loop rather than at the beginning). We restate this as a warning.

WARNING: On some BASIC systems, when the FOR statement beginning a FOR/NEXT loop is executed, at least one pass is made through the loop.

Following are some points concerning the use of FOR/NEXT loops that were not raised explicitly in this section.

1. The initial, terminal, and step values are determined once, when the FOR statement is executed, and cannot be altered within the body of the loop.
2. Although the control variable can be modified inside the loop, don't do it. The resulting program will be very difficult to read.
3. Entry into a loop should be made only by executing the FOR statement.
4. If an exit is made from a loop prior to its completion (an IF or GO TO statement), the current value of the control variable will be retained. (See Example 4.)
5. If an exit is made via the NEXT statement (that is, the loop is satisfied), the value of the control variable is the first value not used. (On systems not conforming to the ANSI standard for minimal BASIC, this may not be the case. Experiment!)
6. Loops may contain loops. (This is the subject of Section 8.4.)

8.2   FLOWCHARTING FOR/NEXT LOOPS

FOR/NEXT loops occur in most BASIC programs. For this reason, many flowchart symbols have been designed for representing such loops. The flowchart symbol presented here is one that we feel is especially appropriate for BASIC programs.

Using only the flowchart symbols given in Chapter 5, the loop

FOR I=1 TO N

.
.
.

NEXT I

may be flowcharted as follows.

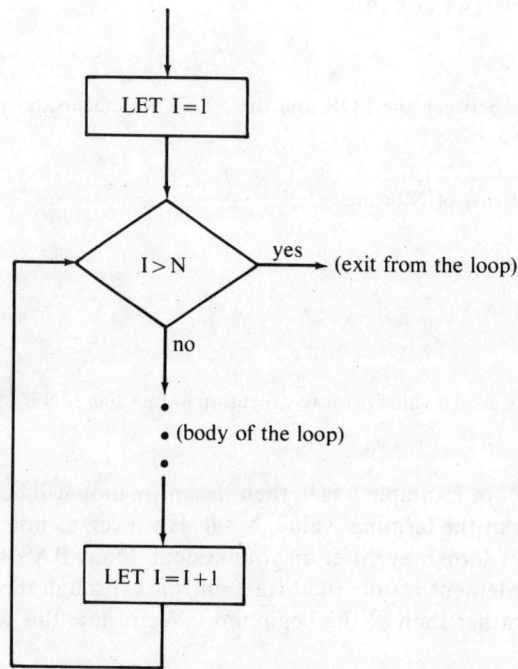

The three symbols in this flowchart are combined to give us the following symbol for representing FOR/NEXT loops.

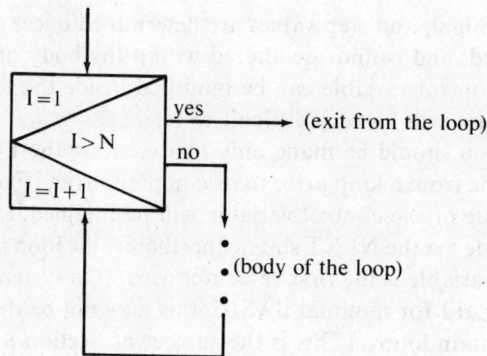

EXAMPLE 7. A flowchart for a program to input ten numbers and print their average.

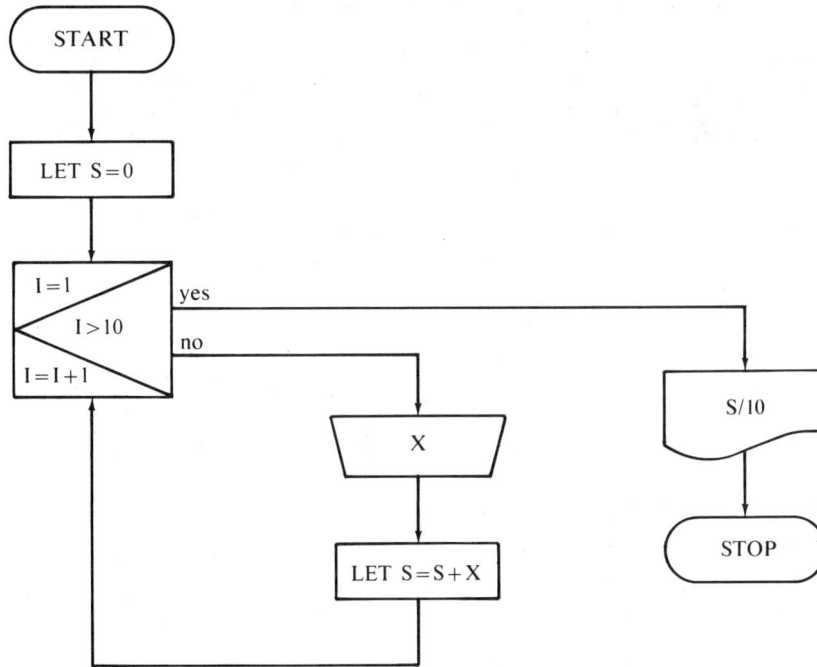

The FOR/NEXT flowchart symbol is easily modified to represent different FOR/NEXT loops. For example, the loop

FOR I=2 TO 9 STEP 3
.
.
.

NEXT I

would be represented as follows.

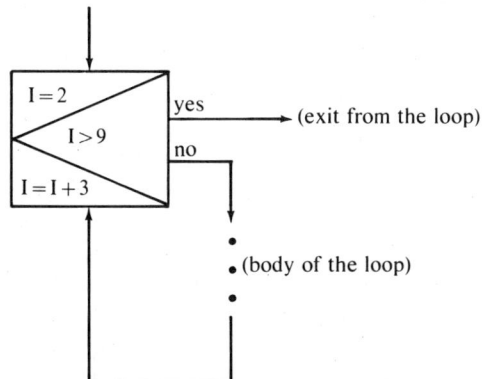

A loop with a negative step causes no difficulty. For example, the loop

FOR X=3 TO 1 STEP −.1
.
.
.
NEXT X

would be represented as follows.

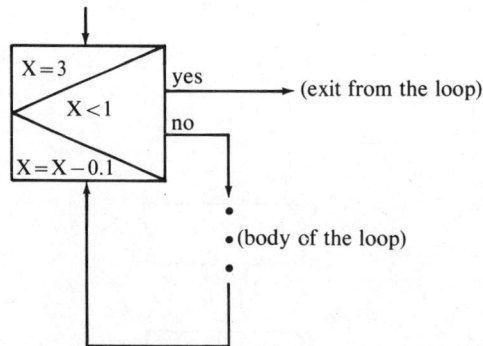

8.3 PROBLEMS

1. What will be printed when each program is run?

a.
```
10 FOR J=2 TO 4
20     PRINT J+2
30 NEXT J
40 END
```

b.
```
10 FOR N=5 TO -3 STEP -4
20     PRINT N
30 NEXT N
40 END
```

c.
```
10 LET C=0
20 LET X=1
30 FOR Q=1 TO 4.9 STEP 2
40     LET C=C+1
50     LET X=X*Q
60 NEXT Q
70 PRINT "TIMES THROUGH LOOP=";C
80 PRINT X
90 END
```

d.
```
10 FOR I=1 TO 3
20     PRINT "+";
30 NEXT I
40 FOR J=5 TO 7
50     PRINT "/";
60 NEXT J
70 END
```

2. Each of the following programs contains an error—either a syntax error that will cause an error message to be printed or a programming error that the computer will not recognize but that will cause incorrect results. In each case find the error and tell which of the two types it is.

a.
```
10 REM 6% PROGRAM
20 FOR N=1 TO 6
30     READ X
40     PRINT X,.06*X
50 NEXT X
60 DATA 85,90,95
70 DATA 70,75,85
80 END
```

b.
```
10 REM COUNT THE POSITIVE
20 REM NUMBERS TYPED
30 FOR I=1 TO 10
40     LET C=0
50     INPUT N
60     IF N<=0 THEN 80
70     LET C=C+1
80 NEXT I
90 PRINT C;"ARE POSITIVE"
99 END
```

```
c.  10 REM SUMMING PROGRAM        d.  10 REM PRINT THE NUMBERS
    20 LET S=0                        20 REM 1 3 6 10 15
    30 FOR X=1 TO 4                   30 LET S=1
    40    READ X                      40 FOR N=1 TO 15 STEP S
    50    LET S=S+X                   50    PRINT N
    60 NEXT X                         60    LET S=S+1
    70 DATA 18,25,33,41               70 NEXT N
    80 END                           80 END
```

Write the programs called for in Problems 3–11. In each case a single FOR/NEXT loop is to be used.

3. Twenty numbers are to be typed at the terminal. Determine the sum of those that are positive.
4. Twenty numbers are to be entered at the terminal. Determine how many of these numbers are negative, how many are positive, and how many are zero.
5. Print the integers from 1 to 72, eight to the line.
6. Print the integers from 1 to 72, eight to the line, equally spaced. (Use the TAB function.)
7. A program is desired that will continually request (INPUT statement) that numbers be typed until ten numbers have been typed that lie in the range from 5 to 25. The average of these ten numbers is then to be printed.
8. A program is desired to assist third-grade students with their fives multiplication table. In particular, the student should be asked to answer the questions $2 \times 5 = ?$, $3 \times 5 = ?$, ..., $12 \times 5 = ?$ If a question is answered correctly, the next question should be asked; if not, the question should be repeated. However, if the same question is answered incorrectly twice, the correct answer should be printed and then the next question should be asked.
9. Evaluate the following sums S. If a value for N is required, it is to be supplied by the user.

   a. $S = 1 + 2 + 3 + \ldots + N$
   b. $S = (-12) + (-9) + (-6) + \ldots + (48)$
   c. $S = 1 + 1/2 + 1/3 + \ldots + 1/N$
   d. $S = (.06) + (.06)^2 + (.06)^3 + \ldots + (.06)^N$
   e. $S = 1 - 1/2 + 1/3 - 1/4 + \ldots - 1/100$

10. The following DATA lines show the salaries for all salaried employees in a small firm. (The first value (10) denotes how many salaries are listed.)

```
800 DATA 10
810 DATA 9923, 10240, 10275, 11390, 12560
820 DATA 12997, 13423, 14620, 19240, 22730
```

Prepare a report showing the effect of a flat across-the-board raise of I dollars in addition to a percentage increase of P%. I and P are to be input. Include three columns labeled PRESENT SALARY, RAISE, and NEW SALARY.

11. The following DATA lines show the annual salaries for all salaried employees in a firm. Each salary amount is followed by a count of the number of employees earning that amount. (This firm has a salary step schedule.)

```
800 DATA 8
810 DATA 9020, 4, 10250, 8, 12330, 16, 12940, 30
820 DATA 13570, 21, 14840, 86, 15920, 28, 16520, 7
```

Prepare a three-column report as in Problem 10. In addition, conclude the report by printing the total cost to the owners of the old salary package, the total cost of the new salary package, the total dollar amount of all raises (the difference of the previous two figures), and the overall percent increase this amount represents.

8.4   NESTED LOOPS

It is permissible, and often desirable, to have one FOR/NEXT loop contained in another. When nesting loops in this manner, there is one rule that must be observed:

If the body of one FOR/NEXT loop contains either the FOR or the NEXT statement of another loop, it must contain both of them (see Figure 8.1).

```
┌─ FOR I= . . .                      ┌─ FOR R= . . .
│       .                            │       .
│       .                            │       .
│  ┌─ FOR J= . . .                   │  ┌─ FOR S= . . .
│  │      .                          │  │      .
│  │      .                          │  │      .
│  └─ NEXT J                         │  └─ NEXT R
│       .                            │       .
│       .                            │       .
└─ NEXT I                            └─ NEXT S
   a.  Correct                          b.  Incorrect


┌─ FOR X= . . .                      ┌─ FOR I= . . .
│       .                            │       .
│       .                            │       .
└─ NEXT X                            │  ┌─ FOR J= . . .
                                     │  │      .
   .                                 │  │      .
   .                                 │  │  ┌─ FOR K= . . .
┌─ FOR X= . . .                      │  │  │      .
│       .                            │  │  │      .
│       .                            │  │  └─ NEXT K
│  ┌─ FOR Y= . . .                   │  │      .
│  │      .                          │  │      .
│  │      .                          │  └─ NEXT J
│  └─ NEXT Y                         │       .
│       .                            │       .
│       .                            └─ NEXT I
└─ NEXT X
   c.  Correct                          d.  Correct
```

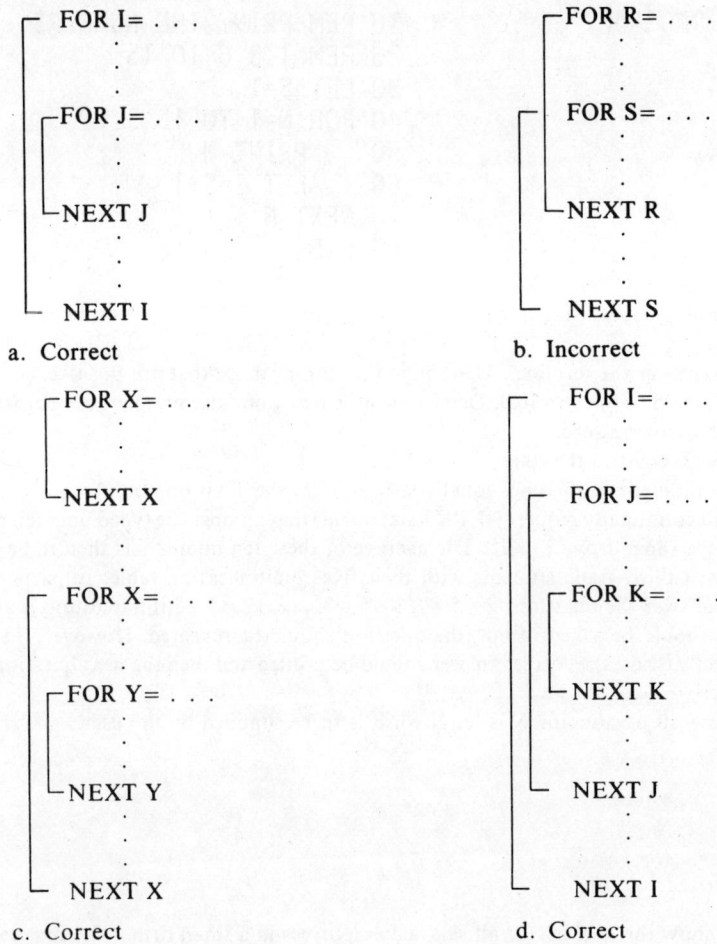

FIGURE 8.1 Correctly and incorrectly nested loops.

EXAMPLE 8. Let's write a program whose output is the following addition table for all possible sums of the integers 1 through 5.

```
2  3  4  5  6
3  4  5  6  7
4  5  6  7  8
5  6  7  8  9
6  7  8  9  10
```

Problem Analysis: The sum 3 + 4 is to be printed in the third row and fourth column. More generally, the sum I + J is to be printed in the Ith row and Jth column. Since an entire row must be printed before we go on to the next row, the following algorithm is suggested.

a. Let I = 1.
b. Print I + J for J = 1, 2, . . . , 5.
c. Let I = I + 1 and, if I ≤ 5, go to step (b).
d. Stop.

Programming this procedure will indeed print the sums in the order specified but not in the format shown. A semicolon following the PRINT instruction

PRINT I + J;

will supress the carriage return but will print too many numbers on one line. This problem can be rectified by using the instruction

$$PRINT$$

each time a row is completed (that is, each time J exceeds 5).

The Flowchart

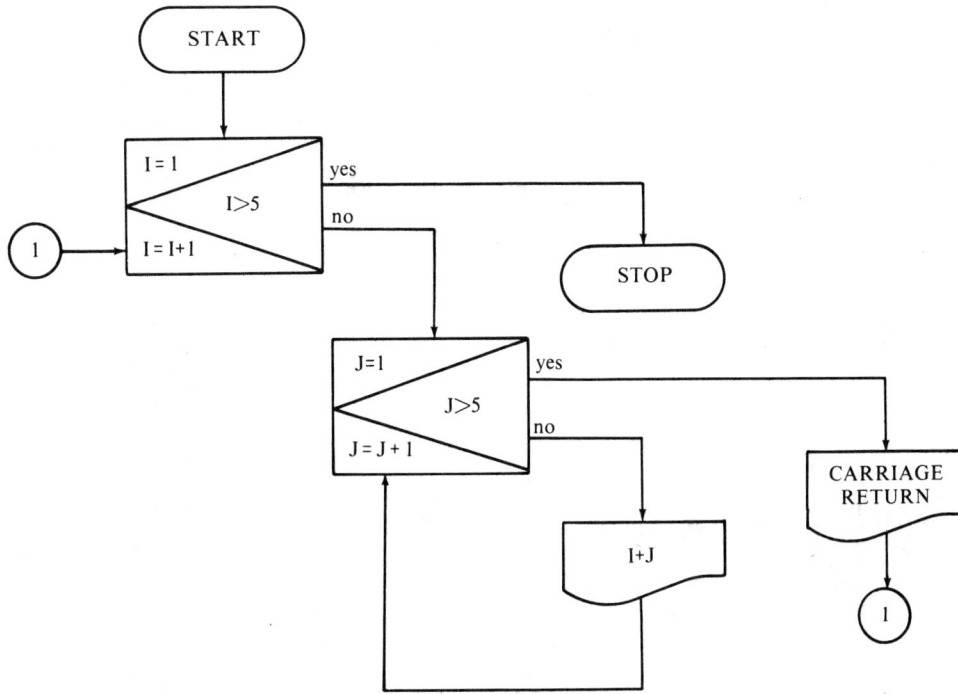

The Program

```
100 REM I DENOTES A ROW; J A COLUMN
110 FOR I=1 TO 5
120     REM THE J LOOP PRINTS THE ITH ROW
130     FOR J=1 TO 5
140         PRINT I+J;
150     NEXT J
160     PRINT
170 NEXT I
180 END
RUN

   2  3  4  5  6
   3  4  5  6  7
   4  5  6  7  8
   5  6  7  8  9
   6  7  8  9 10
READY
```

EXAMPLE 9. A program to print an array of asterisks with 5 rows and 12 columns.

```
10 FOR I=1 TO 5
20    FOR J=1 TO 12
30       PRINT "*";
40    NEXT J
50    PRINT
60 NEXT I
70 END
RUN

************
************
************
************
************
READY
```

After lines 20–40 (the J loop) print a row of 12 asterisks, line 50 causes the print mechanism to return to the left margin so that the next line can be printed.

EXAMPLE 10. A program to print five rows of asterisks, one in the first row, two in the second, and so on.

```
10 FOR I=1 TO 5
20    FOR J=1 TO I              (Observe the use of I in this line.)
30       PRINT "*";
40    NEXT J
50    PRINT
60 NEXT I
70 END
RUN

*
**
***
****
*****
READY
```

To center this design on the page, you should use the TAB function. For example, to cause the printing of each row to begin in column position 20, simply replace the PRINT instruction in line 30 with

PRINT TAB(19+J);"*";

Nested FOR/NEXT loops are especially useful when tables must be prepared in which the rows and columns each correspond to equally spaced data values. We conclude this chapter with an example illustrating one such application of nested loops.

EXAMPLE 11. Prepare a table showing the possible raises for salaried employees whose salaries are $10000,

$11000, $12000, ..., $17000. A raise is to consist of a flat across-the-board increase of I dollars and a percentage increase of either 1%, 2%, 3%, or 4%.

Problem Analysis: Let's agree on the following variable names.

S = Present salary ($10000, $11000, ..., $17000).
I = Flat across-the-board increase (to be input).
P = Percentage increase (1%, 2%, 3%, 4%).
R = Amount of the raise for a given S, I, and P.

The formula governing this situation is

R = (P/100)*S+I

For each salary S, we must display four possible raises R, one for each of the indicated percentages P. Thus, a five-column table is appropriate, the first showing the present salary S and the other four showing the four possible raises. The following program segment can be used to print these values.

```
FOR S=10000 TO 17000 STEP 1000
    PRINT S,
    FOR P=1 TO 4
        LET R=(P/100)*S+I
        PRINT R,
    NEXT P
NEXT S
```

All that remains is to include an INPUT statement, so that a value can be typed for I, and the PRINT statements needed to print a title for the table and appropriate column headings.

The Program

```
100 PRINT "                    SALARY INCREASE SCHEDULE"
110 PRINT
120 PRINT "ACROSS THE BOARD INCREASE";
130 INPUT I
140 PRINT
150 PRINT "SALARY              -----ADDITIONAL PERCENTAGE INCREASE-----"
160 PRINT TAB(14);"1 PERCENT"; TAB(29);"2 PERCENT";
170 PRINT TAB(44);"3 PERCENT"; TAB(59);"4 PERCENT"
180 PRINT
190 FOR S=10000 TO 17000 STEP 1000
200     PRINT S,
210     FOR P=1 TO 4
220         LET R=(P/100)*S+I
230         PRINT R,
240     NEXT P
250 NEXT S
260 END
RUN
```

SALARY INCREASE SCHEDULE

ACROSS THE BOARD INCREASE ? 550

SALARY	-----ADDITIONAL PERCENTAGE INCREASE-----			
	1 PERCENT	2 PERCENT	3 PERCENT	4 PERCENT
10000	650.	750.	850.	950.
11000	660.	770.	880.	990.
12000	670.	790.	910.	1030.
13000	680.	810.	940.	1070.
14000	690.	830.	970.	1110.
15000	700.	850.	1000.	1150.
16000	710.	870.	1030.	1190.
17000	720.	890.	1060.	1230.

READY

8.5   PROBLEMS

1. What will be printed when each program is run?

a.
```
10 FOR I=1 TO 3
20     FOR J=2 TO 3
30         PRINT J
40     NEXT J
50 NEXT I
60 END
```

b.
```
10 FOR J=9 TO 7 STEP -2
20     FOR K=4 TO 9 STEP 3
30         PRINT J+K;
40     NEXT K
50 NEXT J
60 END
```

c.
```
10 FOR X=1 TO 3
20     FOR Y=1 TO 5
30         PRINT X;
40     NEXT Y
50     PRINT
60 NEXT X
70 END
```

d.
```
10 FOR X=1 TO 4
20     FOR Y=X+1 TO 5
30         PRINT Y;
40     NEXT Y
50     PRINT
60 NEXT X
70 END
```

e.
```
10 LET X=0
20 FOR P=1 TO 6
30     FOR Q=2 TO 7
40         FOR R=2 TO 4
50             LET X=X+1
60         NEXT R
70     NEXT Q
80 NEXT P
90 PRINT X
99 END
```

f.
```
10 FOR I=0 TO 6
20     FOR J=0 TO 6
30         IF I=J THEN 70
40         IF I+J=6 THEN 70
50         PRINT " ";
60         GO TO 80
70         PRINT "*";
80     NEXT J
90     PRINT
95 NEXT I
99 END
```

2. Each of the following programs contains an error—either a syntax error that will cause an error message to be printed or a programming error that the computer will not recognize but that will cause incorrect results. In each case, find the error and tell which of the two types it is.

a.
```
10 REM PRINT PRODUCTS
20 FOR I=1 TO 3
30 FOR J=2 TO 4
40 PRINT I;"TIMES";J;"=";I*J
50 NEXT I
60 NEXT J
70 END
```

b.
```
10 REM PRINT SUMS
20 FOR A=3 TO 1
30 FOR B=4 TO 1
40 PRINT A;"PLUS";B;"=";A+B
50 NEXT B
60 NEXT A
70 END
```

c. A program to print:

```
1  2
1  3
1  4
2  3
2  4
3  4
```

```
10 FOR I=1 TO 4
20 FOR J=2 TO 4
30 IF I=J THEN 50
40 PRINT I;J
50 NEXT J
60 NEXT I
70 END
```

d. A program to print:

```
XXXXX
 XXXX
  XXX
   XX
    X
```

```
10 FOR R=1 TO 5
20 FOR C=1 TO 5
30 IF R>=C THEN 60
40 PRINT " ";
50 GO TO 70
60 PRINT "X";
70 NEXT C
80 PRINT
90 NEXT R
99 END
```

3. Produce the following designs. Each time a PRINT statement is executed, no more than one character should be printed. (Do not use the TAB function.)

a.
```
1
2 2
3 3 3
4 4 4 4
5 5 5 5 5
```

b.
```
5 5 5 5 5
  4 4 4 4
    3 3 3
      2 2
        1
```

c.
```
    *   *
    *   *
* * * * * * *
    *   *
* * * * * * *
    *   *
    *   *
```

d.
```
********
********
  ***
  ***
  ***
  ***
  ***
  ***
```

Write a program to perform each task specified in Problems 4–7.

4. Produce a tax-rate schedule showing the 4%, 5%, 6%, and 7% tax on the dollar amounts $1, $2, $3, . . . , $25.

5. Prepare a table showing the interest earned on a $100 deposit for the rates .05 to .08 in increments of .01 and for times 1, 2, . . . , 8 years. Interest is compounded annually ($I = P(1 + R)^N - P$).

6. Prepare the table for Problem 5 except that rates are to be in increments of .005 instead of .01. (The TAB function is necessary.)

7. Present the information required in Problem 6 by producing seven short tables, one for each interest rate specified. Each of these tables should be labeled, as should the information contained in the tables. (No TAB function is required.)

8.6 REVIEW TRUE OR FALSE QUIZ

1. If a group of instructions is to be executed several times in a program, it is always a good practice to use a FOR/NEXT loop.   T   F
2. In any one program the number of FOR statements and the number of NEXT statements must be equal.   T   F
3. The IF statement often provides a convenient way to transfer control out of a FOR/NEXT loop.   T   F
4. If a loop begins with the instruction FOR I=1 TO 35, the variable I must occur in some statement before the NEXT I statement is encountered.   T   F
5. If an exit is made from a loop via an IF statement in the body of the loop, the current value of the control variable will be retained.   T   F
6. If an exit is made from a loop via the NEXT statement, the value of the control variable will be reset to zero.   T   F
7. The instruction FOR J=X TO 10 STEP 3 is valid even though X may have a value that is not an integer.   T   F
8. In the statement FOR N=15 TO 200 STEP C, C must be a positive integer.   T   F
9. The initial, terminal, and step values in a FOR/NEXT loop cannot be modified in the body of the loop.   T   F
10. The control variable in a FOR/NEXT loop can be modified in the body of the loop; moreover, doing so represents a good programming practice.   T   F
11. The control variable of a loop containing a loop may be used as the initial, terminal, or step value of the inner loop.   T   F

9 ARRAYS

If we wish to examine all numbers in a data list to determine counts of those less than 50 and those greater than 50, and then to perform some calculation on these counts, two variable names must be used to store the two counts. If more than two counts are involved, more than two variables must be used. This situation poses a real problem when only the simple BASIC variables considered to this point are available. Imagine the complexity of a program using as many as 100 different simple variables. To be useful, a programming language must provide the means for handling such problems efficiently. BASIC meets this requirement with the inclusion of **subscripted variables.** These variables may be referenced simply by specifying their numerical subscripts. They not only resolve the difficulty cited but also greatly simplify numerous programming tasks involving large quantities of data. In this chapter the BASIC subscripted variables will be described and illustrated.

9.1 ONE-DIMENSIONAL ARRAYS

A **one-dimensional array,** or **list,** is an ordered collection of items in the sense that there is a first item, a second item, and so on. For example, if you have taken five quizzes during a semester and received grades of 71, 83, 96, 77, and 92, you have a list in which the first grade is 71, the second grade is 83, and so forth. In mathematics we might use the following subscripted notation.

$$g_1 = 71$$
$$g_2 = 83$$
$$g_3 = 96$$
$$g_4 = 77$$
$$g_5 = 92$$

However, since the BASIC character set does not include subscripts, the notation is changed.

$$G(1) = 71$$
$$G(2) = 83$$
$$G(3) = 96$$
$$G(4) = 77$$
$$G(5) = 92$$

We say that the *name* of the list is G, that G(1), G(2), G(3), G(4), and G(5) are *subscripted* variables, and that 1, 2, 3, 4, and 5 are the *subscripts* of G. G(1) is read **G sub 1,** and in general G(I) is read **G sub I.** G(1), G1, and G are all different variables and can be used in the same program; the computer has no problem distinguishing among them, even though people often do.

EXAMPLE 1. A loop to assign values to G(1), G(2), G(3), G(4), and G(5).

```
100 FOR I=1 TO 5
110    READ G(I)
120 NEXT I
130 DATA 71,83,96,77,92
```

On each pass through the loop, the index I of the loop serves as the subscript. The first time through the loop, I has the value 1; hence the instruction in line 110 assigns the value 71 to G(1). Similarly, G(2) through G(5) are assigned their respective values during the remaining four passes through the loop.

Subscripted variables are treated the same as simple variables. They may be assigned values by LET and INPUT statements, as well as by the READ statement. For example, the loop

```
FOR I=1 TO 5
    INPUT G (I)
NEXT I
```

can be used to input values for G(1) through G(5) during program execution.

Values assigned to subscripted variables are retained until changed in another programming line, just as for simple variables.

EXAMPLE 2.

```
100 FOR I=1 TO 5
110    READ G(I)
120 NEXT I
130 PRINT G(1),G(3)
140 LET G(3)=G(5)
150 PRINT G(2),G(3)
160 DATA 71,83,96,77,92
170 END
RUN

71              96
83              92
READY
```

Lines 130, 140, and 150 show that a subscript may be a BASIC constant as well as a variable.

Remark: Lists must have names. Any single letter may be used for this purpose (G was used in this example). Many systems allow a letter followed by a single digit, but this practice is not recommended. Notations such as Q7(7) and A5(3) can be confusing.

The subscript that appears within the parentheses to indicate the position in a list may be any BASIC numerical expression. Thus, the following are all admissible.

A(7)	X(I+1)
B(7+3/2)	Z(100-N)

When the computer encounters a subscript, the subscript is evaluated; if it is not an integer, it is rounded to the nearest integer (some systems truncate instead of rounding off). The smallest subscript allowed on your system will be either 0 or 1. In this text we will assume that it is 1 so that the programs presented will perform as indicated on all systems. If the computer encounters a subscript smaller than the smallest subscript allowed, an error diagnostic will be printed and the program run will terminate. The largest subscripts allowed will be discussed in the next section. For now, assume the top limit to be 10.

EXAMPLE 3. The appearance of the same list name (G in the following program) in two FOR/NEXT loops, each of which uses a different indexing variable name (I and J in the program), causes some difficulty for the beginning programmer.

```
10 FOR I=1 TO 5
20    READ G(I)
30 NEXT I
40 FOR J=1 TO 5
50    LET B(J)=G(6-J)
60 NEXT J
70 DATA 71,83,96,77,92
80 END
```

The first loop (the I loop) assigns the five data values to G(1), ..., G(5) as before. The second loop (the J loop) then creates a new list B with the values B(1) = 92, B(2) = 77, B(3) = 96, B(4) = 83, and B(5) = 71. Note that this program reads a list of five numbers from DATA lines and then stores these same five numbers in a second list B, but in the reverse order.

Remark 1: Modifying lists to create new lists is a common programming task. In this example the terms in list G were rearranged to create a second list B.

Remark 2: Although it is common practice to refer to the symbols G(I) and B(J) as variables, remember that the actual variable names are G(1), G(2), G(3), ..., B(3), B(4), and B(5). Each time lines 20 and 50 are executed, I and J have particular values indicating which of these ten variables is being referenced.

9.2   THE **DIM** STATEMENT

Whenever a subscripted variable—say Z(1)—appears in a program, ten memory locations (11 if zero subscripts are allowed) are automatically reserved for the list Z. These locations are used to store values for Z(1), Z(2), ..., Z(10). If subscripts larger than 10 are needed, you must see to it that more space is reserved in memory. This is accomplished with the DIM statement, which is illustrated as follows.

EXAMPLE 4. A program segment to read values for the N variables B(1), B(2), ..., B(N).

```
100 DIM B(35)
110 INPUT N
120 FOR I=1 TO N
130    READ B(I)
140 NEXT I
```

Line 100 reserves 35 memory locations for the list B. If 35 is input for N at line 110, the FOR/NEXT loop will read values from DATA lines for B(1), B(2), ..., B(35). If 20 is input for N, the FOR/NEXT loop will assign values only to the variables B(1), B(2), ..., B(20); the remaining variables, B(21), ..., B(35), although available, are simply not used. However, if a value larger than 35 is input for N, the attempt to read a value for B(36) will cause an error message to be printed, indicating that a subscript is out of range, and the program run will terminate.

The DIM statement is also called the **dimension statement,** because it determines the dimension (that is, the length) of a list. When a program contains a DIM statement—for example, DIM B(35)—we say that the list B has been **dimensioned.**

More than one DIM statement may appear in a program, and each DIM statement may be used to dimension more than one list. The programming line

5 DIM A(100), X(50), Z(5)

is acceptable and will reserve 155 memory locations: 100 for the list A, 50 for the list X, and 5 for the list

Z. Specifying dimensions smaller than 10 is not necessary but may be useful when space is at a premium.*

The general form of the DIM statement, as it applies to lists, is

ln DIM a(e), b(f), ..., c(g)

where **a, b, c** denote single letters (names of lists) and **e, f, g** are positive-integer constants. DIM statements must appear before any reference is made to the lists being dimensioned. The customary practice (and a good one at that) is to place all DIM statements near the beginning of a program. If a DIM statement is encountered during program execution, control simply passes to the next line.

EXAMPLE 5. A list of integers, all between 1 and 100, is contained in DATA lines. Let's write a program to determine how many of each integer are included. We assume that 9999 terminates the list.

Problem Analysis: We must determine 100 counts: the number of 1s, the number of 2s, and so on. Let's use $C(1), C(2), ..., C(100)$ to store these counts. Now, each value appearing in the DATA lines must be read to determine which of the 100 integers it is. If it is 87, then $C(87)$ must be increased by 1; if it is 24, then $C(24)$ must be increased by 1. Using X to denote the value being read, we may write the following procedure.

   a. Initialize: $C(I) = 0$ for $I = 1$ to 100.
   b. Read a value for X.
   c. If X = 9999, print the results and stop.
   d. Add 1 to $C(X)$ and go to step (b).

Let's conserve paper by printing two columns, containing I and $C(I)$, but suppressing the printout whenever $C(I) = 0$ (that is, if I is not in the given list).

The Flowchart (shown on page 109)

The Program

```
100 REM INITIALIZE COUNTERS
110 DIM C(100)
120 FOR I=1 TO 100
130    LET C(I)=0
140 NEXT I
150 REM PRINT COLUMN HEADINGS
160 PRINT "DATA VALUE","FREQUENCY"
170 PRINT
180 REM READ X AND ADD 1 TO C(X) UNTIL
190 REM THE EOD TAG 9999 IS READ
200 READ X
210 IF X=9999 THEN 240
220 LET C(X)=C(X)+1
230 GO TO 200
240 REM PRINT THE TABLE VALUES
250 FOR I=1 TO 100
260    IF C(I)=0 THEN 280
270    PRINT I,C(I)
280 NEXT I
500 DATA 80.80,80,80,80,60,60,50
510 DATA 50,50,45,45,50,50,50,32
```

*Some systems require you to dimension all subscripted variables, and some do not require you to dimension any. Experiment!

```
998 DATA 9999
999 END
RUN
```

DATA VALUE   FREQUENCY

32	1
45	2
50	6
60	2
80	5

READY

The Flowchart

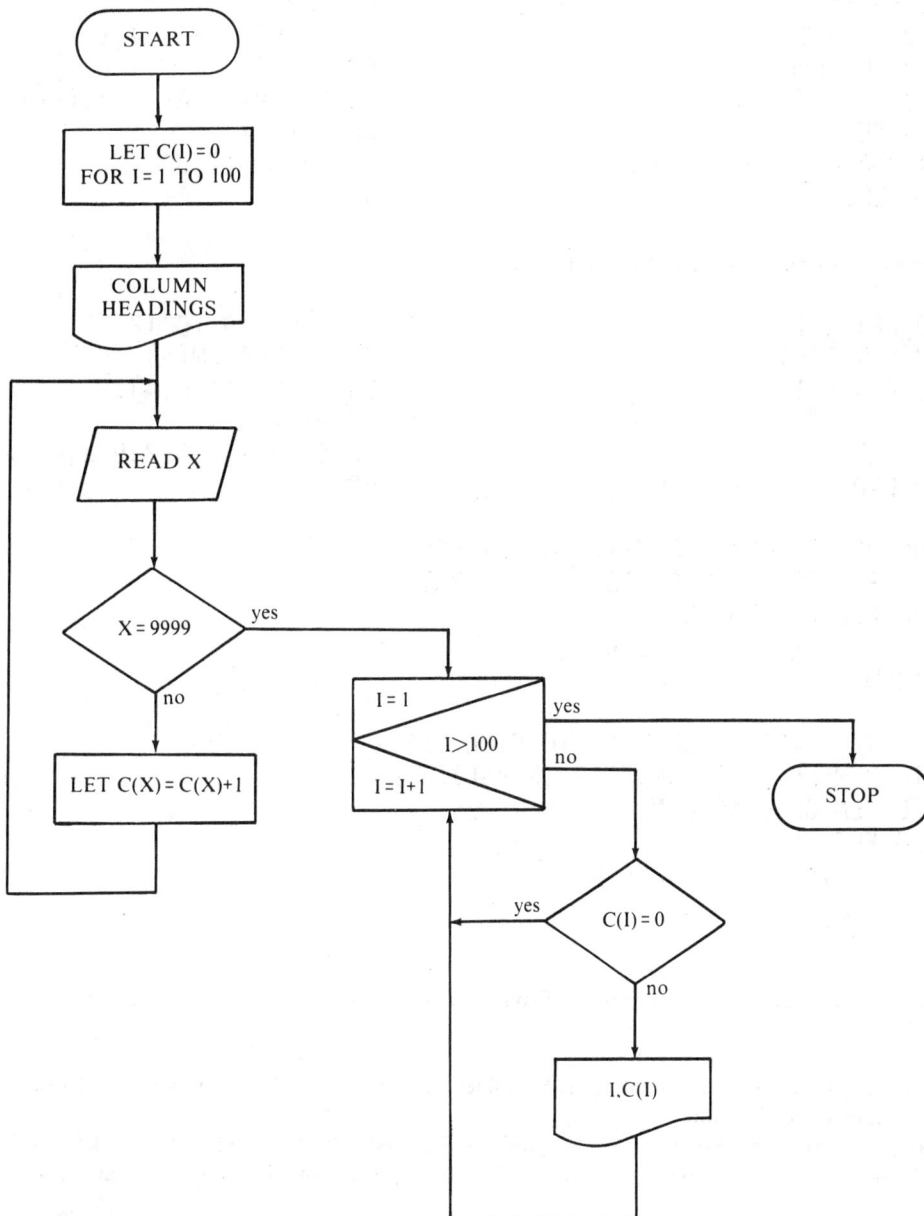

9.3   PROBLEMS

1. What will be printed when each program is run?

a.
```
10 LET I=2
20 READ X(I),X(1)
30 FOR I=1 TO 2
40    PRINT X(I)
50 NEXT I
60 DATA 4,5,7,3
70 END
```

b.
```
10 LET J=1
20 READ X(J)
30 FOR I=1 TO 3
40    READ X(I+1)
50    PRINT X(I);
60 NEXT I
70 DATA 3,1,5,6,8
80 END
```

c.
```
110 READ J
120 FOR J=5 TO 7
130    READ M(J)
140 NEXT J
150 READ B,C
160 FOR K=B TO C
170    PRINT M(K);
180 NEXT K
190 DATA 2,9,8,4,6,6,3
200 END
```

d.
```
10 FOR I=1 TO 3
20    READ A(I)
30 NEXT I
40 FOR I=1 TO 2
50    LET A(I)=A(I+1)
60    LET A(I+1)=A(I)
70    PRINT A(I),A(I+1)
80 NEXT I
90 DATA 7,8,3
99 END
```

2. Explain what is wrong with each of the following.

a.
```
10 LET N=12
20 DIM A(N)
30 FOR I=1 TO N
40    LET A(I)=I
50 NEXT I
60 END
```

b.
```
10 FOR A=9 TO 12
20    READ M(A)
30    PRINT M(A);
40 NEXT A
50 DATA 7,3,5,2,9,1,-3,-2
60 END
```

c.
```
300 REM PROGRAM SEGMENT TO REVERSE THE
310 REM ORDER IN A LIST L OF LENGTH 10
320 FOR K=1 TO 10
330    LET L(11-K)=L(K)
340 NEXT K
```

d.
```
400 REM PROGRAM SEGMENT TO FIND THE
410 REM LARGEST NUMBER S IN A LIST L
420 REM OF LENGTH N
430 FOR J=1 TO N
440    IF S>L(J) THEN 460
450    LET L(J)=S
460 NEXT J
```

Write a program to perform each task specified in Problems 3–12. The RESTORE statement is not to be used in any of these problems.

3. Read a list A of undetermined length from DATA lines, and print the values in reverse order. Use the EOD tag 9999 to terminate the data list.

4. Five data values are to be read into a list B as follows. The first value is to be assigned to B(1) and B(10), the second to B(2) and B(9), and so on. The list B is then to be printed, and five more values are to be read in the

same manner. This process is to continue until all data values have been processed. Your program is to come to an orderly halt.

5. Ten values are to be read into a list Y. Then a new list X containing 20 values is to be created so that the odd-numbered entries in X contain zeros and the even-numbered entries are the entries of Y in the same order. Print both lists. Do not assume that your BASIC system initializes all variables to zero.

6. Read 20 values into a list A, and print three columns as follows. Column 1 contains the list in the original order; column 2 contains the list in reverse order; column 3 contains the average of the corresponding elements in columns 1 and 2.

7. The following DATA lines show the annual salaries of all the employees in Division 72 of the Manley Corporation. The last value (72) is an EOD tag.

```
500 DATA 14000, 16200, 10195, 18432, 13360
510 DATA 19300, 16450, 12180, 25640,  8420
520 DATA  8900,  9270,  9620,  9940, 11200
530 DATA 72
```

Calculate and print the average salary of all employees in Division 72, and then print a list of those salaries exceeding this average.

8. Read the salary data shown in Problem 7 into a list S. Then create a new list T as follows. T(I) is to be obtained by subtracting S(I) from the average of all the salaries. The lists S and T are then to be printed as a two-column table with appropriate column headings.

9. Use the salary data shown in Problem 7 to create two lists as follows. A is to contain all salaries less than $14,000, and B is to contain the rest. Lists A and B are then to be printed as columns with appropriate column headings.

10. The mean M and standard deviation D of a set of numbers contained in data lines are desired. The following method should be used to compute D. If the numbers are $x_1, x_2, x_3, \ldots, x_n$, then $D = \sqrt{S1/(n-1)}$, where

$$S1 = (x_1 - M)^2 + (x_2 - M)^2 + \cdots + (x_n - M)^2.$$

11. A number of scores, each lying in the range from 0 to 100, are given in a collection of DATA lines. These scores are to be used to create a list C as follows.

C(1) = a count of those scores S satisfying $S \leq 20$
C(2) = a count of those scores S satisfying $20 < S \leq 40$
C(3) = a count of those scores S satisfying $40 < S \leq 60$
C(4) = a count of those scores S satisfying $60 < S \leq 80$
C(5) = a count of those scores S satisfying $80 < S \leq 100$

The results should be printed in tabular form as follows.

INTERVAL	FREQUENCY	
0–20	C(1)	(actually the value of C(1))
20–40	C(2)	
40–60	C(3)	
60–80	C(4)	
80–100	C(5)	

12. Problem 11 asked for a count of the number of scores in each of five equal-length intervals between 0 and 100. Instead of using five intervals, allow a user to type a positive integer N to produce a similar frequency table using N equal-length intervals.

9.4   SORTING

Many programming tasks require *sorting* (arranging) lists according to some specified order. When lists of numbers are involved, this usually means arranging them according to size, from smallest to largest or from largest to smallest. For example, you may be required to produce a salary schedule in which salaries are printed from largest to smallest. When lists of names are involved, we may wish to arrange them in alphabetical order. In this section we will show how lists of numbers can be arranged in ascending or descending order. Lists of strings (for instance, names) will be considered in Chapter 10.

The first sorting algorithm we will describe, called the **bubble sort,** will take any list A(1), A(2), ..., A(N) of numbers and rearrange them so that they are in ascending order—that is, so that

$$A(1) \leq A(2) \leq \cdots \leq A(N).$$

We demonstrate the steps with a short list A containing only four values:

$$4 \quad 3 \quad 5 \quad 1$$

First we compare the values in positions 1 and 2. If they are in the proper order (the first is less than or equal to the second), we leave them alone. If not, we interchange them.

$$\textbf{4} \quad \textbf{3} \quad 5 \quad 1 \qquad \text{becomes} \qquad \textbf{3} \quad \textbf{4} \quad 5 \quad 1.$$

Next we compare the values in positions 2 and 3 in the same manner.

$$3 \quad \textbf{4} \quad \textbf{5} \quad 1 \qquad \text{remains} \qquad 3 \quad \textbf{4} \quad \textbf{5} \quad 1.$$

Then we compare the values in positions 3 and 4.

$$3 \quad 4 \quad \textbf{5} \quad \textbf{1} \qquad \text{becomes} \qquad 3 \quad 4 \quad \textbf{1} \quad \textbf{5}.$$

The effect of these three comparisons was to move the largest value to the last position. This process is now repeated, except that this time the final comparison is omitted because the largest value is already in the last position.

$$3 \quad \textbf{4} \quad \textbf{1} \quad 5 \qquad \text{remains} \qquad 3 \quad \textbf{4} \quad \textbf{1} \quad 5.$$
$$3 \quad \textbf{4} \quad \textbf{1} \quad 5 \qquad \text{becomes} \qquad 3 \quad \textbf{1} \quad \textbf{4} \quad 5.$$

We repeat the process once more, this time noting that the final two comparisons are unnecessary because the correct numbers are already in the last two positions.

$$\textbf{3} \quad \textbf{1} \quad 4 \quad 5 \qquad \text{becomes} \qquad \textbf{1} \quad \textbf{3} \quad 4 \quad 5.$$

The list is now in the proper order.

To summarize, the list A contained four values, and we made the following comparisons.

Compare A(I) with A(I + 1) for I = 1, 2, 3.
Compare A(I) with A(I + 1) for I = 1, 2.
Compare A(I) with A(I + 1) for I = 1.

If the list contained N values instead of 4, the following comparisons would have been made to sort the list.

Compare A(I) with A(I + 1) for I = 1, 2, ..., N – 1.
Compare A(I) with A(I + 1) for I = 1, 2, ..., N – 2.
Compare A(I) with A(I + 1) for I = 1, 2, ..., N – 3.

.
.
.

Compare A(I) with A(I + 1) for I = 1, 2.
Compare A(I) with A (I + 1) for I = 1.

Note that, each time the list is examined, one fewer comparison is made. N – 1 comparisons are made the first time, N – 2 the second, N – 3 the third, and so on. Hence, if J counts the number of times through this list, J will take on the successive values 1 through N – 1, and all necessary comparisons can be accomplished with the nested FOR/NEXT loops.

```
FOR J = 1 TO N – 1
FOR I = 1 TO N – J
         .
         .
         .
NEXT I
NEXT J
```

The actual method of comparison is as follows: if A(I) is greater than A(I + 1), we must interchange them. Using the *temporary* variable T, the three instructions

$$LET\ T = A(I)$$
$$LET\ A(I) = A(I + 1)$$
$$LET\ A(I + 1) = T$$

accomplish this. If A(I) is not greater than A(I + 1), these three lines must be skipped. The flowchart in Figure 9.1 displays the process just described. The corresponding program segment, shown in Figure 9.2, can be used in any program to sort, in ascending order, any list A of N numbers.

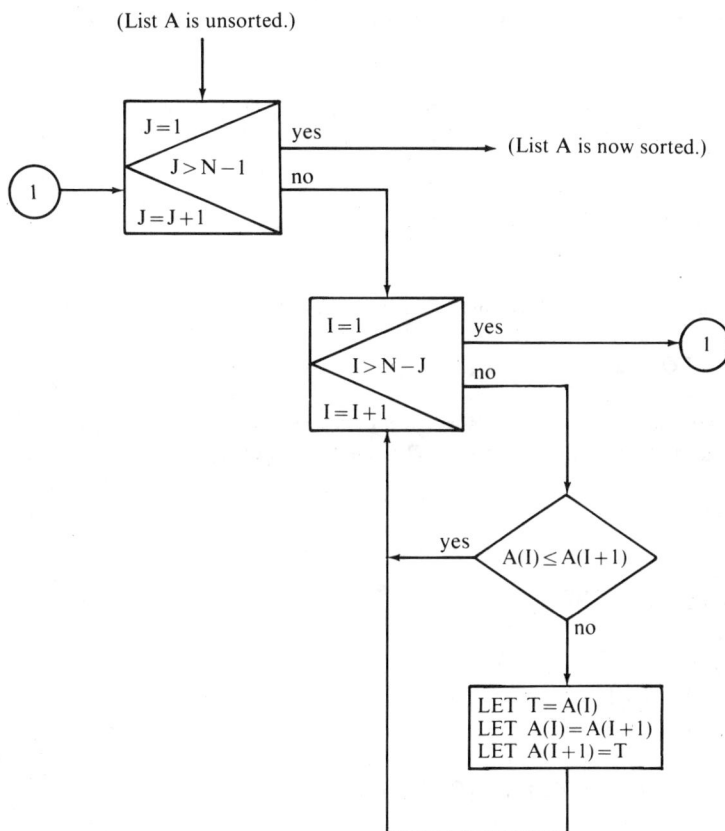

FIGURE 9.1 Flowchart to perform a bubble sort

```
500 REM BUBBLE SORT TO ARRANGE THE N
510 REM TERMS OF LIST A IN ASCENDING ORDER
520 FOR J=1 TO N-1
530    FOR I=1 TO N-J
540       IF A(I)<=A(I+1) THEN 580
550       LET T=A(I)
560       LET A(I)=A(I+1)
570       LET A(I+1)=T
580    NEXT I
590 NEXT J
600 REM LIST A IS SORTED
```

FIGURE 9.2 Program segment to perform a bubble sort

If the comparisons are reversed, with line 540 being changed to

540   IF A(I)>=A(I + 1) THEN 580

the program segment in Figure 9.2 will sort the list in descending rather than ascending order. This accounts for the name *bubble sort*—the smaller or lighter values are "bubbled" to the top.

Many applications requiring lists to be sorted involve more than one list. For example, we may be given lists A and B of length N and asked to sort the list of pairs A(I), B(I) so that $A(1) \leq A(2) \leq \cdots \leq A(N)$. This can be accomplished by modifying the bubble sort so that B(I) and B(I + 1) are interchanged whenever A(I) and A(I + 1) are interchanged. We illustrate with an example.

EXAMPLE 6. Several pairs of numbers are included in DATA lines. The first of each pair is a quality point average (QPA), and the second gives the number of students with this QPA. Write a program to produce a table with the two column headings QPA and FREQUENCY. The frequency counts in the second column are to appear in descending order.

Problem Analysis: Two lists are given in the DATA lines. Let's use Q to denote the list of QPAs and F to denote the frequency counts. The following procedure shows the three subtasks that must be performed.

a. Read lists Q and F.
b. Sort the two lists so that the frequencies appear in descending order.
c. Print the two lists as a two-column table.

To code step (a), we must remember that the lists are presented in DATA lines as pairs of numbers. Thus, we will read values for Q(I) and F(I) for I = 1, 2, and so on, until all pairs have been read. Let's use the dummy pair 0, 0 as an EOD tag.

To code step (b), we will use a bubble sort to sort list F in descending order. However, since a pair Q(I), F(I) must not be separated, we will interchange Q values whenever the corresponding F values are interchanged.

The Program

```
100 REM READ LISTS Q AND F
110 DIM Q(50),F(50)
120 FOR I=1 TO 50
130     READ Q(I),F(I)
140     IF Q(I)=0 THEN 180
150 NEXT I
160 PRINT "I CAN ONLY HANDLE 49 PAIRS"
170 STOP
180 LET N=I-1
190 REM SORT LISTS Q AND F ACCORDING
200 REM TO DECREASING F VALUES
210 FOR J=1 TO N-1
220     FOR I=1 TO N-J
230         IF F(I)>=F(I+1) THEN 300
240         LET T=F(I)
250         LET F(I)=F(I+1)
260         LET F(I+1)=T
270         LET T=Q(I)
280         LET Q(I)=Q(I+1)
290         LET Q(I+1)=T
300     NEXT I
310 NEXT J
320 REM PRINT COLUMN HEADINGS AND TABLE VALUES
330 PRINT "QPA","FREQUENCY"
340 PRINT
```

```
350 FOR I=1 TO N
360    PRINT Q(I),F(I)
370 NEXT I
500 DATA 4.00,  2,3.75, 16,3.40, 41,3.20,38,3.00,92
510 DATA 2.75,162,2.30,352,2.00,280,1.70,81,1.50,27
998 DATA 0,0
999 END
RUN

QPA          FREQUENCY

 2.3         352
 2.          280
 2.75        162
 3.           92
 1.7          81
 3.4          41
 3.2          38
 1.5          27
 3.75         16
 4.            2
READY
```

Lines 270–290 were inserted in the bubble sort to interchange Q values whenever the corresponding F values were interchanged.

Remark: Notice that a FOR/NEXT loop (lines 120–150) is used to read the data values even though the number of values to be read is unknown (an EOD tag terminates the data list). Since Q and F were dimensioned to have length 50, there is no point in attempting to read more than 50 pairs with line 130. If a user includes too many pairs in the DATA lines, line 160 will print the message "I CAN ONLY HANDLE 49 PAIRS" and the user will know what went wrong.

The bubble sort is not a very efficient sorting algorithm. However, it is one of the easiest to understand, to remember, and to code. For this reason beginners, and also many experienced programmers, tend to use it exclusively. This is fine for lists that are not excessively long or for programs that will see only limited use.

Much attention has been given to the problem of sorting, and many sorting algorithms have been developed. The reasons for this activity go deeper than the need to produce well-formated output documents with values printed according to some particular order. A frequently occurrring task is that of searching a list A(1), A(2), ..., A(N) for some specified value V. If the list is not arranged in a known order, the best we can do is to compare V with A(1), then with A(2), and so on, until V is found or until the entire list has been examined. This is called a **sequential search** and is easily coded as follows.

```
500 FOR I=1 TO N
510    IF V=A(I) THEN 550
520 NEXT I
530 PRINT V;"NOT FOUND"
540 STOP
550 PRINT V;"HAS THE INDEX";I
```

If a long list A is to be searched for many different values V (this is the usual situation, in practice), such a sequential search proves to be extremely wasteful of computer time. However, if the list A is sorted (say, in ascending order), a much more efficient search can be made for V. Principally, it is this need for a fast searching algorithm that prompted all the attention given to sorting algorithms.

Figures 9.3 and 9.4 show two very efficient algorithms you may wish to use. The first is a fast sorting algorithm known as the **Shellsort,** * and the second is a most efficient search algorithm called the **Binary Search.** They are presented here as alternatives to the bubble sort and the sequential search, should you have a need for them.†

```
500 REM SHELLSORT TO SORT LIST A WITH N TERMS
510 REM IN ASCENDING ORDER
520 LET S=N
530 LET S=INT(S/2)
540 IF S<1 THEN 670
550 FOR K=1 TO S
560     FOR I=K TO N-S STEP S
570         LET J=I
580         LET T=A(I+S)
590         IF T>=A(J) THEN 630
600         LET A(J+S)=A(J)
610         LET J=J-S
620         IF J>=1 THEN 590
630         LET A(J+S)=T
640     NEXT I
650 NEXT K
660 GO TO 530
670 REM LIST A IS NOW SORTED
```

FIGURE 9.3   Program segment to perform a Shellsort

```
700 REM BINARY SEARCH TO SEARCH LIST A
710 REM OF LENGTH N FOR V.  M IS SET EQUAL
720 REM TO THE INDEX I FOR WHICH A(I)=V.
730 REM M=0 MEANS V WAS NOT FOUND.
740 LET L=1
750 LET R=N
760 LET M=INT((L+R)/2)
770 IF V=A(M) THEN 840
780 IF V<A(M) THEN 810
790 LET L=M+1
800 GO TO 820
810 LET R=M-1
820 IF L<=R THEN 760
830 LET M=0
840 REM SEARCH IS COMPLETE
```

FIGURE 9.4   Program segment to perform a Binary Search

9.5   PROBLEMS

Write a program to perform each task specified in Problems 1–12.

1. Any list of numbers typed at the terminal is to be printed in ascending order. The value 9999, when typed, is to indicate that the entire list has been entered. (Use the bubblesort algorithm.)

*"A High-Speed Sorting Procedure," by Donald L. Shell, *Communications of the ACM,* Vol. 2, July 1959, pp. 30–32.
†A detailed explanation of how and why the two algorithms work may be found in our text *BASIC: An Introduction to Computer Programming* (Monterey, Calif.: Brooks/Cole, 1978).

2. Perform the task described in Problem 1 by the following method. First, input the values into a list A. Then, create a second list B as follows. Find the smallest entry in A, assign it to B(1), and replace this smallest entry of A by a very large number—say, 1E20. Next, find the smallest entry in the modified list A, assign it to B(2), and replace this smallest entry of A by the same large number 1E20. Continue this process until all entries in A have been placed in list B. Finally, print list B; it contains the values typed in ascending order. (Note that the order in which the values were typed is lost; all entries of A are now 1E20.)

3. A list of numbers is to be typed at the terminal to obtain a two-column printout with the column headings TYPED LIST and SORTED LIST. The first column is to contain the list values in the order typed, and the second column is to contain the same values printed from largest to smallest. Use the following algorithm.

   a. Input the list values into identical lists A and B.
   b. Sort list A into descending order (bubblesort).
   c. Print the table as described.

4. Produce a two-column table with the column headings DATA LIST and SORTED DATA LIST. The first column is to contain the data in the order given in DATA lines, and the second column is to contain the same values printed in descending order. Use the following algorithm.

   a. Read list L.
   b. Sort list L into descending order.
   c. Print the column headings.
   d. Read the data list again to print the table values.

   Try your program using the following DATA lines.

       500 DATA 80, 70, 40, 90, 95, 38, 85, 42, 60, 70
       510 DATA 40, 60, 70, 20, 18, 87, 23, 78, 85, 23
       998 DATA 9999

5. Use the following algorithm to perform the task described in Problem 4.

   a. Read the data list into two identical lists A and B.
   b. Sort list B into descending order.
   c. Produce the desired printout.

6. Several numbers, ranging from 0 to 100, are to be typed at the terminal and stored in two lists A and B. A is to contain those numbers that are less than 50, and the others are to be stored in list B. Lists A and B are then to be sorted in descending order and printed side by side with the column headings LESS THAN 50 and 50 OR MORE.

7. Read a list L and sort it in ascending order. Then create a new list M containing the same values as L but with no repetitions. For example, if L(1) = 7, L(2) = L(3) = 8 and L(4) = L(5) = L(6) = 9, then the list M is to have M(1) = 7, M(2) = 8, and M(3) = 9. Print both lists. Run your program using the DATA lines shown in Problem 4.

8. Read a list L and sort it in ascending order. Then modify L by deleting all values appearing more than once. For example, if L(1) = 7, L(2) = L(3) = 8, and L(4) = L(5) = L(6) = 9, then the new list is to have L(1) = 7, L(2) = 8, and L(3) = 9. Run your program using the DATA lines shown in Problem 4.

9. A study of the Tidy Corporation's annual reports for the years 1970–1978 yielded the following statistics.

Year	Gross Sales (in Thousands)	Earnings per Share
1970	19,500	.27
1971	18,350	−.40
1972	18,400	−.12
1973	18,000	−.84
1974	18,900	.65
1975	20,350	.78
1976	24,850	1.05
1977	24,300	.68
1978	27,250	.88

Include the second and third columns of this table in DATA lines for a program to print two columns with the same headings as those shown. However, the Earnings-per-Share figures are to appear in ascending order. (Use the method described in Example 6.)

10. Include all three columns given for the Tidy Corporation (Problem 9) in DATA lines for a program to produce a three-column table with the same headings. However, the Gross-Sales figures are to appear in descending order.

11. N pairs of numbers are to be read from DATA lines so that the first of each pair is in list A and the second in list B. Sort the pairs A(I), B(I) so that $A(1) \leq A(2) \leq \cdots \leq A(N)$ and also so that $B(I) \leq B(I+1)$ wherever $A(I) = A(I+1)$. Print the modified lists in two adjacent columns with the headings LIST A and LIST B.

12. Two lists, whose terms are in ascending order, are given in DATA lines as follows. Each list is terminated with 9999.

$$500 \ DATA \ 3, \ 4, \ 9, \ 16, \ 25, \ 31, \ 37, \ 42, \ 9999$$
$$510 \ DATA \ 2, \ 6, \ 9, \ 13, \ 17, \ 25, \ 29, \ 38, \ 9999$$

The two lists—call them list A and list B—may be *merged* into a single list M, whose terms are also in ascending order, by the following method. First, compare A(1) with B(1) and assign the smaller to M(1). Suppose B(1) is smaller. Then M(1) = B(1), and A(1) is compared with B(2). If this time A(1) is smaller, then M(2) = A(1), and A(2) and B(2) are compared. (If it happens that two values being compared are equal, assign the A entry to list M.) Continue in this manner until all terms in one of the two lists have been stored in M. The remaining terms in the other list are then placed in M as they appear. Before you attempt to write down an algorithm to carry out this task, it may be helpful to use the method to merge the two lists

$$A = 3 \quad 4 \quad 6 \quad 8 \quad 9 \quad 10$$
$$B = 5 \quad 8 \quad 8$$

to obtain

$$M = 3 \quad 4 \quad 5 \quad 6 \quad 8 \quad 8 \quad 8 \quad 9 \quad 10.$$

9.6   TWO-DIMENSIONAL ARRAYS

Data to be processed by the computer are often presented in tabular form. For example, you may wish to write a program to analyze the following data, which summarize the responses of college students to a hypothetical opinion poll concerning the abolition of grades.

	In Favor of Abolishing Grades	Not in Favor of Abolishing Grades	No Opinion
Freshmen	207	93	41
Sophomores	165	110	33
Juniors	93	87	15
Seniors	51	65	8

If you wanted to determine the percentage of sophomores polled who are not in favor of abolishing grades, the entry 110 would be divided by the sum of the entries in the second row. Many such calculations may be desired, and the computer is ideally suited for such tasks. What is needed is a convenient way to present these data to the computer. First, we will introduce some terminology to make it easier to refer to such tables of values.

A **two-dimensional array,** or simply an **array,** is a collection of items arranged in a rectangular fashion. That is, there is a first (horizontal) row, a second row, and so on, and a first (vertical) column, a second column, and so on. Thus, any particular item in an array is specified simply by giving its row number and column number. For example, the item in the third row and second column of the opinion-poll table is 87. By convention, when specifying an item in an array, we give the row number first. Hence, in the opinion-poll table, 33 is in the 2, 3 position and 51 is in the 4, 1 position.

In mathematical notation we could write

$$P_{1,1} = 207, \quad P_{1,2} = 93, \quad \text{and} \quad P_{1,3} = 41$$

to indicate the values in the first row of our table. Since the BASIC character set does not include subscripts, this notation is changed as it was for lists. Thus, the values in the opinion-poll table would be written as follows.

P(1,1) = 207	P(1,2) = 93	P(1,3) = 41
P(2,1) = 165	P(2,2) = 110	P(2,3) = 33
P(3,1) = 93	P(3,2) = 87	P(3,3) = 15
P(4,1) = 51	P(4,2) = 65	P(4,3) = 8

We say that P is the *name* of the array, that P(1,1), P(1,2), . . . are *doubly subscripted* variables, and that the numbers enclosed in parentheses are the *subscripts* of P. The symbol P(I,J) is read "P sub I comma J" or simply "P sub IJ." Since P has 4 rows and 3 columns, it is called a **4-by-3 array** (also written as **4 × 3 array**).

EXAMPLE 7. A program to read the values from the opinion-poll table into an array called P.

Problem Analysis: The variable P(I,J) is to be assigned the value appearing in the Ith row and Jth column of the table. (Recall that we give the row number first and the column number second.) Let's suppose that the 12 numbers are to be included in DATA lines as follows.

```
DATA 207, 93, 41
DATA 165, 110, 33
DATA 93, 87, 15
DATA 51, 65, 8
```

Since READ statements will "read" values in the order in which they appear, the entries of the first row of P must be read first, the second row next, and so on until all values are read. Thus, the variables P(I,J) will be read in the following order of the subscripts.

```
for I = 1
    J = 1   J = 2   J = 3
for I = 2
    J = 1   J = 2   J = 3
for I = 3
    J = 1   J = 2   J = 3
for I = 4
    J = 1   J = 2   J = 3
```

But this is exactly the order specified by the nested FOR/NEXT loops

```
FOR I = 1 TO 4
FOR J = 1 TO 3
    .
    .
    .
NEXT J
NEXT I
```

The Program

```
100 FOR I=1 TO 4
110    REM READ THE ITH ROW.
120    FOR J=1 TO 3
130       READ P(I,J)
140    NEXT J
150 NEXT I
500 DATA 207,93,41
510 DATA 165,110,33
520 DATA 93,87,15
```

```
530 DATA 51,65,8
999 END
```

Remark 1: The data do not have to be given in four lines as was done here. The single line

500 DATA 207, 93, 41, 165, 110, 33, 93, 87, 15, 51, 65, 8

could replace lines 500 through 530. The order in which they appear is all that matters.

Remark 2: The following five lines were used to assign values to P.

```
FOR I=1 TO 4
   FOR J=1 TO 3
      READ P(I,J)
   NEXT J
NEXT I
```

Some BASIC systems allow you to accomplish the same thing with a single statement called a MAT (matrix) statement. (**Matrix** is another name for an array of values.) Proper use of MAT statements can shorten your programs and make them easier to understand. The MAT statements are described in Chapter 14.

EXAMPLE 8. Let's modify the program of Example 7 so that a count is determined of the number of students from each class who participated in the poll.

Problem Analysis: Since all three entries in any one row correspond to students in one of the four classes, our task is to add the three entries in each row. If we let $S(1)$ denote the sum of the entries in the first row, and similarly $S(2)$, $S(3)$, $S(4)$ for the other three rows, we can write the following.

$$S(1) = P(1,1) + P(1,2) + P(1,3)$$
$$S(2) = P(2,1) + P(2,2) + P(2,3)$$
$$S(3) = P(3,1) + P(3,2) + P(3,3)$$
$$S(4) = P(4,1) + P(4,2) + P(4,3)$$

For the first sum we can set $I = 1$ and $J = 1, 2$, and then 3. For the second we can set $I = 2$ and $J = 1, 2$, and 3. Since the order in which the subscripts of P are considered is the same as described in Example 7, the same nested FOR/NEXT loops are applicable to this problem.

Of course, $S(1)$, $S(2)$, $S(3)$, and $S(4)$ should all be initialized to zero. A procedure describing the process follows.

Algorithm

a. Read the array P values (done in Example 7).
b. Let I = 1.
c. Let $S(I) = 0$.
d. Let $S(I) = S(I) + P(I,J)$ for $J = 1, 2, 3$. Then print $S(I)$.
e. Add 1 to I and go to step (c) until I exceeds 4.
f. Stop.

The program is thus obtained by adding the following lines to the program of Example 7.

```
160 FOR I=1 TO 4
170    LET S(I)=0
180    FOR J=1 TO 3
```

```
190        LET S(I)=S(I)+P(I,J)
200     NEXT J
210     PRINT S(I)
220 NEXT I
```

Remark: This program could have been written using only one pair of nested FOR/NEXT loops. Instead of adding the indicated lines 160 through 220 to the program of Example 7, we could have added the following three lines to that program.

```
105 S(I) = 0
135 S(I) = S(I) + P(I,J)
145 PRINT S(I)
```

Although the latter form of this program is shorter, it is not necessarily better. In the first form, each of the two tasks being performed, reading values and counting students, occupies its own part of the program. The program was written this way because the overall task was broken down into two easier tasks. That the resulting program may not be the shortest possible is of little consequence. The longer program obtained by segmenting is easier to read and certainly easier to modify, should that be required.

The variable names that can be used for arrays are the same as those used for lists. However, if a list and an array are both used in the same program, they may not have the same name.

When a subscripted variable such as $B(1,1)$ is used in a program, the largest subscript allowed is 10. However, just as for singly subscripted variables, the DIM statement may be used to specify larger subscripts. For example, if A is to be an array with as many as 50 rows and 20 columns, then the statement

$$DIM\ A(50,20)$$

would be used. Lists and arrays may be dimensioned with the same DIM statement.

$$10\ DIM\ Z(15),\ M(25,30),\ A(20),\ N(100,45)$$

is a proper DIM statement; it reserves 15 locations for list Z, $25 \times 30 = 750$ locations for the array M, 20 locations for list A, and $100 \times 45 = 4500$ locations for the array N.

9.7   PROBLEMS

1. What will be printed when each program is run?

a.
```
100 FOR I=1 TO 4
110     FOR J=1 TO 4
120         LET M(I,J)=I*J
130     NEXT J
140 NEXT I
150 FOR K=1 TO 4
160     PRINT M(K,K);
170 NEXT K
180 END
```

b.
```
100 FOR I=1 TO 3
110     FOR J=1 TO 2
120         READ A(I,J)
130         LET B(J,I)=A(I,J)
140     NEXT J
150 NEXT I
160 PRINT B(2,1);B(2,2);B(2,3)
170 DATA 1,2,3,4,5,6,7,8,9
180 END
```

c.
```
100 FOR K=1 TO 3
110     FOR L=1 TO K
120         READ S(K,L)
130         LET S(L,K)=S(K,L)
```

d.
```
100 DIM M(4,4)
110 FOR I=1 TO 4
120     FOR J=1 TO 4
130         LET M(I,J)=0
```

```
140    NEXT L            140      IF I>J THEN 160
150 NEXT K               150      LET M(I,J)=1
160 FOR N=1 TO 3         160      PRINT M(I,J);
170    PRINT S(N,2);     170   NEXT J
180 NEXT N               180   PRINT
190 DATA 1,1,1,2,2,2,3,3,3  190 NEXT I
200 END                  200 END
```

2. Find and correct the errors in the following program segments. You are to assume that values have already been assigned to the 5-by-5 array A.

a.
```
200 REM PRINT THE SUM S
210 REM OF EACH ROW OF A
220 LET S=0
230 FOR I=1 TO 5
240    FOR J=1 TO 5
250       LET S=S+A(I,J)
260    NEXT J
270    PRINT S
280 NEXT I
```

b.
```
200 REM INTERCHANGE THE ROWS
210 REM AND COLUMNS OF A
220 FOR I=1 TO 5
230    FOR J=1 TO 5
240       LET T=A(I,J)
250       LET A(I,J)=A(J,I)
260       LET A(J,I)=T
270    NEXT J
280 NEXT I
```

Write a program to perform each task specified in Problems 3–14.

3. Values are to be read into an N × N array A. Then the sum of the entries in the upper-left to lower-right diagonal of A is to be printed. This sum is called the *trace* of the array (matrix) A.
4. Read 16 values into the 4 × 4 array M. The array M is then to be printed. In addition, the four column sums are to be printed below their respective columns.
5. Read 16 values into the 4 × 4 array M. Then print the array. Row sums are to be printed to the right of their respective rows and column sums below their respective columns. (Hint: Assign the sum of the entries in row I to M(I,5) and the sum of the entries in column J to M(5,J). Then the entire output can be produced by printing the new 5 × 5 array M.)
6. The *transpose* B of an N × N array A is the N × N array whose rows are the columns of A in the same order. Read the entries of A from DATA lines, and print the transpose B. (You may assume that N will be less than 6.)
7. The *sum* S of two N × N arrays A and B is the N × N array whose entries are the sums of the corresponding entries of A and B. Read A and B from DATA lines, and print the arrays A, B, and S. (You may assume that N will be less than 6.)
8. Repeat Problem 4 for an N × N array M in which N can be any integer up to 10. (Use the TAB function so that columns will line up.)
9. Repeat Problem 5 for an N × N array M in which N can be any number up to 10. (Use the TAB function.)
10. Repeat Problem 6 assuming that N can be as large as 10. (Use the TAB function.)
11. Repeat Problem 7 assuming that N can be as large as 10. (Use the TAB function.)
12. Write a program to read values into a 5 × 7 array B. The computer is then to perform the following tasks.
    a. Create and print a list C whose Ith position contains the average of the 7 elements in the Ith row of B.
    b. Create and print another 5 × 7 array Z whose values are the values of B reduced by the average of all elements in B.
13. Write a program to create the following 5 × 5 array A.

```
 0   1   1   1   1
-1   0   1   1   1
-1  -1   0   1   1
-1  -1  -1   0   1
-1  -1  -1  -1   0
```

The values A(I,J) are to be determined during program execution without using READ or INPUT statements. The array A should be printed as it appears above. (Hint: the value to be assigned to A(I,J) can be determined by comparing I with J.)

14. An N × N array of numbers is called a *magic square* if the sums of each row, each column, and each diagonal are all equal. Write a program to test any N × N array in which N will never exceed 10. Values for N and array values should be read from DATA lines. Be sure to print out and identify all row, column, and diagonal sums, the array itself, and a message indicating whether or not the array is a magic square. Try your program on the following arrays.

a.

11	10	4	23	17
18	12	6	5	24
25	19	13	7	1
2	21	20	14	8
9	3	22	16	15

b.

4	139	161	26	174	147
85	166	107	188	93	12
98	152	138	3	103	157
179	17	84	165	184	22
183	21	13	175	89	170
102	156	148	94	8	143

9.8   REVIEW TRUE OR FALSE QUIZ

1. Dimension statements may appear anywhere in a program as long as they appear before the lists or arrays being dimensioned are used.   T   F

2. If N is assigned the value 25 at line 10, then the programming line 20 DIM A(N) will reserve 25 memory locations for the list A.   T   F

3. If in a list Z the only locations to be used are Z(8), Z(9), Z(10), Z(11), and Z(12), there is no need to dimension Z since only five locations are needed.   T   F

4. Once a list L is assigned values in a program, the instruction PRINT L is sufficient to cause the list to be printed.   T   F

5. The programming line   50 LET A(I + 1) = 7   could never cause an error message to be printed.   T   F

6. If a noninteger subscript is encountered during program execution, an error message will be printed and the program run will terminate.   T   F

7. The statement LET G = 5 may appear in a program that contains the statement DIM G(100).   T   F

8. The expressions *one-dimensional array* and *list* are used synonymously.   T   F

9. Array values may be assigned by LET statements.   T   F

10. Since two-dimensional arrays make use of two subscripts, they must be used in nested loops.   T   F

11. If both one- and two-dimensional arrays are to be used in a program, two DIM statements must be used.   T   F

12. A list must be in ascending order before a sequential search can be made.   T   F

13. The bubble sort is always used to arrange the terms of a list in ascending order.   T   F

14. A FOR / NEXT loop can be used to read values from DATA lines only if a count of how many values are to be read is included.   T   F

The BASIC variables considered thus far are called *numeric* variables, since they may be assigned only values that are numerical constants. BASIC also contains *string* variables, which may be assigned values that are strings. String variables are described and illustrated in this chapter.

10.1 STRING VARIABLES

A **string constant** (or **string**) is a sequence, or string, of BASIC characters enclosed in quotation marks. The following are string constants.

"INCOME"	"NANCY JONES"
"X="	"567"
"19 APRIL 1775"	"*****"

The *value* of a string constant is the sequence of all BASIC characters, including blanks, appearing between the quotes. A string may contain as many characters as will fit on a line.

Variables whose values are string constants are called **string variables.** A string variable is denoted by a single letter followed by a dollar sign: A$, B$, . . . , Z$. (Your system may allow you to use other names in addition to these.) If a string variable appears in a PRINT statement, the string constant previously assigned to this string variable is printed. The following three examples illustrate how string constants can be assigned to string variables using the LET, INPUT, and READ statements.

EXAMPLE 1.

```
10 LET Z$="END"
20 LET Y$="THE"
30 PRINT Y$,Z$
40 LET Y$=Z$
50 PRINT Y$
60 END
RUN

THE             END
END
READY
```

124

Remark: Line 40 replaces the string "THE" with the string "END" in exactly the same manner as the LET statement operates for numerical constants.

EXAMPLE 2.

```
10 LET A$="BILL AND "
20 INPUT B$
30 PRINT A$;B$
40 END
RUN

? "SALLY"                    (Underlined characters are printed by the computer.)
BILL AND SALLY
READY
```

The INPUT statement (line 20) causes a question mark to be printed just as before. Since a string variable (B$) appears in this INPUT statement, a string constant must be typed.

Remark: Had a blank not been included as the last character of the string "BILL AND " (line 10), the output would have been BILL ANDSALLY.

EXAMPLE 3.

```
100 READ A$,B$
110 PRINT B$,A$
120 DATA "FLIES", "TIME"
130 END
RUN

TIME            FLIES
READY
```

Here are some rules governing the assignment of string variables:

1. Only string constants may be assigned to string variables.
2. The maximum length of a string that may be assigned to a string variable varies from system to system. (The proposed ANSI standard specifies 18 as this maximum value.)
3. Quotation marks must be used when a string appears in a LET statement.
4. When strings appear in DATA lines or are typed in response to INPUT statements, the quotation marks are sometimes optional. The rules that apply to such strings may differ among systems. The most common situation is that quotes are required only in the following cases.
   a. Significant blanks begin, terminate, or are embedded in the string. (If such a string is unquoted, the leading, trailing, and embedded blanks are ignored.)
   b. A comma appears in the string. (The comma is used to delimit BASIC constants.)
   c. On some systems, any string beginning with a nonalphabetic character must quoted. (Experiment with your system.)
5. It is always correct to enclose strings in quotation marks.

EXAMPLE 4. Quoted and unquoted strings in DATA lines.

```
100 FOR I=1 TO 5
110    READ Z$
120    PRINT Z$
130 NEXT I
140 DATA VI,"  AL","1234",TO GO,"RICE,JIM"
150 END
RUN

VI
   AL
1234
TOGO
RICE,JIM
READY
```

Quotes are needed for " AL" because of the leading blanks, for "1234" (on some systems) because the first character is nonalphabetic, and for "RICE,JIM" because of the comma.

Numerical and string constants appearing in DATA lines constitute a single data list; no special treatment is given to string constants. The execution of a READ statement will attempt to assign the "next" value in this list to the variable being assigned. If the variable and the data value are not of the same type, an error will result.

EXAMPLE 5.

```
100 READ A$,X,Y
110 READ B$
120 PRINT A$,X,B$,Y
130 DATA AL,7,9,MARY
140 END
RUN

AL              7              MARY              9
READY
```

10.2   STRINGS IN RELATIONAL EXPRESSIONS

Strings may be compared using the IF statement as shown in the following examples.

EXAMPLE 6.

```
10 PRINT "TYPE FINI TO END THIS PROGRAM"
20 INPUT A$
30 IF A$="FINI" THEN 60
40 PRINT A$
50 GO TO 20
60 PRINT "ADIOS"
70 END
RUN

TYPE FINI TO END THIS PROGRAM
? HELLO
```

```
HELLO
? GOODBYE
GOODBYE
? "    FINI"
    FINI
? FINI
ADIOS
READY
```

Remark 1: For two strings to be equal, they must be identical. Thus, "   FINI" is not equal to "FINI", since the first begins with blanks and the second does not.

Remark 2: When strings appear in relational expressions ("FINI" in line 30), quotation marks must be used.

EXAMPLE 7. An agreeable program.

```
10 PRINT "ANSWER YES OR NO"
20 PRINT "DO YOU ENJOY BASIC";
30 INPUT A$
40 IF A$="YES" THEN 70
50 PRINT "I DON'T EITHER."
60 STOP
70 PRINT "SO DO I."
80 END
```

EXAMPLE 8. A program to search a list for any word typed at the terminal. If the word is found, a corresponding message is printed.

```
100 REM---ON MIXING COLORS---
110 PRINT "NAME A COLOR";
120 INPUT C$
130 READ N
140 FOR I=1 TO N
150    READ X$,Y$
160    IF X$=C$ THEN 200
170 NEXT I
180 PRINT C$;" IS NOT IN MY LIST"
190 STOP
200 PRINT Y$
500 DATA 11
510 DATA WHITE,"USED FOR TINTING"
520 DATA BLACK,"USED FOR SHADING"
530 DATA YELLOW,"A PRIMARY COLOR"
540 DATA RED,"A PRIMARY COLOR"
550 DATA BLUE,"A PRIMARY COLOR"
560 DATA ORANGE,"MIX YELLOW AND RED"
570 DATA GREEN,"MIX YELLOW AND BLUE"
580 DATA PURPLE,"MIX RED AND BLUE"
590 DATA PINK,"MIX RED AND WHITE"
600 DATA GRAY,"MIX BLACK AND WHITE"
610 DATA MAGENTA,"MIX RED WITH A SPECK OF BLACK"
999 END
RUN
```

```
NAME A COLOR? MAGENTA
MIX RED WITH A SPECK OF BLACK
READY
```

Remark: Note that the list being searched consists of every other data value. The other values are read (Y\$ in line 150) but are not used unless the corresponding color (X\$ in line 150) is the color (C\$) input at line 120.

Some BASIC systems allow strings to be compared using all six relational operators: $=, <>, <,$ $<=, >,$ and $>=$. The form of a relational expression involving strings is

$$\textbf{a} \quad \textbf{R} \quad \textbf{b}$$

where **a** and **b** denote string constants or string variables and **R** denotes a relational operator.

To understand when one string is less than another string, you should have some knowledge of the method used to store a string in memory. Whenever a program requires the use of a string, each character of the string is assigned a numerical value, called its **numeric code.** It is these numerical values that are compared. As one would expect, the numeric code for the letter A is smaller than that for B, the numeric code for B is smaller than that for C, and so on. But it is not only letters that can be compared; each BASIC character has its own unique numeric code so that any two characters may be compared. One BASIC character is less than a second character if the numeric code of the first is less than the numeric code of the second.

Unfortunately, computer systems differ in their numeric codes. The ordering sequence of the BASIC character set as given by the American Standard Code of Information Interchange (ASCII) is presented in Table 10.1.

TABLE 10.1   ASCII numeric codes for the BASIC character set

Character	Numeric Code	Character	Numeric Code	Character	Numeric Code
(blank)	32	5	53	J	74
!	33	6	54	K	75
"	34	7	55	L	76
#	35	8	56	M	77
$	36	9	57	N	78
%	37	:	58	O	79
&	38	;	59	P	80
'	39	<	60	Q	81
(	40	=	61	R	82
)	41	>	62	S	83
*	42	?	63	T	84
+	43	@	64	U	85
,	44	A	65	V	86
−	45	B	66	W	87
.	46	C	67	X	88
/	47	D	68	Y	89
0	48	E	69	Z	90
1	49	F	70	[	91
2	50	G	71	\	92
3	51	H	72	]	93
4	52	I	73	↑	94

Using these ASCII numeric codes, we can write the following.

$$\text{"G"} < \text{"P"} \text{ since } 71 < 80.$$
$$\text{"4"} < \text{"Y"} \text{ since } 52 < 89.$$
$$\text{"\$"} < \text{"↑"} \text{ since } 36 < 94.$$
$$\text{"8"} < \text{"?"} \text{ since } 56 < 63.$$

If strings containing more than one character are to be compared, they are compared character by character beginning at the left. Strings consisting only of letters of the alphabet are ordered just as they would appear in a dictionary.

EXAMPLE 9. Some relational expressions with their truth values.

Relational Expression	Truth Value
"AMA" > "AM"	True
"XYZW" > "XYZZE"	False
"1234" <= "1234"	True
"13N" > "14A"	False
"M24" <= "M31"	True
"P1" > "M394"	False

EXAMPLE 10. A program to print those words appearing in a data list that begin with the letter "B".

```
100 READ W$
110 IF W$="END OF LIST" THEN 999
120 IF W$<"B" THEN 100
130 IF W$>="C" THEN 100
140 PRINT W$,
150 GO TO 100
500 DATA WHITE,BLACK,YELLOW,RED,BLUE,ORANGE,GREEN,PURPLE
510 DATA PINK,GRAY,MAGENTA,BEIGE,BROWN,VIOLET,LIME,AVACADO
998 DATA "END OF LIST"
999 END
RUN

BLACK           BLUE        BEIGE        BROWN
READY
```

A word from the data list is read into W$ and is immediately compared with the EOD tag "END OF LIST". (We don't want to consider this EOD tag as a member of the list being searched.) If W$<"B"(line 120), control is transferred back to line 100, thus rejecting W$ since its first letter must have been an "A". Similarly, line 130 rejects words beginning with C, D, E, ..., or Z.

10.3 PROBLEMS

1. What will be printed when each program is run?

a.
```
10 LET Z$="JULY "
20 LET Y$="4,17"
30 LET X$="76"
40 PRINT Z$;Y$;X$
50 END
```

b.
```
10 FOR X=2 TO 3
20    READ A,M$,B$
30    PRINT M$;
40 NEXT X
50 DATA 6, CAT, MOUSE
```

```
                                          60 DATA 9,"WOMAN","MAN"
                                          70 END
```

```
c.  10 READ A$,B$,C$            d.  10 FOR I=1 TO 3
    20 RESTORE                      20    READ Z$
    30 READ D$                      30    IF Z$>"ROBERTS" THEN 50
    40 PRINT B$;C$;D$               40    PRINT Z$
    50 DATA HEAD, ROB, IN, HOOD     50 NEXT I
    60 END                         60 DATA ALBERT, ZIP, ROBERT
                                    70 END
```

2. Find and correct the errors.

```
a.  10 LET A$=ABLE              b.  10 READ Y;Z$
    20 LET B$=POT                  20 PRINT Z$;" OF ";Y
    30 PRINT B$;A$                 30 DATA "42",SUMMER
    40 END                         40 END
```

```
c.  10 PRINT "CITY-STATE-ZIP"   d.  10 READ X,X$
    20 FOR I=1 TO 2                20 PRINT X$;X
    30    READ A$                  30 DATA "1";A
    40    PRINT A$;                40 END
    50 NEXT I
    60 DATA LEXINGTON,MA,"02173"
    70 END
```

```
e.  10 READ B$                  f.  10 READ X$,N1
    20 IF B$=HELLO THEN 10         20 IF X$=OFFON THEN 60
    30 PRINT B$                    30 PRINT X$;" CORRESPONDS TO";N1
    40 STOP                        40 GO TO 10
    50 DATA HELLO, GOODBYE         50 DATA OFF,0,ON,1,OFFON
    60 END                         60 END
```

Write programs to perform each task specified in Problems 3–10. Any string comparisons required can be accomplished by using only IF statements that test for equality.

3. A list of numbers appears in DATA lines. The user should be allowed to issue any of the following commands: LIST, to print the list of numbers; SUM, to print the sum of the numbers; AVERAGE, to print the average of the numbers; DONE, to terminate the run. After each command other than DONE is carried out, the user should be allowed to issue another command.

4. Modify the program of Example 8 so that a user can try many colors during a single program run. Arrange things so that the program halts when "DONE" is typed.

5. N names appear in DATA lines. The program should allow a name to be typed at the terminal. If the name is one of those in the DATA lines, the message

_____ IS IN THE LIST.

should be printed. If it is not, the message

_____ IS NOT IN THE LIST.

should be printed. In either case the user should be able to enter another name. The program should terminate when the user types END.

6. A list of words appears in DATA lines. A user should be allowed to type in a word. If the word appears in the list, all words in the list up to but not including it should be printed. If the word doesn't appear, a message to that effect should be printed. In either case the user should be allowed to enter another word. If END is typed, the run should terminate.

7. Using the following table, determine the batting average and slugging percentage for each player. In the table, 1B indicates a single, 2B a double, 3B a triple, HR a homerun, and AB the number of times a player has been at bat. (The table is to be presented in DATA lines, one for each player.)

$$\text{batting average} = \frac{\text{number of hits}}{\text{AB}} \qquad \text{slugging percentage} = \frac{\text{total bases}}{\text{AB}}$$

Player	1B	2B	3B	HR	AB
Gomez	100	22	1	14	444
Boyd	68	20	0	3	301
Jackson	83	15	8	7	395
O'Neil	68	22	1	8	365
Struik	65	11	3	5	310
McDuffy	54	11	4	0	256
Vertullo	78	18	1	15	418
Ryan	25	1	1	0	104
Torgeson	49	15	0	11	301
Johnson	54	5	2	0	246

Print a table listing the players with their batting averages and slugging percentages in two adjacent columns.

8. Read the employee name, hourly rate, and hours worked, and print a report showing the name and gross pay of each worker. The report is to be concluded with a message identifying the person whose pay is the greatest.

Name	Hourly Rate	Hours Worked
Jaime	$4.25	40
Horton	5.95	30
Elison	3.35	36
Sonners	3.75	32
Bellows	4.10	38
Hobson	4.50	40
Janson	4.75	35

9. The following data lines describe an investor's stock portfolio. The four entries on each line show, from left to right, the stock name, the number of shares owned, last week's closing price, and this week's closing price. (Transactions made during the week are not included.)

```
500 DATA "STERLING DRUG",800,16.50,16.125
510 DATA "DATA GENERAL",500,56.25,57.50
520 DATA "OWEN ILLINOIS",1200,22.50,21.50
530 DATA "MATTEL INC",1000,10.75,11.125
540 DATA "ABBOTT LAB",2000,33.75,34.75
550 DATA "FED NATL MTG",2500,17.75,17.25
```

Prepare reports as follows. Each report is to have a title, and each column is to be labeled.

a. A printed report displaying precisely the information contained in the DATA lines.

b. A five-column report, with the first four columns as in part (a) and a fifth column showing the percentage increase or decrease for each security.

c. A four-column report showing the stock name, the equity at the close of business last week, the equity this week, and the dollar change in equity. The report should be concluded with a message showing the total net gain or loss during the week.

10. A wholesaler carries two types of items, type A and type B. The following DATA lines show, from left to right, the item code (ITEM1, ITEM2, ...), the item type (A or B), the number of units on hand, the average cost per unit, and the sale price per unit.

```
500 DATA ITEM1,A,20500,1.55,1.95
510 DATA ITEM2,A,54000,0.59,0.74
520 DATA ITEM3,B, 8250,3.40,4.10
530 DATA ITEM4,B, 4000,5.23,6.75
540 DATA ITEM5,A,15000,0.60,0.75
550 DATA ITEM6,A,10500,1.05,1.35
560 DATA ITEM7,B, 6000,7.45,9.89
```

Prepare reports as follows. Each report is to have a title, and each column is to be labeled.
a. A printed report displaying precisely the information contained in the DATA lines.
b. Two separate reports, the first displaying the given information for type-A items and the second for type-B items.
c. A printed five-column report showing the item code, the number of units on hand, and the total cost, total sales price, and total income these units represent (income = sales – cost). The report is to be concluded with a message showing the total cost, total sales price, and total income represented by the entire inventory.

Write a program to perform each task specified in Problems 11–14. These programs will require string comparisons that do more than simply test for equality.

11. A list of English words is presented in DATA lines. Print those whose first two letters are "TO".
12. A list of English words is presented in DATA lines with the EOD tag ZZZ. Print those that begin with a letter from D to M, and then print a message telling how many words were printed and how many were in the given list.
13. A list of N names appears in DATA lines ("Last,First"). Separate the names into three lists. The first list is to contain all names A through K, the second all names L through Q, and the third all names R through Z. The three lists are to be printed one under the other with the three headings A–K, L–Q, and R–Z.
14. For any string typed at the terminal, the computer is to print "THE FIRST CHARACTER IS A LETTER" or "THE FIRST CHARACTER IS NOT A LETTER", whichever message is correct. A user should be allowed to type many strings during a single program run, and the program should halt when "DONE" is typed.

10.4 SUBSCRIPTED STRING VARIABLES

BASIC systems that provide *subscripted* string variables allow us to process lists of strings, such as names, rather than just lists of numbers. The symbols A$, B$, ..., Z$ are used as the names of such lists.

EXAMPLE 11. A program to read ten names into a list A$ and then search this list for any names typed in at the terminal. The program will terminate when the word "DONE" is typed.

```
100 REM READ THE LIST A$ OF NAMES
110 FOR I=1 TO 10
120     READ A$(I)
130 NEXT I
140 REM SEARCH A$ FOR ANY NAME TYPED AT THE TERMINAL
150 PRINT "TYPE NAMES EXACTLY AS FOLLOWS"
160 PRINT "FIRST NAME (SINGLE SPACE) LAST NAME"
170 PRINT "TYPE 'DONE' WHEN FINISHED"
180 INPUT N$
190 IF N$="DONE" THEN 999
200 FOR I=1 TO 10
210     IF N$<>A$(I) THEN 240
```

```
220     PRINT N$;" IS IN THE LIST."
230     GO TO 180
240 NEXT I
250 PRINT N$;" IS NOT IN THE LIST."
260 GO TO 180
500 DATA "ABRAHAM LINCOLN","ANDREW JOHNSON"
510 DATA "ULYSSES GRANT","RUTHERFORD HAYES"
520 DATA "JAMES GARFIELD","CHESTER ARTHUR"
530 DATA "GROVER CLEVELAND","BENJAMIN HARRISON"
540 DATA "WILLIAM MCKINLEY","THEODORE ROOSEVELT"
999 END
RUN

TYPE NAMES EXACTLY AS FOLLOWS
FIRST NAME (SINGLE SPACE) LAST NAME
TYPE 'DONE' WHEN FINISHED
? LINCOLN
LINCOLN IS NOT IN THE LIST.
? ABRAHAM LINCOLN
ABRAHAM LINCOLN IS IN THE LIST.
? DONE
READY
```

It is often necessary to arrange lists of strings in some specified order (for example, lists of names in alphabetical order). The sorting algorithms shown in Section 9.4 can also be used with lists of strings. The only change needed is to replace the variable names with string-variable names.

EXAMPLE 12. A program to alphabetize any list of words typed at the terminal. The list is to be terminated by typing FINI.

```
100 REM BUBBLE SORT AS APPLIED TO STRINGS
110 DIM A$(50)
120 PRINT "ENTER YOUR LIST. TYPE FINI TO END"
130 FOR I=1 TO 50
140     INPUT A$(I)
150     IF A$(I)="FINI" THEN 190
160 NEXT I
170 PRINT "I CAN ONLY HANDLE 49 WORDS"
180 STOP
190 LET N=I-1
200 REM ALPHABETIZE THE N WORD LIST A$.
210 FOR J=1 TO N-1
220     FOR I=1 TO N-J
230         IF A$(I)<=A$(I+1) THEN 270
240         LET T$=A$(I)
250         LET A$(I)=A$(I+1)
260         LET A$(I+1)=T$
270     NEXT I
280 NEXT J
290 REM PRINT THE ALPHABETIZED LIST
300 FOR I=1 TO N
310     PRINT A$(I)
320 NEXT I
```

```
330 END
RUN

? LINCOLN
? JOHNSON
? GRANT
? HAYES
? GARFIELD
? ARTHUR
? CLEVELAND
? FINI
ARTHUR
CLEVELAND
GARFIELD
GRANT
HAYES
JOHNSON
LINCOLN
READY
```

Note that the temporary variable in lines 240 and 260 is T$ and not T. *Strings* must be assigned to string variables and *numbers* to numerical variables.

Remark: Notice that a FOR/NEXT loop (lines 130–160) was used to input data values even though the number of values to be input was unknown. See the remark following Example 6 of Section 9.4.

10.5 PROBLEMS

Write a program to perform each task specified in Problems 1–6.

1. Read N words into a list B$. The user should then be allowed to issue any of the following commands: LIST, to print the list B$; SORT, to alphabetize the list B$; DONE, to terminate the program run. After each command other than DONE is carried out, the user should be allowed to issue another command.
2. Last year's sales report of the J. T. Pencil Company reads as follows.

January	$32,350	July	$22,000
February	$16,440	August	$43,500
March	$18,624	September	$51,400
April	$26,100	October	$29,000
May	$30,500	November	$20,100
June	$28,600	December	$27,500

Produce a two-column report with the headings MONTH and SALES. Sales figures are to appear in descending order.
3. Compute the semester averages for all students in a psychology class. A separate DATA line should be used for each student and should contain the student's name and five grades. A typical DATA line might read

700 DATA "LINCOLN JOHN",72,79,88,97,90

The output should be in tabular form, with the two column headings STUDENT and SEMESTER AVERAGE. Semester averages are to appear in descending order.
4. Modify Problem 3 so that the table is printed with the students' names in alphabetical order.
5. Modify Problem 3 as follows. A letter grade should be given according to the following table.

Average	Grade
90–100	A
80–89	B
70–79	C
60–69	D
Below 60	E

The five strings A, B, C, D, and E should be read into a list N$. The output should be in tabular form with the two column headings STUDENT and LETTER GRADE. (No sorting is required for this problem.)

6. Allow a user to create a list L$ of words as follows. The computer is to request (INPUT statement) that a word be typed. If the word has not already been typed, it should be added to the list; if it has, then it should be ignored. In either case the user should then be allowed to enter another word. However, if the user types the word LIST, the list L$ created to that point should be printed and another request made. If the user types END, the program run should terminate.

10.6 REVIEW TRUE OR FALSE QUIZ

1. A semicolon between two variable names in a PRINT statement will always cause at least one space to be skipped. T F
2. It now makes sense to use the condition A<"B" in an IF statement. T F
3. It is sometimes advisable to assign values to string variables and numeric variables using the same INPUT or READ statement. T F
4. It is always correct to use quotes on string constants. T F
5. Quotation marks are always necessary when we assign a value to a string variable with a LET statement. T F
6. When we assign values to a string variable with the READ or INPUT statement, quotation marks are sometimes necessary. T F
7. String constants appearing in relational expressions must be quoted. T F
8. The EOD tag used in reading long lists of data must be a numeric constant, even though all other data values appearing in the DATA lines are string constants. T F
9. An instruction such as INPUT C$ can often be used as an effective means for issuing commands to a running program. T F
10. The ASCII numeric codes given in Table 10.1 are used by all BASIC systems as the numeric codes assigned to the BASIC character set. T F

11 BASIC FILES

Although DATA statements provide the means for presenting large quantities of data to the computer, situations do arise in which they prove to be inadequate. For example, it may happen that the output values of one program are required as the input values of another program, or even of several other programs. For this reason many BASIC systems allow for input data to come from a source external to the program and for the output to be stored on some peripheral device for later use. This is accomplished by the use of files.

A BASIC file is a named collection of related data that can be referenced by a BASIC program.

Methods for creating and reading files and the BASIC statements needed to perform these tasks are described in this chapter. You should be forewarned, however, that BASIC systems vary in the form of the statements used to manipulate files. Your BASIC manual will give you the exact form used on your system.

11.1 THE **INPUT#** AND **PRINT#** STATEMENTS (BCD FILES)

One method for creating a file is to type the data values at the terminal. For example, to create a file containing the values 5, 3, 7, 9, 7, 8, 4, 6, and 5, you might type the following.

```
10,  5,  3,  7
20,  9,  7,  8
30,  4,  6,  5
```

The numbers 10, 20, and 30 are line numbers, just as in an ordinary BASIC program. When creating a file at the terminal, you name it in the same way that you name your programs. (A program is a file.) Let's assume that the name of this file is DATA5.

EXAMPLE 1. A program to use the nine values in file DATA5 as input values.

```
10 FILE#1="DATA5"
20 FOR I=1 TO 3
30    INPUT#1,N,X,Y,Z
40    PRINT X;Y;Z
```

```
50 NEXT I
60 END
RUN

   5   3   7
   9   7   8
   4   6   5
READY
```

The FILE# statement at line 10 assigns the integer 1 as the **file designator** (also called the **file ordinal**) for the file DATA5. Any unsigned integer may be used for the designator. Whenever a file is used in a BASIC program, it is referenced by its designator and not by its name.

Remark: Your system may require you to use the statement

10 OPEN "DATA5" FOR INPUT AS FILE 1

in place of line number 10. This statement also assigns the integer 1 as the file designator for the file DATA5. In addition, it specifies that DATA5 is to be used only as an input file.

The INPUT# statement at line 30 inputs four values from DATA5 that are assigned to N, X, Y, and Z. (Note that the line numbers are assigned to the variable N but that N is not used in the program for any other purpose. The INPUT# statement does not make a distinction between line numbers and your data values.)

Some BASIC systems provide an **end-of-file statement** that can be used to detect whether or not more data values are available for input. We illustrate by rewriting the program of Example 1.

EXAMPLE 2.

```
10 FILE#1="DATA5"
20 IF END#1 THEN 60
30 INPUT#1,N,X,Y,Z
40 PRINT X;Y;Z
50 GO TO 20
60 END
RUN

   5   3   7
   9   7   8
   4   6   5
READY
```

Line 20 checks whether more values are available on DATA5. There is a *pointer* associated with a file, just as with a data list. If there are no more values (that is, if the pointer is at the end of file #1), this statement causes control to be transferred to line 60, which in this program terminates the run.

Remark: Using an end-of-file statement as in line 20 obviates the need to use an EOD tag to terminate or a data count to precede your data list.

It is not uncommon for a single program to produce many printed reports. Rather than having the output printed during a program run, you can use the PRINT# statement to "print" it on a file. Printing at the terminal is a time-consuming operation, whereas printing on a file takes very little time.

Then, at some later time when the computer is not busy, you can obtain a printed copy of the output by listing the file using the LIST command.

EXAMPLE 3. A program to create a file containing whatever numbers are input during program execution.

```
10 FILE#2="DATA"
20 INPUT S
30 IF S=999 THEN 60
40 PRINT#2,S
50 GO TO 20
60 END
RUN

? 255.13
? 620.07
? 143.86
? 999
READY
```

Line 10 designates a file with ordinal 2 and name DATA. Assuming that a file named DATA had not already been created, this file will be blank.

Remark: Your system may require you to use the statement

10 OPEN "DATA" FOR OUTPUT AS FILE 2

in place of line number 10. This statement also designates a file with ordinal 2 and name DATA. However, it specifies that DATA is to be used only as an output file.

The PRINT# statement at line 40 "prints" whatever values are input for S on file #2 instead of at the terminal. If the file DATA is listed, you will obtain

LIST
255.13
620.07
143.86
READY

Note that the file DATA contains no line numbers. Line numbers need not appear in files created by BASIC programs.

Files typed at the terminal and those created by a BASIC program using a PRINT# statement are sometimes referred to as *display files* or *terminal files,* since they can be displayed at the terminal by the LIST command. The contents of files that can be listed in this manner appear as a sequence of BCD (*binary coded decimal*) characters. This means that a numerical value such as 38 will appear as two separate codes, one for 3 and one for 8, and not as the binary-number representation of the decimal number 38.

The INPUT# statement can be used to input data from any BCD file, whether it is typed at the terminal or created by a BASIC program using the PRINT# statement. However, if you do so, you must take some care while creating the file. In particular, if several values are printed on one line of the file, they must be separated by commas, just as they would be if they were being typed in response to an INPUT statement. Thus, to print two values on one line of file #1, you would use

PRINT#1,A;",";B

rather than

PRINT#1,A,B

That is, the comma must actually be "printed" on the file.

EXAMPLE 4. A program to create a short BCD file and then read it.

```
10 FILE#5="INV35"
20 LET A$="NEEDLES"
30 LET M=4300
40 LET N=.62
50 PRINT#5,A$;",";M;",";N
60 RESTORE#5
70 INPUT#5,B$,X,Y
80 PRINT B$;X;Y
90 RESTORE#5
99 END
RUN

NEEDLES 4300  .62
READY
```

Line 10 creates a blank file whose name is "INV35" and whose designator is 5.

Line 50 prints the values of A$, M, and N on file #5 with a comma printed between successive values.

Line 60 "restores" the pointer to the first value on file #5 so that the three values just printed can be assigned to B$, X, and Y by the INPUT# statement in line 70.

If the file "INV35" is listed, you will obtain the following printout:

LIST

NEEDLES, 4300 , .62
READY

Remark 1: It is a good policy to *restore* all files with the RESTORE# statement just before the run terminates. If you do not, you may have trouble listing your files after the program run.

Remark 2: If your system requires the statement

10 OPEN "INV35" FOR OUTPUT AS FILE 5

in place of the FILE# statement at line 10, you must use the following two lines in place of the RESTORE#5 statement at line 60:

60 CLOSE 5
61 OPEN "INV35" FOR INPUT AS FILE 5

In addition, you should CLOSE all files before the run terminates. In the present case, the line 90 CLOSE 5 will suffice. (Consult your manual.)

Maintaining and updating existing data files are common business applications. We conclude this section with an example illustrating this practice. The example involves updating a short, simplified inventory file. However, it should be remarked that, in practice, data files usually are not short and require rather complicated programs to maintain them. Our objective is simply to show that file maintenance is possible. A complete discussion of the many techniques used in file-maintenance programs is beyond the scope of an introductory text such as this one.

EXAMPLE 5. A BCD file named INVTRY contains the following data.

A10010, 2000
A10011, 4450
C22960, 1060
D40240, 2300
X99220, 500
X99221, 650
Y88000, 1050
Y88001, 400
END, 0

The first entry in each line denotes an item code, and the second entry gives the quantity on hand. The last line END, 0 terminates the file. Our task is to write a program to allow a user to update INVTRY to reflect all transactions since the last update.

Problem Analysis: Let's assume that the user must specify, for each item to be changed, the item code, the number of units shipped since the last update, and the number of units received since the last update. Thus, the user will come to the terminal armed with a list such as the following.

Item Code	Shipped	Received
A10010	1200	1000
A10011	1000	550
D40240	1800	2000
Y88000	300	0

A person carrying out this task by hand might proceed as follows.

a. Read an item code.
b. Search the file INVTRY for this code, and change the units-on-hand figure as required.
c. If more changes are to be made, go to step (a).
d. Have the updated copy of INVTRY typed.

This procedure is not suitable for a BASIC program. Step (b) says to change a *single* number appearing on the file INVTRY, and this cannot be done in BASIC. We must first input the data from INVTRY into lists (subscripted variables) and then make the necessary changes in these lists. After this has been done for each item requiring a change, step (d) will involve creating a new copy of INVTRY using the PRINT# statement. Before rewriting this procedure in a form suitable for a BASIC program, let's choose variable names.

C$ = the list of item codes from file INVTRY.
Q = the corresponding list of quantities from INVTRY.
N = the number of lines in the file INVTRY.
X$ = the item code to be typed.
S = the quantity shipped.
R = the quantity received.

In the following algorithm we require the user to type END after all changes have been made.

The Algorithm

a. Input lists C$ and Q from the file INVTRY.
b. Enter an item code X$.
c. If X$ = END, make a new copy of INVTRY and stop.

d. Find I such that C$(I) = X$. If X$ is not in the list, go to step (b).
e. Enter the quantities S and R corresponding to item X$.
f. Let Q(I) = Q(I) + R − S, and go to step (b).

The Program

```
100 REM INVENTORY UPDATE PROGRAM
110 REM    C$ = LIST OF ITEM CODES FROM INVTRY FILE
120 REM    Q  = LIST OF QUANTITIES FROM INVTRY FILE
130 REM    N  = NUMBER OF LINES IN INVTRY FILE
140 REM    X$ = ITEM CODE TO BE INPUT
150 REM    S  = QUANTITY SHIPPED (OF ITEM X$)
160 REM    R  = QUANTITY RECEIVED (OF ITEM X$)
170 FILE#1="INVTRY"
180 REM INPUT LISTS C$ AND Q FROM FILE 1
190 DIM C$(50),Q(50)
200 LET N=1
210 INPUT#1,C$(N),Q(N)
220 IF C$(N)="END" THEN 250
230 LET N=N+1
240 GO TO 210
250 REM UPDATE LISTS C$ AND Q
260 PRINT "ITEM CODE";
270 INPUT X$
280 IF X$="END" THEN 430
290 REM SEARCH LIST C$ FOR X$
300 FOR I=1 TO N-1
310    IF C$(I)=X$ THEN 350
320 NEXT I
330 PRINT X$;" IS NOT A CORRECT ITEM CODE"
340 GO TO 260
350 REM ENTER THE QUANTITIES S AND R TO UPDATE Q(I)
360 PRINT "UNITS SHIPPED";
370 INPUT S
380 PRINT "UNITS RECEIVED";
390 INPUT R
400 LET Q(I)=Q(I)+R-S
410 PRINT
420 GO TO 260
430 REM UPDATE THE FILE INVTRY
440 RESTORE#1
450 FOR I=1 TO N
460    PRINT#1,C$(I);",";Q(I)
470 NEXT I
480 PRINT "INVTRY IS UPDATED"
490 REM PRINT THE UPDATED INVENTORY
500 PRINT
510 PRINT "ITEM CODE","UNITS ON HAND"
520 FOR I=1 TO N-1
530    PRINT C$(I),Q(I)
540 NEXT I
550 RESTORE#1
560 END
```

Lines 490 to 540 are included so that the contents of the updated file INVTRY will be displayed at the terminal.

```
RUN
ITEM CODE ? A10010
UNITS SHIPPED ? 1200
UNITS RECEIVED? 1000

ITEM CODE ? A10011
UNITS SHIPPED ? 1000
UNITS RECEIVED? 550

ITEM CODE ? D40240
UNITS SHIPPED ? 1800
UNITS RECEIVED? 2000

ITEM CODE ? Y88000
UNITS SHIPPED ? 300
UNITS RECEIVED? 0

ITEM CODE ? END
INVTRY IS UPDATED

ITEM CODE        UNITS ON HAND
A10010           1800
A10011           4000
C22960           1060
D40240           2500
X99220           500
X99221           650
Y88000           750
Y88001           400
READY
```

11.2   THE **READ#** AND **WRITE#** STATEMENTS (BINARY FILES)

A second type of BASIC file—one that must be created by a BASIC program—is called a **binary file**—numbers are stored in their binary form instead of in the BCD form mentioned in Section 11.1. For this reason, programs using binary files will execute more quickly than programs using BCD files; the computer must translate numerical values in BCD files to their binary form before any calculations can take place. A disadvantage of using binary files is that they should not be listed at the terminal; since numerical values are stored in binary form, the printout will not be readable.

To create a binary file under program control, you must use the WRITE# statement to create it and the READ# statement to read it. The awkward "comma" situation encountered with the PRINT# and INPUT# statements does not occur.

EXAMPLE 6.   A program to create a short binary file.

```
10 FILE#2="DATA"
20 INPUT X,Y
30 IF X=9999 THEN 60
40 WRITE#2,X,Y
50 GO TO 20
60 END
```

```
RUN

? 2, 3
? 4, 8
? 5, 18
? 9999, 0
READY
```

Line 40 "writes" two values on file #2—the two values typed in response to the INPUT statement at line 20. When X = 9999, after the fourth pair of values is entered, the program terminates without any output.

EXAMPLE 7. A program to examine the contents of the binary file DATA created by the program in Example 6.

```
10 FILE#1="DATA"
20 RESTORE#1
30 IF END#1 THEN 70
40 READ#1,A,B
50 PRINT A;B
60 GO TO 30
70 END
RUN

   2   3
   4   8
   5  18
READY
```

Line 40 reads two values from file #1, and line 50 prints them at the terminal. This process is continued until the end-of-file is reached.

If a program is to read data from an existing file, it is a good policy to restore the pointer associated with the file before using the file. On some systems, files are not automatically restored when you type RUN. The RESTORE# statement in line 20 assures that the reading begins at the first value.

This example illustrates that files created with the WRITE# statement (binary files) must be read with the READ# statement, just as files created at the terminal or with the PRINT# statement (BCD files) must be read with the INPUT# statement.

We conclude this chapter with an example of a program that updates an existing binary file.

EXAMPLE 8. The ID numbers and names of all employees of the Land Foundry Company are stored on the binary file EMPLOY. The file begins with a count of the number of employees, and a typical line is

23501 AHEARN JOHN F.

Let's write a program to allow a user to add new employees to this file.

Problem Analysis: The name and ID number of a new employee will be typed at the terminal. Let's use the following variables to denote these two items.

E$ = the name being typed.
I = the ID number being typed.

Generally, BASIC systems do not allow you to add data to a file. You must first read the entire file into lists (subscripted variables), then include any new items in these lists, and finally make a new copy of the file. We will use the following variable names to read the data contained in the file EMPLOY.

C = the count of how many employees are included (first value on the file).
L = the list of ID numbers.
N$ = the corresponding list of names.

Using these variable names, we can write the following procedure for updating the file EMPLOY. The details are left for the coding process.

The Algorithm

a. Read the count C from the file EMPLOY.
b. Read the ID numbers and names into lists L and N$.
c. Input an ID number I and name E$ (an ID of 0 will end the input session).
d. If I = 0, make a new copy of EMPLOY and stop.
e. If I is already in list L, print an appropriate message and go to step (c).
f. Add 1 to C, I to list L, and E$ to list N$.
g. Go to step (c).

The Program

```
100 REM PROGRAM TO UPDATE THE FILE "EMPLOY".
110 FILE#1="EMPLOY"
120 RESTORE#1
130 REM READ THE LISTS L AND N$ FROM FILE#1
140 REM C COUNTS THE NUMBER OF EMPLOYEES INCLUDED
150 DIM L(100),N$(100)
160 READ#1,C
170 FOR K=1 TO C
180    READ#1,L(K),N$(K)
190 NEXT K
200 PRINT "FOLLOWING EACH ? TYPE AN ID NUMBER AND NAME AS FOLLOWS."
210 PRINT "    ID NUMBER, LAST (SPACE) FIRST (SPACE) MIDDLE INITIAL"
220 PRINT "    (TYPE 0,X TO END THIS SESSION.)"
230 PRINT
240 INPUT I,E$
250 IF I=0 THEN 370
260 REM SEARCH LIST L FOR THE ID NUMBER I
270 FOR K=1 TO C
280    IF I=L(K) THEN 350
290 NEXT K
300 REM ADD I AND E$ TO THE LISTS L AND N$
310 LET C=C+1
320 LET L(C)=I
330 LET N$(C)=E$
340 GO TO 230
350 PRINT "THE ID";I;"IS ASSIGNED TO   ";N$(K)
360 GO TO 230
370 REM UPDATE FILE#1
380 RESTORE#1
390 WRITE#1,C
400 FOR K=1 TO C
410    WRITE#1,L(K),N$(K)
```

```
420 NEXT K
999 END
```

This program writes the updated lists on the file EMPLOY but causes no output at the terminal. In order to check whether the new names are actually written on EMPLOY, let's add the following program segment to read the updated file and print it at the terminal.

```
430 RESTORE#1
440 READ #1,C
450 PRINT
460 PRINT "ID NUMBER","EMPLOYEE'S NAME"
470 PRINT
480 FOR K=1 TO C
490    READ#1,I,E$
500    PRINT I,E$
510 NEXT K
RUN
```

```
FOLLOWING EACH ? TYPE AN ID NUMBER AND NAME AS FOLLOWS.
     ID NUMBER, LAST (SPACE) FIRST (SPACE) MIDDLE INITIAL
     (TYPE 0,X TO END THIS SESSION.)

? 63334, MANN HEATHER A

? 23501, JACKSON SUSAN A
THE ID 23501 IS ASSIGNED TO AHEARN JOHN F

? 33501, JACKSON SUSAN A

? 0,X

ID NUMBER        EMPLOYEE'S NAME

  23501          AHEARN JOHN F
  53241          ANDERSON ALBERT G
  15653          SIMPSON DONALD C
  37671          HENDRIX SAMUEL D
  49313          POST EDWARD L
  44446          MURRAY HAROLD N
  83817          CONNORS FRANK J
  23786          SILVA JOSE R
  23619          SEMPLE ALBERT J
  63334          MANN HEATHER A
  33501          JACKSON SUSAN A
READY
```

The file statements introduced in this chapter will be most useful when you want to create files and save them on some peripheral device for later use. The methods used to save and retrieve files differ from system to system. For example, before running the program of Example 8, you may have to type a system command such as

GET, EMPLOY

so that the previously created file EMPLOY will be available for your program. After running the program, you may be required to type a command such as

REPLACE, EMPLOY

to save the updated version for use at another time. The manual for your system will show you the precise forms of these commands to use.

11.3   PROBLEMS

1. The following programs do not work. Explain why. Also explain what each program was meant to do. The files ABC1 and ABC2 referenced in these programs contain the following information.

ABC1 (BCD file)	ABC2 (Binary file)
10, JOAN, 78	SAL, 64
20, SAM, 75	JILL, 72
30, GREG, 86	JACK, 88
40, ALICE, 81	JANE, 95
50, MARK, 93	PETE, 79

a.
```
10 FILE#1="ABC1"
20 FOR I=1 TO 5
30    INPUT#1,A$,S
40    PRINT A$,S
50 NEXT I
60 END
```

b.
```
10 FILE#2="ABC2"
20 FOR I=1 TO 5
30    INPUT#2,A$,S
40    PRINT A$,S
50 NEXT I
60 END
```

c.
```
10 FILE#3="ABC1"
20 READ#3,N,A$,S
30 FOR I=1 TO 4
40    READ#3,N,B$,T
50    IF S>=T THEN 80
60    LET S=T
70    LET A$=B$
80 NEXT I
90 PRINT A$,S
99 END
```

d.
```
10 FILE#1="ABC1"
20 FILE#2="ABC2"
30 FOR I=1 TO 5
40    INPUT#1,N,A$(I),S(I)
50    READ#2,A$(5+I),S(5+I)
60 NEXT I
70 FOR I=1 TO 10
80    PRINT#1,A$(I),S(I)
90 NEXT I
99 END
```

Problems 2–7 refer to the BCD file INFO maintained by the Libel Insurance Company. The contents of INFO are as follows.

(Line No.)	Name	Sex	Age	Years of Service	Annual Salary
100	Ingers John	M	47	13	20200
110	Arthur Susan	F	33	6	14300
120	Smith Ann	F	41	15	23900
130	Jarvis Peter	M	22	2	11400
140	Kent Donald	M	59	7	19200
150	Toland Mary	F	25	3	13000
160	Holland John	M	33	13	21500
170	Doane Susan	F	28	4	13400
180	Smith Harry	M	68	30	25500
190	Arthur Andrew	M	35	6	14300
200	Smith Silvia	F	21	3	9200

2. Print a five-column report with a title and appropriate column headings displaying the employee information contained in the file INFO.

3. Print two reports showing the employee information contained in INFO by sex. Each report is to be titled and is to have four appropriately labeled columns.

4. Print a list of all employees whose salaries exceed $15,000, and also give the total salary earned by these employees.

5. Print a report showing the names, years of service, and salaries of all employees who have been with the firm for more than five years.

6. Print a report showing the names and salaries of all Libel employees. Salaries are to be listed from largest to smallest.

7. Print a report as in Problem 6 with the names in alphabetical order.

Problems 8–10 refer to the following product survey.

A manufacturing company sends a package consisting of eight new products to each of ten families and asks each family to rate each product on the following scale.

0 = poor   1 = fair   2 = good   3 = very good   4 = excellent

Here are the results in tabular form.

					Product Number				
		1	2	3	4	5	6	7	8
	1	0	2	1	3	0	4	1	2
	2	1	3	3	4	1	4	3	2
	3	1	3	4	2	3	4	1	3
	4	2	0	4	4	2	3	3	4
Family	5	1	3	4	3	2	2	2	2
Number	6	2	2	1	1	2	1	4	2
	7	2	2	4	3	1	4	1	3
	8	1	3	2	4	3	4	4	4
	9	0	4	3	2	0	1	3	2
	10	1	1	2	4	1	1	4	3

8. Create a file RATE at the terminal containing the information in this table. Then use this file to print a two-column report showing the product numbers and the average rating for each product.

9. Use the file RATE to print a report as in Problem 8. However, the average ratings are to appear from smallest to largest.

10. Use the file RATE to print a two-column report as follows. The first column is to give the product numbers receiving at least six ratings of 3 or better. The second column is to give the number of these ratings obtained.

Problems 11–13 refer to the following files maintained by the Sevard Company.

File SST (Binary file)				*File WEEKLY (Created at the terminal)*		
Employee ID	Year-to-Date Income	Hourly Rate		Line Number	Employee ID	This Week's Hours
24168	12442.40	7.35		10	24168	40
13725	17250.13	11.41		20	13725	36
34104	10425.00	6.50		30	34104	32
28636	11474.25	6.75		40	28636	40
35777	15450.35	10.45		50	35777	40
15742	14452.00	10.05		60	15742	30

11. A Social Security tax deduction of 5.85% is taken on the first $13,200 earned by an employee. Once this amount

is reached, no further deduction is made. Using the binary file SST and the BCD file WEEKLY, produce a report giving the ID number, the current week's gross pay, and this week's Social Security deduction for each employee.

12. Modify the program written for Problem 11 to update the year-to-date income in the file SST.

13. Using the files SST and WEEKLY, print a list of the ID numbers of all employees who have satisfied the Social Security tax requirement for the current year. With each ID number printed, give the year-to-date income figure.

14. The binary file NAMES contains a list of names. Write a program to allow a user to issue any of the following commands: LIST, to list the names at the terminal; ADD, to add a name to the list; DELETE, to delete a name from the list; ALPHA, to alphabetize the list of names; DONE, to update the file NAMES and terminate the run. After each command other than DONE is carried out, the user should be allowed to issue another command. (You should be able to use your program to create the file NAMES as well as to update an existing file.)

15. A binary file GRADE contains the following information.

2		
Edwards	75	93
Lebak	91	65
Myers	41	83
Nolan	89	51
Post	78	63
Sovenson	56	87
Block	82	82

The two numbers following each name represent grades, and the first value, the number 2, tells how many grades have previously been recorded on the file for each student. Write a program to allow a user to enter any of the following commands.

LIST: to obtain a printout of the current contents of the file GRADE.
AVERAGE: to obtain a listing of student names and averages.
ADD: to add an additional grade for each student. (Each student's name should be printed to allow the user to enter the next grade.)
DONE: to terminate the run. When this command is issued, an updated file GRADE should be created.

11.4   REVIEW TRUE OR FALSE QUIZ

1. The line numbers in a file typed at the terminal do not conflict with the line numbers in a program using this file. Hence, the data in such a file can be processed by many different programs.   T F

2. It is often desirable to use a PRINT# statement in place of a PRINT statement in programs that produce a great deal of output.   T F

3. You may use either the INPUT# or the READ# statement to access the values in any file.   T F

4. Binary files must be accessed with the READ# statement and BCD files must be accessed with the INPUT# statement. However, files typed at the terminal may be accessed with either of these two statements.   T F

5. At most two files can be referenced in a program, one for input data and one for output data.   T F

6. The BASIC instruction RESTORE#3 will set the pointer associated with the file whose ordinal is 3 to the beginning of the file.   T F

7. If the file DATA is to be used as an input file to a program, it is advisable to follow the statement FILE#1="DATA" by the statement RESTORE#1.   T F

8. Line numbers must be used in BCD files but are not needed in binary files.   T F

9. The contents of a binary file are easily examined using the LIST command.   T F

12 FUNCTIONS AND SUBROUTINES

Since BASIC is a problem-solving language, and since problems are often formulated in mathematical terms, two types of functions are included in the language. In Section 12.1 the so-called *built-in* functions, or functions supplied with your BASIC system, are described. Then, in Section 12.3, you will learn how to define other functions, ones that you may need but that are not included in your system. In addition, BASIC *subroutines* are introduced in Section 12.5. The subroutine statements allow you to include an entire program segment just once in a program, even though it must be executed at more than one point in the program.

12.1   BASIC FUNCTIONS

The **built-in functions** (also called BASIC **functions** or LIBRARY **functions**) are an integral part of the BASIC language and may be used in any program. In this section we'll describe some of the more familiar of these and show how they are used. A list of the most common BASIC functions is provided at the end of this section.

The BASIC Function **ABS**

Let **e** denote any BASIC numerical expression. If ABS(**e**) appears in a BASIC program, its value is the absolute value of the value of the expression **e**. For example, ABS(3) = 3, ABS(–3) = 3, and ABS(4 – 9) = 5. For this reason, ABS is called the **absolute-value function.** The following examples illustrate its use.

EXAMPLE 1. A program to print the absolute value of the sum of any two numbers.

```
10 INPUT X,Y
20 IF X=0 THEN 60
30 LET Z=ABS(X+Y)
40 PRINT Z
50 GO TO 10
60 END
RUN

? 7,3
 10
```

```
? 5,-9
 4
? 0,0
READY
```

Remark: This program could have been written without using the ABS function. For example, if line 30 were replaced by the lines

```
30 LET Z=X+Y
32 IF Z>= 0 THEN 40
34 LET Z=-Z
```

the resulting program would function in the same way as the original. Clearly the first version is more desirable; its logic is transparent, whereas the logic of the second version is somewhat obscure. As a general rule you should use the BASIC functions supplied with your system. Your programs will be not only easier to write but also easier to understand and hence easier to debug or modify.

EXAMPLE 2. A data list contains the monthly sales figures for each of ten retail stores. Each of these ten figures is preceded by a store-identification code number. Let's write a program to identify those stores whose sales deviate from the figure $17,500 by more than $3750.

Problem Analysis: We choose variable names as follows.

S = the sales figure being read.
C = the code number for the store whose sales are S dollars.

To find the deviation of S from 17,500, we subtract S from 17,500 or 17,500 from S, depending on whether 17,500 is larger or smaller than S. Since we are interested only in how close S is to 17,500, not in which is larger, we simply examine the absolute value of S – 17,500. The store code C will be printed if ABS(S – 17500) is greater than 3750. This process must be repeated ten times, once for each store.

The Flowchart (shown on page 151)

The Program

```
100 FOR I=1 TO 10
110    READ C,S
120    IF ABS(S-17500)>3750 THEN 140
130    GO TO 150
140    PRINT "STORE";C;"SALES";S
150 NEXT I
160 DATA 240,21000,280,16000,290,12500,320,25740,340,14480
170 DATA 380,28700,410,20400,420,14200,440,10200,520,17850
180 END
RUN

STORE 290 SALES 12500
STORE 320 SALES 25740
STORE 380 SALES 28700
STORE 440 SALES 10200
READY
```

The Flowchart

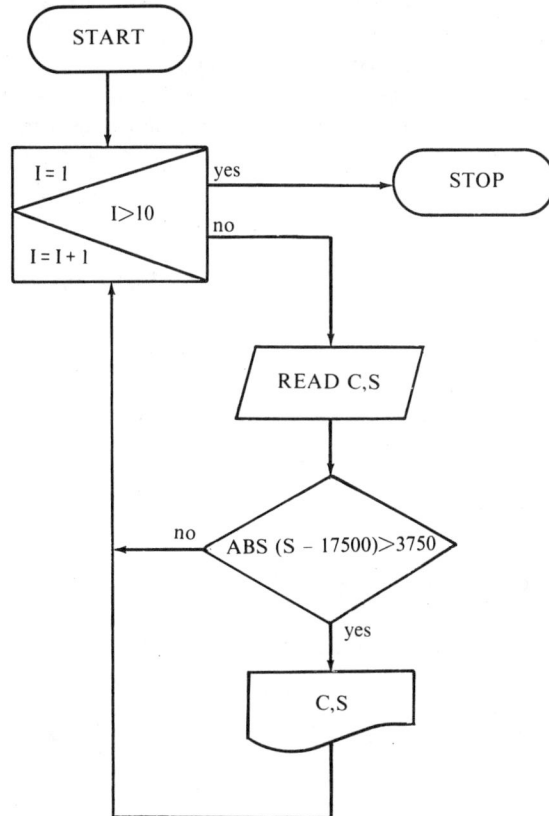

Remark: The logic of this program would be easier to follow if the GO TO statement at line 130 were removed. How should this be accomplished?

The BASIC Function **INT**

If INT(**e**) is used in a BASIC program, its value is the greatest integer less than or equal to the value of the expression **e**. For example, INT(2.6) = 2, INT(7) = 7, INT(7 – 3.2) = 3, and INT(–4.35) = –5. For this reason INT is called the **greatest-integer function.**

The INT function can be used to round off numbers. For example, suppose X satisfies the inequalities

$$36.5 \leq X < 37.5.$$

Then X + 0.5 satisfies the inequalities

$$37 \leq X + 0.5 < 38,$$

and we see that

$$INT(X + 0.5) = 37.$$

That is, to round a number X to the nearest integer, use the BASIC expression INT(X + 0.5).

EXAMPLE 3. Let's find an expression to round any amount X to two decimal places.

Any value of X such that

$$127.135 \leq X < 127.145$$

must be rounded to 127.14. This can be accomplished by multiplying X by 100, then rounding to the nearest integer as shown above, and dividing again by 100. Thus, to round X to two decimal places, we use

$$INT(100 * X + 0.5)/100.$$

The following program prints 7 1/8% of the amounts $1, $2, $3, $4, and $5. Values are rounded to the nearest cent.

```
10 FOR X=1 TO 5
20    LET A=7.125/100*X
30    PRINT INT(100*A+0.5)/100
40 NEXT X
50 END
RUN

 .07
 .14
 .21
 .29
 .36
READY
```

EXAMPLE 4. A program to tell whether or not a value input is an integer.

```
100 INPUT A
110 IF A=INT(A) THEN 130
120 PRINT "NOT ";
130 PRINT "AN INTEGER"
140 END
```

The condition A = INT(A) is true only when A is an integer. If it is, line 120 is skipped and the message AN INTEGER is printed.

Remark: If a program calls for an integer A to be input (for example, if A denotes a count), an IF statement with the condition A $<>$ INT(A) can be used to reject values typed that are not integers. The following three lines illustrate this use of the INT function.

```
10 PRINT "HOW MANY VALUES ARE THERE";
20 INPUT A
30 IF A <> INT(A) THEN 10
```

Just as the condition A = INT(A) is true only when A is an integer, so too will the condition A/2 = INT(A/2) be true when A/2 is an integer—that is, when A is divisible by 2. Also, A/3 = INT(A/3) is true only when A is divisible by 3; moreover, in general, if N denotes any nonzero integer, then A/N = INT(A/N) is true only when A is divisible by N. We illustrate with an example.

EXAMPLE 5. A program to print every fourth value appearing in the DATA lines.

```
10 FOR I=1 TO 16
20    READ X
30    IF I/4<>INT(I/4) THEN 50
40    PRINT X;
50 NEXT I
60 DATA 8,3,4,22,1,6,9,36
70 DATA 8,4,1,49,2,2,7,33
80 END
RUN

 22  36  49  33
READY
```

I counts the number of values read. I/4 will be an integer for I = 4, 8, 12, and 16—that is, for every fourth value. Thus, line 30 will cause a jump around the print statement at line 40 for every value read other than these four.

Caution: Using relational expressions of the form

$$N/D = INT(N/D)$$

can lead to unexpected difficulties. A computer stores numbers and does arithmetic in the binary number system. This means that a calculation involving a number that cannot be represented exactly as a binary number may be only approximate; hence, exact comparisons may not be possible. The same situation occurs in the decimal number system. For instance, 1/3 cannot be represented exactly as a finite decimal. Thus, working with decimals, you could obtain

$$INT(6/3) = INT(6*0.3333333) = INT(1.9999998) = 1$$

and not 2, which is the correct value. If your BASIC system does not behave as it should, you can always fudge things so that it will. For instance, you can choose a small number F, such as F = 1E – 10, and use the relational expression

$$N/D = INT(N/D + F).$$

TABLE 12-1 The most common BASIC functions

Function	Purpose
ABS(x)	Gives the absolute value of x.
INT(x)	Gives the greatest integer less than or equal to x.
SGN(x)	Returns the value 1 if x is positive, -1 if x is negative, and 0 if x is zero.
SQR(x)	Calculates the principal square root of x if $x \geq 0$. Results in an error if x is negative.
RND(x)	Returns a pseudo-random number between 0 and 1. (Consult manual of the system being used for the precise form required for x.)
SIN(x)	Calculates the sine of x where x is in radian measure.
COS(x)	Calculates the cosine of x where x is in radian measure.
TAN(x)	Calculates the tangent of x where x is in radian measure.
ATN(x)	Calculates the arctangent of x; $-\pi/2 \leq ATN(x) < \pi/2$.
LOG(x)	Calculates the natural logarithm $\ln(x)$. x must be positive.
EXP(x)	Calculates the exponential e^x, where $e = 2.71828\ldots$ is the base of the natural logarithms.

12.2 PROBLEMS

1. Evaluate the following BASIC expressions.
   a. ABS(3*(2–5))   b. ABS(–3*(–2))   c. ABS(2–30/3*2)
   d. INT(26.1+0.5)   e. INT(–43.2+0.5)   f. INT(10*2.37+0.5)/10
   g. 100*INT(1235.7/100+0.5)   h. ABS(INT(–3.2))   i. INT(ABS(–3.2))
2. Evaluate the following with A = –4.32, B = 5.93, and C = 2864.7144.
   a. INT(ABS(A))   b. ABS(INT(A))   c. INT(B+0.5)
   d. INT(A+0.5)   e. INT(C+0.5)   f. 10*INT(C/10+0.5)
   g. 100*INT(C/100+0.5)   h. 1000*INT(C/1000+0.5)   i. INT(1000*C+0.5)/1000
3. What will be printed when each program is run?

a.
```
100 LET N=0
110 IF N>4 THEN 170
120 LET X=N*(N-1)
130 LET Y=ABS(X-8)
140 PRINT N,Y
150 LET N=N+1
160 GO TO 110
170 END
```

b.
```
100 LET X=1.1
110 LET Y=X
120 LET Z=INT(Y)
130 PRINT Y,Z
140 LET Y=X*Y
150 IF Y<=1.5 THEN 120
160 END
```

c.
```
100 LET S=13.99
110 IF S>14 THEN 160
120 LET R=INT(100*S+0.5)/100
130 PRINT S,R
140 LET S=S+0.003
150 GO TO 110
160 END
```

d.
```
100 LET N=63
110 LET D=1
120 LET D=D+1
130 IF D>N/2 THEN 170
140 IF N/D<>INT(N/D) THEN 120
150 PRINT D
160 GO TO 120
170 END
```

4. Using the INT function, write the programming line that will round off the value of X:
   a. to the nearest tenth.
   b. to the nearest hundredth.
   c. to the nearest thousandth.
   d. to the nearest hundred.
   e. to the nearest thousand.

Write a program to perform each task specified in Problems 5–20. Where appropriate, messages should be printed to identify values to be typed and also to label the output values. A user should be able to input several different sets of numbers without having to rerun the program.

5. Two positive integers are to be input to determine if the first is divisible by the second.
6. Two numbers are to be input to determine if the absolute value of their sum is equal to the sum of their absolute values.
7. Three positive integers are to be typed to determine whether the first is divisible only by the second, only by the third, by both the second and third, or by neither.
8. Determine and print all positive factors of a positive integer N input at the terminal. (Include the factors 1 and N.)
9. Print the exact change received from a purchase of P dollars if an amount D is presented to the salesclerk. Assume that D is at most $100. The change should be given using the largest possible denominations of bills and coins. For example, if P = 17.43 and D = 100, the change should be as follows.

                    1 $50 bill
                    1 $20 bill
                    1 $10 bill
                    1 $2 bill

1 50¢ coin
1 nickel
2 pennies

10. The *deviation* of a number N from a number M is defined to be ABS(M − N). Print a two-column table, with the first column containing all values in the DATA lines and the second column showing the deviations of these numbers from whatever value is input for M. The table should be concluded with a message giving the sum of all the deviations. Run your program for the data list 2, 5, 3, 7, 12, −8, 43, and −16, and for the input value M = 6.

11. Produce a two-column table as follows. The first column is to contain all values in the DATA lines, and the second column is to show the deviation of each number X in the first column from the integer INT(X). The table is to be concluded with a message giving the sum of all the deviations.

12. Each salesperson for the Mod Dress Company is paid $140 a week plus 4.875% of all sales. Using the following sales figures, produce a five-column report showing the name, total sales, base pay, commission, and gross pay for each salesperson. All money amounts are to be rounded to the nearest cent. (If your system does not allow string variables, use employee ID numbers instead of names.)

Total Sales for the Week

Name	Type-1 Items	Type-2 Items
Barnes, James	$ 726.28	$1198.42
Colby, Irene	415.92	2092.50
Cole, Bruce	2606.95	700.40
Drew, Nancy	350.42	301.27
Hilton, Lynn	1300.23	1521.32
Moore, Warren	268.92	399.92
Rich, Steven	2094.50	227.03
Skinner, Kerry	1102.37	303.52

13. Assume that a salesperson for the Mod Dress Company is paid $140 a week plus a commission of 3.125% on all Type-1 sales and 5.875% on all Type-2 sales. However, a salesperson whose total sales do not exceed $700 receives only the base pay of $140. Using the sales figures given in Problem 12, produce a five-column report showing the name, base pay, Type-1 commission, Type-2 commission, and gross pay for each salesperson. All money amounts are to be rounded to the nearest cent.

14. Produce a report as described in Problem 12 with the amounts in the gross-pay column being printed from largest to smallest.

15. Produce a report as described in Problem 13 with the amounts in the gross-pay column being printed from smallest to largest.

16. A positive integer N ≥ 2 is said to be **prime** if its only positive-integer factors are 1 and N. Determine if a positive integer N typed at the terminal is prime. (If N has a factor, then it will have one between 2 and SQR(N), inclusive.)

17. Determine and print all prime numbers between 10 and 78.

18. Determine and print all prime numbers between A and B. A and B are to be input and are to be rejected if either is not a positive integer or if B is not greater than A.

19. Add the digits in any three-digit positive integer. For example, if 378 is input, then 18 (3 + 7 + 8) should be printed. (Hint: 3 = INT(378/100) and 7 = INT(78/10).) The program should reject typed-in values that are not integers greater than 99 and less than 1000. (If your program does not behave as you think it should, you should reread the paragraph labeled "Caution" following Example 5 in the text.)

20. Add the digits in any positive integer. (See Problem 19.)

12.3 USER-DEFINED FUNCTIONS: THE **DEF** STATEMENT

In addition to providing the built-in functions, BASIC allows you to define and name your own functions. These functions, called **user-defined functions,** can be referenced in any part of your program. There are several advantages in doing so: a function need be defined only once, even though it is used many times in a program; programs can be written so that they are easier to read and their logic is easier to follow; and a program containing a user-defined function is easily modified to treat different functions.

The function names allowed are FNA, FNB, ..., FNZ. The means for defining functions is the DEFINE statement (abbreviated DEF), which we will illustrate by example.

EXAMPLE 6. The statement

$$100 \text{ DEF FNR(X)} = \text{INT}(100*X+0.5)/100$$

defines a function whose *name* is FNR (also called the function R, since the FN in FNR is an abbreviation for function). Recall that the expression INT(100*X+0.5)/100 rounds X to two decimal places. Thus, if the expression FNR(943.828) appears in a program, its value will be 943.83. Similarly, if Y has been assigned the value 943.828, then FNR(Y) will again have the value 943.83. The following short program uses this user-defined function to print P% of any value V. P and V are to be input, and the result is rounded to two decimal places.

```
100 DEF FNR(X)=INT(100*X+0.5)/100
110 INPUT P,V
120 IF P=0 THEN 160
130 LET A=P/100*V
140 PRINT P;"PERCENT OF";V;"IS";FNR(A)
150 GO TO 110
160 END
RUN

? 6, 154.49
  6 PERCENT OF 154.49 IS 9.27
? 7.25, 9834
  7.25 PERCENT OF 9834 IS 712.97
? 0,0
READY
```

Remark 1: The variable name X used in the definition in line 100 could have been any simple BASIC variable name. It is called a "dummy" variable because it serves only to define the function; if used later in the program, it is treated the same as any other variable. For example, if the DEF statement in this program were changed to

$$100 \text{ DEF FNR(P)} = \text{INT}(100*P+0.5)/100$$

the program would function just as before. No conflict would arise because of the appearance of the variable P elsewhere in the program.

Remark 2: Changing line 100 to

$$100 \text{ DEF FNR(X)} = \text{INT}(1000*X+0.5)/1000$$

will cause the results to be rounded to *three* decimal places. Everything else stays the same.

The general form of the DEF statement is

ln DEF FNa(b) = e

where **a** denotes any letter of the English alphabet, **b** denotes a simple BASIC variable, and **e** denotes a BASIC numerical expression defining a function of the variable **b**.

The following rules govern the use of the DEF statement and of the user-defined functions.

1. A function definition should be given in a lower-numbered line than any program statement that references the function.
2. The BASIC expression used in a DEF statement may involve built-in functions and user-defined functions. However, a function may not be defined in terms of itself. A statement such as DEF FNC(Y) = 2 + FNC(Y) is not allowed.
3. A function that has been defined by a DEF statement may be used anywhere in the program, in the same way that the built-in BASIC functions are used.
4. If **e** denotes any BASIC numerical expression, and if a function such as FNA has been defined, then FNA(**e**) is a valid expression.

EXAMPLE 7. Salaried employees are to receive an end-of-year bonus of $100 plus 1% of their annual salaries. The following program calculates the bonus amounts for the salary figures given in the DATA lines.

```
100 DEF FNB(S)=100+(.01)*S
110 DEF FNR(X)=INT(X+0.5)
120 PRINT "SALARY","BONUS"
130 READ S
140 IF S=0 THEN 999
150 LET B=FNB(S)
160 PRINT S,FNR(B)
170 GO TO 130
500 DATA 13028,12560,14520,15250,22580
998 DATA 0
999 END
RUN
```

```
SALARY     BONUS
 13028      230
 12560      226
 14520      245
 15250      253
 22580      326
READY
```

This program shows that more than one user-defined function can be included in a single program. Here, FNB calculates the bonus amount and FNR is used to round this figure to the nearest whole-dollar amount.

Remark: Lines 150 and 160 can be replaced by the single line

150 PRINT S,FNR(FNB(S)).

The program will behave exactly as before.

Your BASIC system may allow you to use the DEF statement to define functions of from 0 to 5 variables. In this case the same function names, FNA, FNB, ..., FNZ, should be used. For example, the statement

10 DEF FNC(X,Y)=X↑2+Y↑2

defines a function whose value for any numbers x and y is $x^2 + y^2$. If the expression FNC(2,3) is used in the program, its value will be $2^2 + 3^2 = 13$. Similarly, if the variables A and B have the values 2 and 3, respectively, then FNC(A,B) will again have the value 13.

EXAMPLE 8. Charges at a car-rental agency are $14 a day plus 12¢ a mile. The following program calculates the total charge if the number of days D and the total mileage M are typed at the terminal.

```
100 DEF FNC(D,M)=14*D+(.12)*M
110 INPUT D,M
120 LET C=FNC(D,M)
130 PRINT "CHARGE: $";C
140 END
RUN


? 3,523
CHARGE: $ 104.76
READY
```

12.4   PROBLEMS

1. Each of these short programs contains an error—either a syntax error that will cause an error message to be printed or a programming error that the computer will not recognize but that will cause incorrect results. In each case, find the error and tell which of the two types it is.

a.
```
10 REM PRINT 6 PERCENT
20 REM OF ANY NUMBER
30 DEF FNZ(U)=.06*U
40 INPUT X
50 LET V=FNZ(U)
60 PRINT V
70 END
```

b.
```
10 REM A TABLE OF SQUARES
20 DEF FNS(I)=X↑2
30 FOR I=1 TO 9
40    LET S=FNS(I)
50     PRINT I,S
60 NEXT I
70 END
```

c.
```
10 REM BONUS CALCULATION
20 DEF FCN(S)=200+0.02*S
30 PRINT "SALARY";
40 INPUT S
50 LET B=FCN(S)
60 PRINT "BONUS IS";B
70 END
```

d.
```
10 REM PRINT RECIPROCALS
20 REM OF 1,2,3,...,10
30 DEF FNR(X)=X/I
40 LET X=1
50 FOR I=1 TO 10
60    PRINT FNR(I)
70 NEXT I
80 END
```

2. What will be printed when each program is run?

a.
```
10 DEF FNR(X)=100*INT(X/100+0.5)
20 FOR I=1 TO 3
30    READ S
40    PRINT FNR(S)
50 NEXT I
60 DATA 227.376,1382.123,7.125
70 END
```

b.
```
10 DEF FNY(X)=1+1/X
20 LET X=2
30 FOR I=1 TO 3
40    LET X=FNY(X)-1
50    PRINT X;
60 NEXT I
70 END
```

c.
```
10 DEF FNA(X,Y)=X/Y
20 FOR I=1 TO 2
30    FOR J=1 TO 4
40       PRINT FNA(J,I),
```

d.
```
10 DEF FNI(P,R,T)=P*R/100*T
20 LET T=1/2
30 LET P=1000
40 FOR R=2 TO 5
```

```
50    NEXT J              50    PRINT FNI(P,R,T)
60    PRINT               60 NEXT R
70 NEXT I                 70 END
80 END
```

3. Write a user-defined function that:
   a. converts degrees Celsius to degrees Fahrenheit (F = 9/5C + 32).
   b. converts degrees Fahrenheit to degrees Celsius.
   c. converts feet to miles.
   d. converts kilometers to miles (1 mi = 1609.3 m).
   e. converts miles to kilometers.
   f. gives the average of two numbers.
   g. gives the average speed for a trip of D miles that takes T hours.
   h. gives the selling price if an article whose list price is X dollars is selling at a discount of Y%.
   i. gives the cost of a trip of X miles in a car that averages 15 miles per gallon if gasoline costs Y cents per gallon.

Write a program to perform each task specified in Problems 4–9.

4. Produce a three-column table showing the conversions from feet F to miles, and then to kilometers, for the values F = 1000, 2000, 3000, ..., 20,000. All output values are to be rounded to three decimal places. Write user-defined functions to perform the two conversions required and to do the rounding.
5. Produce a four-column table as follows. The first column is to contain the mileage figures 10 miles, 20 miles, ..., 200 miles. The second, third, and fourth columns are to give the time in minutes required to travel these distances at the respective speeds 45 mph, 50 mph, and 55 mph. All output values are to be rounded to the nearest minute. Write user-defined functions to calculate the times and to do the rounding.
6. Following is the weekly inventory report of a sewing-supply wholesaler.

Item	Batches on Hand Monday	Batches Sold during Week	Cost per Batch	Sales Price per Batch
Bobbins	220	105	8.20	10.98
Buttons	550	320	5.50	6.95
Needles—1	450	295	2.74	3.55
Needles—2	200	102	7.25	9.49
Pins	720	375	4.29	5.89
Thimbles	178	82	6.22	7.59
Thread—A	980	525	4.71	5.99
Thread—B	1424	718	7.42	9.89

Produce a three-column report showing the item names, the number on hand at the end of the week, and the income per item. Denoting the markup by M and the quantity sold by Q, use a function FNP(M,Q) to calculate the income figures. (If your system does not allow string variables, replace the item names by code numbers.)
7. Produce a three-column report as in Problem 6. However, the income column is to appear in decreasing order. (You will need subscripted variables.)
8. Using the inventory report shown in Problem 6, produce a five-column report showing the item names, the cost per batch, the sales price per batch, the dollar markup per batch, and the percent markup per batch. Denoting the markup by M and the sales price by S, use a function FNA(M,S) to calculate the percent figures in the fifth column (M/S × 100 gives the required percentage). In addition, use a function to round the percentages to the nearest whole number.
9. Prepare the five-column report described in Problem 8. However, the percentages in the fifth column should appear in decreasing order. (Subscripted variables are required.)

12.5   SUBROUTINES

In Section 12.3 you saw that, when a function is needed in a program, it is sufficient to define the function once in a DEF statement. The function may then be referenced as many times as necessary. Very often you will find that the same *sequence* of instructions is needed in two or more places within a program. BASIC also allows you to include this sequence of instructions just once in a program, even though it is to be used in several different parts of the program. Such a sequence of instructions is called a **subroutine subprogram** or, more simply, a **subroutine.** In this section the **GOSUB** and **RETURN** statements, which allow you to write and use BASIC subroutines, are described and illustrated.

The GOSUB statement is used to transfer control to a subroutine, and the RETURN statement is used to transfer control back from the subroutine. A BASIC subroutine is any sequence of BASIC programming lines to carry out a specific task. It *must* contain at least one RETURN statement. The following program illustrates the use of a subroutine.

EXAMPLE 9. A program to print the average of any two input values and also the average of their squares.

```
100 INPUT A,B
110 GOSUB 300
120 LET A=A↑2
130 LET B=B↑2
140 GOSUB 300
150 STOP
300 REM SUBROUTINE TO PRINT THE AVERAGE OF A AND B
310 LET S=A+B
320 PRINT S/2
330 RETURN
999 END
RUN

? 3,4

  3.5
  12.5
READY
```

The subroutine consists of lines 300–330. Line 110 transfers control to line 300, and 3.5, the average of 3 and 4, is printed. The RETURN statement then transfers control back to line 120, the line following the GOSUB statement just used. Lines 120 and 130 assign the new values to be averaged (9 and 16) to A and B. When line 140 is encountered, a second transfer to the subroutine is made and 12.5, the average of 9 and 16, is printed. This time the RETURN statement transfers control back to line 150, which follows the most recent GOSUB statement executed. Following is a schematic representation of the action described.

```
100 INPUT A,B
110 GOSUB 300 ────────────────────────►  300 REM SUBROUTINE
120 LET A=A↑2 ◄────────────────────►     310 LET S=A+B
130 LET B=B↑2                             320 PRINT S/2
140 GOSUB 300 ─ ─ ─ ─ ─ ─ ─ ─ ─ ─ ─ ───  330 RETURN
150 STOP      ◄─ ─ ─ ─ ─ ─ ─ ─ ─ ─
999 END
```

Remark 1: The program segment on the left is referred to as the **main program** or the **calling program,** and we say that the main program "calls" the subroutine.

Remark 2: The stop statement (line 150) is used to ensure that the subroutine is entered only under the control of a GOSUB instruction.

Remark 3: The GOSUB statement differs from the GO TO statement in that it causes the computer to "remember" which statement to execute next when it encounters a RETURN statement. As described, this is the statement immediately following the GOSUB statement used to "call" the subroutine.

The general forms of the GOSUB and RETURN statements are as follows.

ln_1 GOSUB ln_2 (ln_2 is the line number of the first statement of the subroutine.)

ln RETURN

Line ln_1 transfers control to line ln_2, and program execution continues as usual. When the first RETURN statement is encountered, control transfers back to the line following line ln_1.

In the preceding chapters we have attempted to stress the importance of segmenting programming tasks into smaller, more manageable subtasks. A program can often be made more readable if such subtasks are performed by subroutines, even though they may be executed only once in a program run. We illustrate this practice with an example.

EXAMPLE 10. A bank computes the interest charges for early payment of a 12-month installment loan by the "rule of 78." Let's write a program to find the single payment needed to pay off such a loan at any time during the year.

Problem Analysis: The "rule of 78" states that 12/78 of the total interest is charged to the 1st month, 11/78 to the 2nd month, 10/78 to the 3rd, and so on. Thus, if the loan is paid off during the 3rd month, the bank charges the fraction

$$12/78 + 11/78 + 10/78 = 33/78$$

of the total interest amount. $(12 + 11 + 10 + \cdots + 2 + 1 = 78$; hence, if the loan is paid off during the 12th month (that is, is not paid off early), the charge is the total interest amount.)

In practice, a bank does not calculate the actual interest charges. The total interest for the year is included in the amount of the loan, and the portion of the interest that is saved by early payment is considered a rebate. For example, for prepayment during the 3rd month (after two payments), the interest charged to the 4th through 12th months must be rebated. Thus, the fraction of the total interest to be rebated is

$$1/78 + 2/78 + 3/78 + \cdots + 9/78 = \frac{1 + 2 + 3 + \cdots + 9}{78}$$

—that is, 1/78 of the interest for the 12th month, 2/78 for the 11th, 3/78 for the 10th, and so on.

More generally, if prepayment is made during the Nth month (after N – 1 payments), the fraction of the total interest to be rebated is

$$F = 1/78 + 2/78 + 3/78 + \cdots + (12 - N)/78 = \frac{1 + 2 + 3 + \cdots + (12-N)}{78}.$$

The following subroutine determines the fraction F needed to calculate the interest rebate if prepayment is made during the Nth month of the loan.

```
500 REM SUBROUTINE TO CALCULATE THE FRACTION F
510 LET F=0
520 FOR K=1 TO 12-N
530    LET F=F+K
540 NEXT K
550 LET F=F/78
560 RETURN
```

To determine the final payment by hand, a bank officer could proceed as follows.

Algorithm

a. Determine the loan amount (amount borrowed + interest for one year).
b. Subtract the payments already made to obtain the amount due.
c. Determine the interest rebate (F × total interest for the year) and the final payment
   (amount due − rebate).

The individual steps in this algorithm are not difficult to code. What is required is a choice of variable names and a meaningful choice of PRINT statements. The following program shows one way to code this algorithm. The variable names chosen are shown in lines 110–180. The function FNR defined in line 190 is used to round off values to the nearest cent.

```
100 REM PREPAYMENT OF 12 MONTH INSTALLMENT LOAN
110 REM      N=NUMBER OF MONTH IN WHICH PREPAYMENT IS MADE
120 REM      B=AMOUNT BORROWED
130 REM      R=ANNUAL INTEREST RATE
140 REM      A=LOAN AMOUNT (B+INTEREST FOR THE YEAR)
150 REM      P=MONTHLY PAYMENT (P=A/12)
160 REM      T=TOTAL AMOUNT PAID TO DATE
170 REM      F=FRACTION TO CALCULATE THE INTEREST REBATE
180 REM      I=INTEREST REBATE
190 DEF FNR(X)=INT(100*X+0.5)/100
200 REM DETERMINE THE LOAN AMOUNT
210 PRINT "AMOUNT BORROWED";
220 INPUT B
230 PRINT "INTEREST RATE";
240 INPUT R
250 PRINT "MONTH NUMBER";
260 INPUT N
270 PRINT
280 LET A=FNR(B+R*B)
290 PRINT "LOAN AMOUNT",A
300 REM DETERMINE THE AMOUNT DUE
310 LET P=FNR(A/12)
320 PRINT "MONTHLY PYMT",P
330 LET T=(N-1)*P
340 PRINT "AMOUNT PAID",T
350 PRINT "AMOUNT DUE",A-T
360 REM DETERMINE THE INTEREST REBATE AND FINAL PAYMENT
370 GOSUB 500
380 LET I=FNR(F*B*R)
390 PRINT "INT. REBATE",I
400 PRINT "AMOUNT DUE",A-T-I
410 STOP
500 REM SUBROUTINE TO CALCULATE THE FRACTION F
510 LET F=0
520 FOR K=1 TO 12-N
530     LET F=F+K
540 NEXT K
550 LET F=F/78
560 RETURN
999 END
```

```
RUN

AMOUNT BORROWED ? 1000
INTEREST RATE ? .10
MONTH NUMBER ? 7

LOAN AMOUNT      1100
MONTHLY PYMT     91.67
AMOUNT PAID      550.02
AMOUNT DUE       549.98
INT. REBATE      19.23
AMOUNT DUE       530.75
READY
```

Including the programming lines that calculate the fraction F in a subroutine makes the main program, lines 100–410, easier to follow. The REM statement in line 500 tells exactly the purpose of the GOSUB 500 statement in line 370. Note also that the REM statements in lines 200, 300, and 360 correspond to the three steps in the algorithm. The importance of writing program segments that correspond exactly to the steps in an algorithm cannot be overemphasized.

Following are some comments on the use of subroutines.

1. The first line (or lines) of a subroutine should describe the task being performed.
2. A subroutine must contain one or more RETURN statements.
3. A subroutine must be entered only by using a GOSUB statement. You should use a STOP statement as the last line of your main program to avoid inadvertently entering a subroutine.
4. A subroutine should be used if it will make your program easier to read and understand.
5. A subroutine can contain a GOSUB statement transferring control to another subroutine. However, a subroutine should not call itself.

We conclude this chapter with an example further illustrating the use of subroutines.

EXAMPLE 11.   An airline charter service estimates that ticket sales of $1000 are required to break even on a certain excursion. It thus makes the following offer to an interested organization. If ten people sign up, the cost will be $100 per person. However, for each additional person, the cost per person will be reduced by $3.00. Produce a table showing the cost per customer and the profit to the airline for N = 10, 11, 12, . . . , 30 customers. In addition, a message is to be printed giving the number of customers that will maximize the profit for the airline. Column headings, underlined by a row of dashes, are to be used, and a row of dashes is to precede and follow the final message.

Problem Analysis: Let's use the following variable names.

N = number of people who sign up for the excursion (N will be between 10 and 30, inclusive).
C = cost per person (if N people sign up, C = 130 – 3N).
P = profit to the airline (if N people sign up, P = NC – 1000).
N1 = number of people yielding a maximum profit to the airline.
P1 = maximum profit to the airline (initially, P1 = 0).

Producing a table of values with column headings is not new to us. We can use the instruction

PRINT "NO. OF PEOPLE", "COST/PERSON", "AIRLINE PROFIT"

to print the column headings and a FOR/NEXT loop initiated with FOR N = 10 TO 30 to produce the table values. However, if we wish our columns to be centered under the column headings, the TAB function must be used.

$$\text{PRINT TAB(5);N;TAB(18);C;TAB(33);P}$$

According to the problem statement, three rows of dashes are to be printed. Rather than write the loop that does this three times, we will use a subroutine.

```
500 REM SUBR TO PRINT A ROW OF DASHES
510 FOR I=0 TO 46
520    PRINT "-";
530 NEXT I
540 PRINT
550 RETURN
```

Finally, the number N1 of customers that yields a maximum profit P1 to the airline must be determined. Each time a new P value is computed, it will be compared with P1, the largest profit obtained to that point. If P is larger, we will let P1 = P and N1 = N. If not, N1 and P1 will not be changed. To keep our program as straightforward as possible, we also do this in a subroutine.

```
600 REM SUBR TO RECORD THE NUMBER N1 OF CUSTOMERS
610 REM YIELDING THE MAXIMUM PROFIT P1.
620 IF P<=P1 THEN 650
630 LET P1=P
640 LET N1=N
650 RETURN
```

The Program

```
100 REM PROGRAM TO PRINT A TABLE OF AIRLINE EXCURSION RATES
110 REM AND DETERMINE THE MAXIMUM PROFIT TO THE AIRLINE.
120 LET P1=0
130 PRINT "NO. OF PEOPLE","COST/PERSON","AIRLINE PROFIT"
140 GOSUB 500
150 REM COMPUTE AND PRINT THE TABLE VALUES
160 FOR N=10 TO 30
170    LET C=130-3*N
180    LET P=N*C-1000
190    PRINT TAB(5);N;TAB(18);C;TAB(33);P
200    GOSUB 600
210 NEXT N
220 GOSUB 500
230 PRINT N1;"CUSTOMERS YIELD MAX PROFIT OF";P1;"DOLLARS."
240 GOSUB 500
250 STOP
500 REM SUBR TO PRINT A ROW OF DASHES
510 FOR I=0 TO 46
520    PRINT "-";
530 NEXT I
540 PRINT
550 RETURN
600 REM SUBR TO RECORD THE NUMBER N1 OF CUSTOMERS
610 REM YIELDING THE MAXIMUM PROFIT P1.
```

```
620 IF P<=P1 THEN 650
630 LET P1=P
640 LET N1=N
650 RETURN
999 END
RUN
```

NO. OF PEOPLE	COST/PERSON	AIRLINE PROFIT
10	100	0
11	97	67
12	94	128
13	91	183
14	88	232
15	85	275
16	82	312
17	79	343
18	76	368
19	73	387
20	70	400
21	67	407
22	64	408
23	61	403
24	58	392
25	55	375
26	52	352
27	49	323
28	46	288
29	43	247
30	40	200

```
22 CUSTOMERS YIELD MAX PROFIT OF 408 DOLLARS.
```

READY

12.6 PROBLEMS

1. What will be printed when each program is run?

a.
```
100 FOR I=1 TO 3
110     READ X,Y
120     GOSUB 300
130 NEXT I
140 STOP
300 PRINT I;X;Y;X+Y
310 RETURN
500 DATA 3,5,8
510 DATA 6,-2,1
999 END
```

b.
```
110 LET M=5
120 GOSUB 300
130 PRINT M
140 STOP
300 LET M=M+1
310 GOSUB 400
320 RETURN
400 LET M=(M+1)*(M+1)↑2
410 RETURN
999 END
```

c.
```
100 FOR I=1 TO 4
110     GOSUB 200
120     PRINT S
130 NEXT I
```

d.
```
110 LET A=5
120 LET B=3
130 IF A<B THEN 150
140 GOSUB 200
```

```
140 STOP                   150 GOSUB 300
200 LET S=0                160 GO TO 999
210 FOR J=1 TO I           200 PRINT A-B
220    LET S=S+J           210 RETURN
230 NEXT J                 300 PRINT B-A
240 RETURN                 400 RETURN
999 END                    999 END
```

2. Write a program to print all numbers in a data list and then print them again, this time in ascending order. Assume that the first datum is a count of how many numbers are included. Use the following algorithm.

   a. Read the count N and the list A.
   b. Print list A.
   c. Sort list A into ascending order.
   d. Print the sorted list A and stop.

Since the list must be printed twice, use a subroutine for this task. Also, to keep the main program as simple as possible, do the sorting in a subroutine. Use the given algorithm to guide your choice of REM statements.

3. A data list contains many sets of scores S1, S2, and S3. The three values 0, 0, 0 are used to terminate the data list. Write a program to print a four-column report as follows. The three scores are to be printed in the first three columns, and the fourth is to contain the larger of the two values $(S1 + S2 + S3)/3$ and $(S1 + S2 + 2*S3)/4$. Use a subroutine to process S1, S2, and S3 to obtain the larger of these two "averages." The subroutine is to contain no print statements. (Subscripted variables are not required.)

4. A list of numbers is to be processed to obtain a two-column printout. The first column is to contain the numbers in the order given, and the second is to contain a count of how many numbers in the list are strictly less than the number appearing in the first column. Write a program to allow a user to input any list of numbers to obtain the printout described. Use the following algorithm.

   a. Input list A.
   b. For each number A(I) in the list, determine the count C(I) of how many numbers are less than A(I).
   c. Print lists A and C side by side.

Use a subroutine to carry out step (b). Choose REM statements so that your program is easy to understand. (You are not to assume that the numbers will be typed in increasing order.)

5. Write a program for the following game. There are two players, player A and player B, who alternate in choosing a whole number from 1 to 5. (Players should lose their turns if the choice is not between 1 and 5.) Although the players are not aware of it, each number chosen is assigned a point value according to the following table.

Number Chosen	Point Value
1	3
2	2
3	2
4	1
5	2

The first player to accumulate a total of 15 points wins. Messages should be printed to indicate whose turn it is and, of course, who the winner is when the game is over. The point value for the number chosen by a player is to be determined in a subroutine.

6. An apple orchard occupying one acre of land now contains 25 apple trees, and each tree yields 450 apples per season. For each new tree planted, the yield per tree will be reduced by 10 apples per season. How many additional trees should be planted so that the total yield is as large as possible? Produce a table showing the yield per tree and the total yield if N = 1, 2, 3, . . . , 25 additional trees are planted. Use column headings underlined by a row of dashes, and also separate the message, telling how many additional trees to plant, from the table by a row of dashes.

7. An organization can charter a ship for a harbor cruise for $9.75 a ticket provided that at least 200 people agree to go. However, the ship's owner agrees to reduce the cost per ticket by 25¢ for each additional 10 people signing

up. Thus, if 220 people sign up, the cost per person will be $9.25. Write a program to determine the maximum revenue the ship's owner can receive if the ship's capacity is 400 people. In addition, prepare a table showing the cost per person and the total amount paid for N = 200, 210, 220, ..., 400 people. Use column headings underlined by a row of dashes. The maximum revenue the ship's owner can receive should be printed following the table and separated from it by a row of dashes.

8. A merchant must pay the fixed price of $1.00 a yard for a certain fabric. From experience it is known that 1000 yards will be sold each month if the material is sold at cost and also that each 10-cent increase in price will mean that 50 fewer yards will be sold each month. Write a program to produce a table showing the merchant's profit for each selling price from $1.00 to $3.00 in increments of 10¢. In addition, a message giving the selling price that will maximize the profit is to be printed. Column headings underlined with a row of dashes are to be used, and a row of dashes is to separate the table from the final message.

9. Consider the following three print statements.

```
320 PRINT "XXX     XXX     XXX     XXX"
420 PRINT "    XXX     XXX     XXX"
520 PRINT "XXXXXXXXXXXXXXXXXXXXXX"
```

In what follows, XXX   XXX   XXX   XXX is referred to as the *pattern* of line 320, and similarly for lines 420 and 520.

a. Write three subroutines: the first to print the pattern of line 320 L times, the second to print the pattern of line 420 M times, and the third to print the pattern of line 520 N times.

b. Write a calling program to allow a user to input values for L, M, and N so that L + M + N lines will be printed: L lines of the first pattern, M of the second, and N of the third.

c. Write a second program to allow a user to input seven integers A(1), B(1), A(2), B(2), A(3), B(3), and C. A(1), A(2), and A(3) are to be the integers 1, 2, or 3. The computer is then to print

pattern number A(1) on B(1) successive lines;
pattern number A(2) on B(2) successive lines;
pattern number A(3) on B(3) successive lines.

The entire process is to be repeated C times.

d. Alter the patterns specified in lines 320, 420, and 520. (Note: the process described in this problem is not unlike the method used to design intricate patterns in weaving.)

12.7 REVIEW TRUE OR FALSE QUIZ

1. If there is a BASIC function that performs a needed task, you should use it unless it is a simple matter to write your own programming lines to perform this task. T F

2. To determine whether or not the positive integer M is divisible by the positive integer N, we must use an IF statement with the condition INT(M/N) = M/N and not the condition INT(M/N) <> M/N. T F

3. INT(5/2) <> 5/2. T F

4. ABS(INT(–2.3)) = INT(ABS(–2.3)). T F

5. If A = ABS(INT(A)), then A is a positive integer. T F

6. It is a good practice to write our programs so that meaningless values typed in by a user will be rejected. T F

7. The BASIC functions are also referred to as LIBRARY functions. T F

8. The relational expression INT(N) = N is true if N is either zero or a positive integer and is false in all other cases. T F

9. If the statement 1 DEF FNC(P) = 2*P↑2 appears in a program, then the function FNC may be referenced as often as desired and in exactly the same way as any built-in function is referenced. T F

10. If the variable Y is used as the dummy variable in a DEF statement, then Y may also be used as a variable in the program. T F

11. If FNF(X) is defined using a DEF statement, the expression FNF(SQR(A)) is valid but the expression SQR(FNF(A)) is not. T F

12. If FNF(X) is defined in a program, we may also define the function FNC(X) = 2 + FNF(X).   T   F
13. There is nothing wrong with the statement 80 DEF FNA(Y) = 2 + FNA(Y).   T   F
14. If functions FNA and FNB have been defined, the instruction PRINT FNA(I,FNB(I)) will necessarily result in an error when the program is run.   T   F
15. A program need not contain the same number of GOSUB statements as RETURN statements.   T   F
16. The GOSUB statement is really unnecessary, since the GO TO statement will accomplish the same thing.   T   F
17. A STOP statement should appear on the line that immediately precedes the first line of each subroutine.   T   F
18. If one subroutine calls a second subroutine, the first must appear in the program before the second.   T   F
19. Subroutines should be used only when a group of instructions is to be performed more than once.   T   F
20. If a variable appears both in a subroutine and in the main program, it can be assigned any value in the subroutine without changing its value in the main program.   T   F

13 RANDOM NUMBERS AND THEIR APPLICATION

If a coin is tossed several times, a sequence such as HTTHTHHHTTH, where H denotes a head and T a tail, is obtained. We call this a **randomly generated sequence** because each letter is the result of an experiment (tossing a coin) and could not have been determined without actually performing the experiment. Similarly, if a die (a cube with faces numbered 1 through 6) is rolled several times, a randomly generated sequence such as 5315264342 is obtained. The numbers in such a randomly generated sequence are called **random numbers.**

BASIC contains a built-in function called RND, which is used to generate sequences of numbers that have the appearance of being randomly generated. Although these numbers are called random numbers, they are more accurately referred to as **pseudo-random numbers** because the RND function does not perform an experiment such as tossing a coin to produce a number; rather, it uses an algorithm carefully designed to generate sequences of numbers that emulate random sequences. This ability to generate such sequences makes it possible for us to use the computer in many new and interesting ways. Using "random-number generators," people have written computer programs to simulate the growth of a forest, to determine the best location for elevators in a proposed skyscraper, to assist social scientists in their statistical studies, to simulate game playing, and to perform many other tasks.

13.1 THE **RND** FUNCTION

The RND function is used somewhat differently than the other BASIC functions. If the expression RND(X) appears in a program, its value will be a number from 0 up to, but not including, 1:

$$0 \leq RND(X) < 1.$$

The particular value assumed by RND(X) is unpredictable. It will appear to have been selected randomly from the numbers between 0 and 1.

EXAMPLE 1. A program to generate and print eight random numbers lying between 0 and 1.

```
100 FOR I=1 TO 8
110    PRINT RND(X)
120 NEXT I
130 END
RUN
```

```
  1.78311E-2
   .597702
   .986238
   .526585
   .302629
   .619982
   .899148
   .184081
READY
```

Observe that each time line 110 is executed a different number is printed even though the same expression RND(X) is used.

The value of X in RND(X) has different meanings on different systems. We will use the RND function in the form RND(0). Your system may allow or even require you to use RND(1), RND(–1), or some other form of the RND function. The proposed ANSI standard for minimal BASIC specifies that the abbreviated form RND be used; however, since this form has yet to be widely implemented on BASIC systems, we will not use it.

EXAMPLE 2. A program to generate 1000 random numbers between 0 and 1 and determine how many are in the interval from 0.3 to 0.4, inclusive.

```
10 LET C=0
20 FOR I=1 TO 1000
30    LET X=RND(0)
40    IF X<0.3 THEN 70
50    IF X>0.4 THEN 70
60    LET C=C+1
70 NEXT I
80 PRINT C
90 END
RUN

 104
READY
```

Each time line 30 is executed, RND(0) takes on a different value, which is then assigned to X. The two lines 40 and 50 determine whether X lies in the specified interval. In this example it was necessary to assign the value of RND(0) to a temporary variable X so that the comparisons could be made. If we had written

```
30 IF RND(0)<.3 THEN 70
40 IF RND(0)>.4 THEN 70
```

the two occurrences of RND(0) would have different values, which is not what was wanted in this situation.

The numbers generated by the RND function are nearly uniformly distributed between 0 and 1. For example, if many numbers are generated, approximately as many will be less than .5 as greater than .5, approximately twice as many will be between 0 and 2/3 as between 2/3 and 1, approximately 1/100th of the numbers will be between .37 and .38, and so on. The examples throughout the rest of this chapter illustrate how this property of random-number sequences can be put to use by a programmer.

EXAMPLE 3. Write a program to simulate tossing a coin 20 times. An H is to be printed each time a head occurs and a T each time a tail occurs.

Problem Analysis: Since RND(0) will be less than .5 approximately half the time, let's say that a head is tossed whenever RND(0) is less than .5. The following program is then immediate.

```
10 FOR I=1 TO 20
20    IF RND(0)<.5 THEN 50
30    PRINT "T";
40    GO TO 60
50    PRINT "H";
60 NEXT I
70 END
RUN

HHTHTTTHTTHTHTHHHTTH
READY
```

Remark: If we wish to simulate tossing a bent coin that produces a head twice as often as a tail, we could say that a head is the result whenever RND(0) < .66667. Thus, one change in line 20 allows the same program to work in this case.

Normally, if a program containing RND(0) is run a second time, exactly the same sequence of random numbers is generated and used. Although this result can be useful during the debugging process, it does not reflect what actually happens in real-life situations. The BASIC statement **RANDOMIZE** is designed to cause different and unpredictable sequences to be generated each time a program is run.* Its form is

ln RANDOMIZE

as illustrated in the following program.

EXAMPLE 4. Two "runs" of a program using RANDOMIZE.

```
100 RANDOMIZE
110 FOR I=1 TO 5
120    PRINT RND(0)
130 NEXT I
140 END
RUN

 .182351
 .400231
 .909222
 .612347
 .338525
READY
RUN

 .621112
 .121235
6.71728E-2
 .425276
 .882146
READY
```

*Some systems do not allow the RANDOMIZE statement but do provide the means for causing different sequences of random numbers to be generated. The BASIC manual for your system will describe how to do this.

We conclude this section with an example of how the RND function can be used to simulate a real-life situation.

EXAMPLE 5. A professional softball player has a lifetime batting average of .365. Assuming she will come to bat four times in each of her next 100 games, estimate in how many games she will go hitless, have one hit, have two hits, have three hits, and have four hits.

Problem Analysis: To simulate one time at bat, we will generate a number RND(0) and concede a hit if RND(0) < 0.365. For any one game we will compare four such numbers with 0.365. If in a particular game K hits are made ($0 \le K \le 4$), we will record this by adding 1 to the counter C(K + 1). Thus, C(1) counts the number of hitless games, C(2) the games in which one hit is made, and so on.

The Flowchart

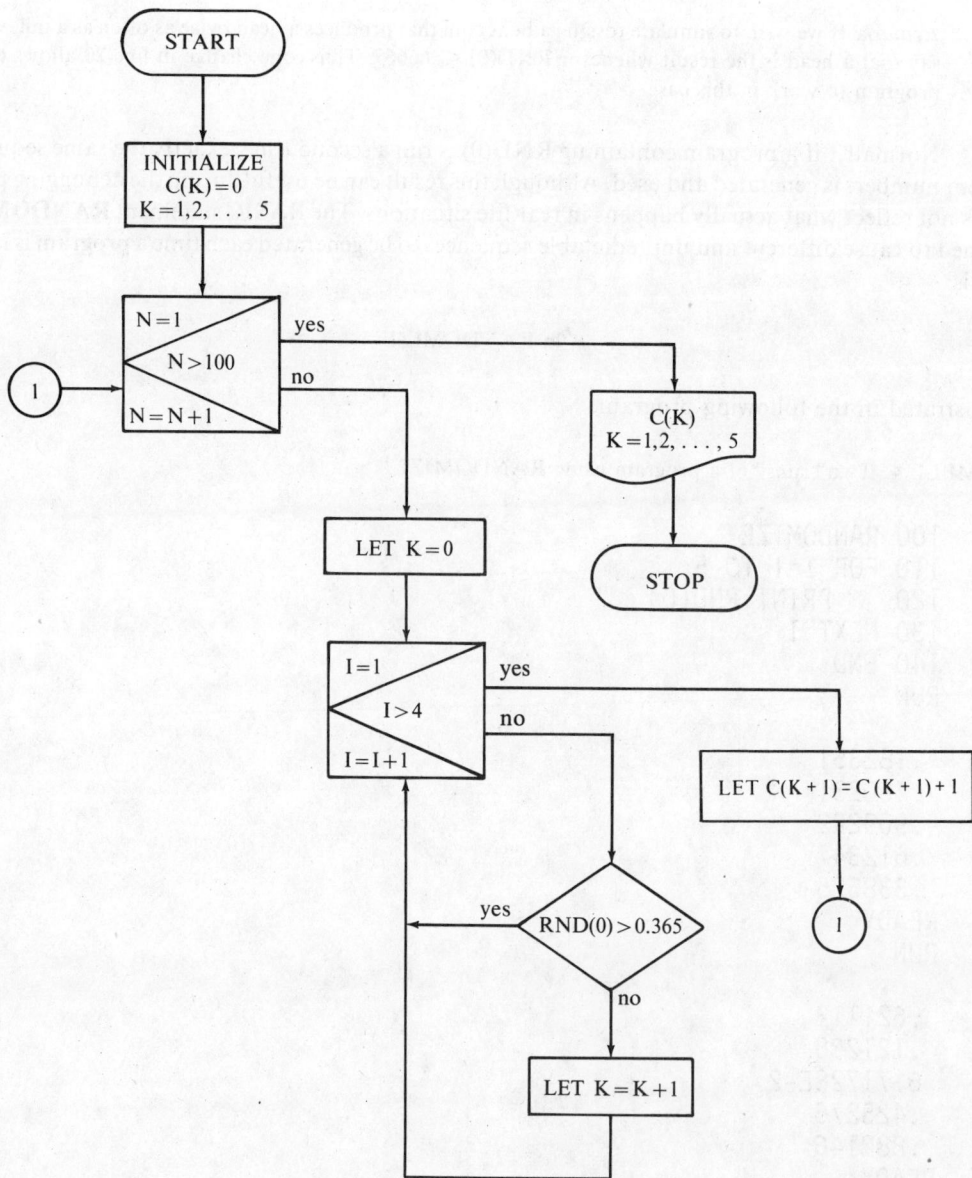

The Program

```
100 REM INITIALIZE COUNTERS TO ZERO
110 FOR K=1 TO 5
120     LET C(K)=0
130 NEXT K
140 REM N LOOP COUNTS THE NUMBER OF GAMES
150 FOR N=1 TO 100
160     REM I LOOP DETERMINES NUMBER K OF HITS IN EACH GAME
170     LET K=0
180     FOR I=1 TO 4
190         IF RND(0)>0.365 THEN 210
200         LET K=K+1
210     NEXT I
220     LET C(K+1)=C(K+1)+1
230 NEXT N
240 PRINT "HITS PER GAME","FREQUENCY"
250 PRINT
260 FOR K=1 TO 5
270     PRINT TAB(6);K-1;TAB(18);C(K)
280 NEXT K
290 END
RUN
```

```
HITS PER GAME   FREQUENCY

      0             16
      1             39
      2             35
      3             9
      4             1
READY
```

13.2 PROBLEMS

Write a program to perform each task specified in Problems 1–9.

1. Print approximately one-fourth of all values appearing in DATA lines. A decision to print or not to print should be made as the number is read.
2. Print approximately 1% of all integers from 1000 to 9999, inclusive. They are to be selected randomly.
3. Simulate tossing three coins ten times. The output should be a list of ten terms such as HHH, HTH, HHT, and so on.
4. Simulate tossing K coins N times. The output should be a list of N terms in which each term is a sequence of K Hs and Ts. N and K are to be input.
5. A game between players A and B is played as follows. A coin is tossed three times or until a head comes up, whichever occurs first. As soon as a head comes up, player A collects $1 from player B. If no head comes up on any of the three tosses, player B collects $6 from player A. In either case, the game is over. Your program is to simulate this game 1000 times to help decide whether A or B has the advantage, or if it is a fair game.
6. Generate a list L of 1000 random numbers between 0 and 1. Using L, determine a list C as follows. C(1) is a count of how many entries of L are between 0 and .1, C(2) a count of those between .1 and .2, and so on. The list C should then be printed.
7. Create a list B of approximately 20 different integers from 1 to 100. The integers are to be chosen randomly. List B should be printed, but only after it has been completely determined.

8. Read 20 different names into a list L$. Create and print a list R$ containing approximately 10 different names selected randomly from L$. Do not print list R$ until after it has been completely determined.

9. The first three hitters in the Bears' batting order have lifetime batting averages of .257, .289, and .324, respectively. Simulate their first trip to the plate for the next 100 games, and tabulate the number of games in which they produce zero, one, two, and three hits.

13.3   RANDOM INTEGERS

Many computer applications require generating random *integers* rather than just random numbers between 0 and 1. For example, suppose a manufacturer estimates that a proposed new product will sell at the rate of 10 to 20 units each week and wants a program to simulate sales figures over an extended period of time. To write such a program, we must be able to generate random integers from 10 to 20 to represent the estimated weekly sales. To do this, we can multiply RND(0), which is between 0 and 1, by 11 (the number of integers from 10 to 20) to obtain

$$0 \leq 11*RND(0) < 11.$$

If many numbers are obtained using 11*RND(0), they will be nearly uniformly distributed between 0 and 11. This means that the value of INT(11*RND(0)) will be one of the integers 0, 1, 2, . . . , 10. Thus, if we add 10 to this expression, we will get an integer from 10 to 20.

$$10 \leq INT(11*RND(0)) + 10 \leq 20.$$

The important thing here is that integers generated in this manner will appear to have been chosen randomly from the set of integers {10, 11, 12, . . . , 20}.

In general, if A and B are integers with A < B,

$$INT((B - A + 1)*RND(0))$$

will generate an integer from 0 to B – A. (Note that B – A + 1 gives the number of integers between A and B, inclusive.) Thus, adding A to this expression, we obtain

$$INT((B - A + 1)*RND(0)) + A$$

whose value is an integer chosen randomly from the set {A, A + 1, A + 2, . . . , B}.

EXAMPLE 6.   Write a program to generate 20 numbers randomly from the set {1, 2, 3, 4, 5}.

Problem Analysis: From the preceding discussion we know that the expression INT(5*RND(0)) will be an integer from 0 to 4. Thus, INT(5*RND(0)) + 1 will be an integer from 1 to 5, as required.

```
10 FOR I=1 TO 20
20    PRINT INT(5*RND(0))+1;
30 NEXT I
40 END
RUN

 1 2 5 1 5 5 4 3 5 3 3 4 2 4 2 2 1 5 4 1
READY
```

EXAMPLE 7.   Write a program to generate 20 numbers randomly from the set {100, 101, 102, . . . , 199}.

Problem Analysis: The technique used in Example 6 is also applicable here. Since INT(100*RND(0)) is an integer from 0 to 99, we must add 100 to obtain an integer from the specified set. Thus, the program required is that of Example 6 with the instruction in line 20 changed to

20 PRINT INT(100*RND(0)) + 100

13.4 SIMULATION

The speed of modern computing machines, together with their ability to generate rather good random sequences, allows us to approach many problems in ways not previously possible. The simulation of future events based on data obtained by observing the results of similar or related previous events is now a common computer application. Example 5 of Section 13.1, concerning the estimation of a ball player's future performance, is one illustration of the simulation of a real-life situation. In this section we give two examples showing how this technique may be used in a business setting.

EXAMPLE 8. A retail store will soon handle a new product. A preliminary market survey indicates that between 500 and 1000 units will be sold each month. (The survey is no more specific than this.) Write a program to simulate sales for the first six months. The retail store management is to be allowed to experiment by specifying the periodic (monthly) inventory purchase.

Problem Analysis: The problem statement does not specify the nature of the output. Let's agree to print a table showing the following items.

P = monthly inventory purchase (to be input).
M = the month (1, 2, ..., 6).
B = quantity on hand at the beginning of the month.
S = estimated sales (500–1000) for one month.
E = quantity on hand at the end of a month.

For each month we must generate a random integer S from 500 to 1000. There are 501 integers to choose from (501 = 1000 – 500 + 1). Thus, we can use the expression

INT(501*RND(0)) + 500

to select an integer randomly from 500 to 1000.

As soon as the monthly inventory purchase P is input, we can calculate B, S, and E as follows.

B = E + P (E will initially be 0).
S = INT(501*RND(0)) + 500.
E = B – S if B ≥ S. Otherwise, E = 0.

The Program

```
100 REM NEW PRODUCT SIMULATION
110 REM    P=MONTHLY INVENTORY PURCHASE
120 REM    M=MONTH (1,2,...,6)
130 REM    B=ON HAND-BEGINNING OF MONTH
140 REM    S=SALES FOR ONE MONTH (500-1000)
150 REM    E=ON HAND-END OF MONTH
160 PRINT "MONTHLY INVENTORY PURCHASE";
170 INPUT P
180 PRINT
190 PRINT "MONTH","ON HAND","EST. SALES","ON HAND AT END OF MONTH"
200 PRINT
```

```
210 LET E=0
220 FOR M=1 TO 6
230     LET B=E+P
240     LET S=INT(501*RND(0))+500
250     IF S>B THEN 280
260     LET E=B-S
270     GO TO 290
280     LET E=0
290     PRINT M,B,S,E
300 NEXT M
310 END
RUN

MONTHLY INVENTORY PURCHASE? 1000
```

MONTH	ON HAND	EST. SALES	ON HAND AT END OF MONTH
1	1000	533	467
2	1467	699	768
3	1768	953	815
4	1815	589	1226
5	2226	906	1320
6	2320	939	1381

READY

Remark 1: The large values in the last column suggest that this program should be run again using something less than 1000 as the monthly inventory-purchase figure.

Remark 2: An unnecessary GO TO statement appears in line 270. How can it be eliminated?

EXAMPLE 9. The owner of a drive-in theater is planning a $5.00-per-car special for Tuesday nights. Previous experience indicates that between 150 and 200 cars enter the theater on Tuesdays and that the number of people arriving in each car varies from one to five. Approximately one-half of the cars have two passengers, approximately one-fourth have four, and the remaining one-fourth have either one, three, or five passengers, with each of these last three counts being equally likely. Experience also indicates that a special of the type being planned will result in a 30% to 50% increase in the number of cars arriving on any one night. Assuming that the regular admission price is $2.50 per person, simulate the admissions for the next five Tuesdays to compare the revenue under the special price with what would be taken in at the regular price.

Problem Analysis: The problem statement does not specify the precise form of the output. Let's agree to produce a five-column printout showing the following values for each of the five Tuesdays.

N1 = the number of cars under the regular admission price.
C = the total number of passengers in the N1 cars.
R1 = the total revenue represented by these C people (R1 = C*2.50).
N2 = the number of cars under the special admission price.
R2 = the total revenue represented by these N2 cars (R2 = N2*5).

The specification of "what" is to be printed leads us directly to the following algorithm.

The Algorithm

a. Choose N1 (a random integer from 150 to 200).
b. Determine the total number C of passengers in the N1 cars.

c. Multiply 2.50 by C to obtain the revenue R1.
d. Increase N1 by from 30% to 50% to obtain N2.
e. Multiply 5.00 by N2 to obtain the revenue R2.
f. Print the values N1, C, R1, N2, R2 on one line.
g. Go to step (a) until five lines have been printed.

Steps (a), (c), (e), and (f) can each be accomplished with one programming line, whereas step (g) simply involves setting up a FOR/NEXT loop.

Step (b) is more complicated. To determine the count C, we must determine the number of people in each of the N1 cars and add these N1 numbers together. Since one-half of the cars have two passengers, we will generate a random number R using RND(0) and add 2 to C if $R < .5$. Similarly, since approximately one-fourth of the cars have four passengers, we will add 4 to C if $1/2 \leq R < 3/4$. However, if $R \geq 3/4$, we must select a number from the set $\{1, 3, 5\}$ and add it to C. You may check that the BASIC expression

$$2*INT(3*RND(0)) + 1$$

has a value from the set $\{1, 3, 5\}$ and that each of these three numbers is equally likely to occur. The following partial flowchart displays the method just described for finding the count C.

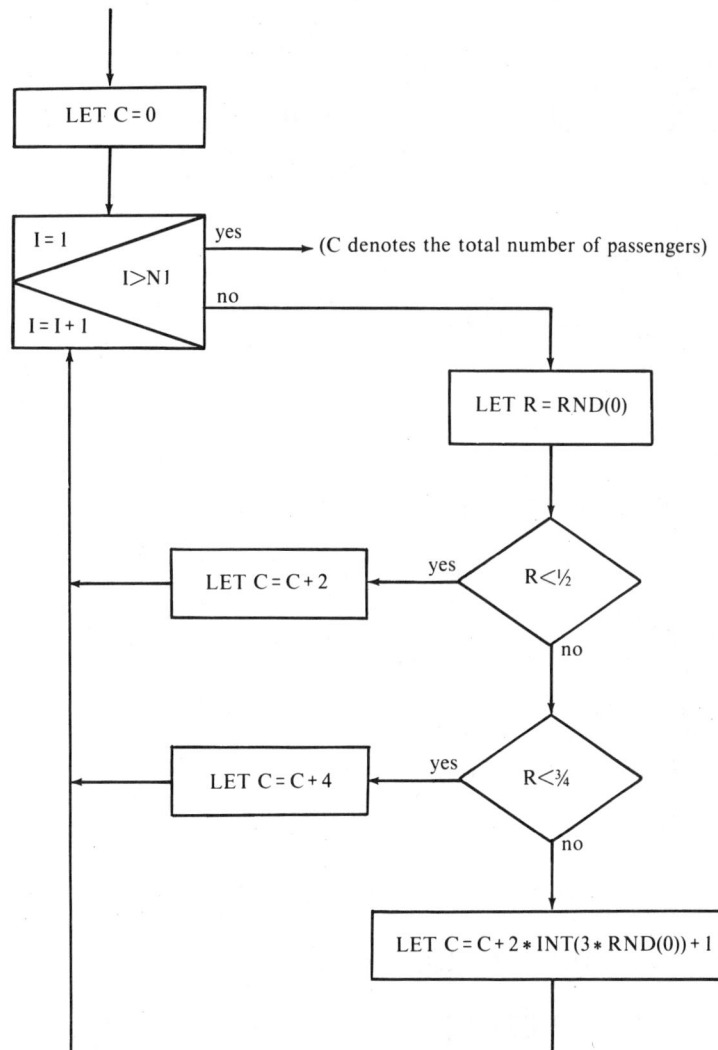

Step (d) requires that we generate a number from 30 to 50 to represent the percentage by which N1 must be increased to obtain N2. Letting P denote this percentage, step (d) can be accomplished as follows.

$$\text{LET P} = \text{INT}(21*\text{RND}(0)) + 30$$
$$\text{LET N2} = \text{N1} + (\text{P}/100)*\text{N1}$$
$$\text{LET N2} = \text{INT}(\text{N2} + .5)$$

The third line rounds N2 to a whole number since it is a count.

The Program

```
100 PRINT "                        DRIVE-IN SIMULATION"
110 PRINT
120 PRINT "REGULAR ADMISSION - $2.50 PER PERSON"
130 PRINT "SPECIAL ADMISSION - $5.00 PER CAR"
140 PRINT
150 PRINT "          REGULAR ADMISSION                    SPECIAL ADMISSION"
160 PRINT "------------------------------------    -----------------------"
170 PRINT "NO. OF CARS","NO. OF PEOPLE","REVENUE","NO. OF CARS","REVENUE"
180 PRINT
190 REM SIMULATE ADMISSIONS FOR FIVE TUESDAYS
200 FOR T=1 TO 5
210    REM N1 = NUMBER OF CARS AT REGULAR ADMISSION PRICE
220    LET N1=INT(51*RND(0))+150
230    REM C = TOTAL NUMBER OF OCCUPANTS OF THE N1 CARS
240    LET C=0
250    FOR I=1 TO N1
260       LET R=RND(0)
270       IF R<.5 THEN 310
280       IF R<.75 THEN 330
290       LET C=C+2*INT(3*RND(0))+1
300       GO TO 340
310       LET C=C+2
320       GO TO 340
330       LET C=C+4
340    NEXT I
350    REM R1 = REVENUE REPRESENTED BY THE C CUSTOMERS
360    LET R1=C*2.50
370    REM N2 = NUMBER OF CARS AT SPECIAL ADMISSION PRICE
380    LET P=INT(21*RND(0))+30
390    LET N2=N1+(P/100)*N1
400    LET N2=INT(N2+.5)
410    REM R2 = REVENUE REPRESENTED BY THE N2 CARS
420    LET R2=N2*5.00
430    REM PRINT ONE ROW OF THE REPORT
440    PRINT TAB(3);N1;TAB(18);C;TAB(30);R1;TAB(47);N2;TAB(60);R2
450 NEXT T
460 END
RUN
```

                          DRIVE-IN SIMULATION

REGULAR ADMISSION - $2.50 PER PERSON
SPECIAL ADMISSION - $5.00 PER CAR

REGULAR ADMISSION			SPECIAL ADMISSION	
NO. OF CARS	NO. OF PEOPLE	REVENUE	NO. OF CARS	REVENUE
153	395	987.5	211	1055
197	538	1345	288	1440
197	539	1347.5	292	1460
167	450	1125	235	1175
196	554	1385	257	1285

READY

13.5   PROBLEMS

1. Write BASIC statements to print the following.
   a. a nonnegative random number (not necessarily an integer) less than 4.
   b. a random number less than 11 but not less than 5.
   c. a random number less than 3 but not less than –5.
   d. a random integer between 6 and 12, inclusive.
   e. a random number from the set {0, 2, 4, 6, 8}.
   f. a random number from the set {1, 3, 5, 7, 9}.
2. Which of these relational expressions are always true? Which are always false? Which may be true or false?
   a. RND(0) >= 0
   b. 4*RND(0) <= 4
   c. INT(7*RND(0)) <= 6
   d. INT(2*RND(0) + 4) < 6
   e. RND(0) <= RND(0)
   f. INT(RND(0)) <= RND(0)
   g. RND(0) + 1 > RND(0)
   h. RND(0) + RND(0) = 2*RND(0)
3. What values can be assumed by each of the following expressions? For each expression, tell whether the possible values are all equally likely to occur.
   a. INT(2*RND(0) + 1)
   b. 3*INT(RND(0))
   c. INT(5*RND(0)) – 2
   d. INT(2*RND(0)+1) + INT(2*RND(0)+1)
   e. INT(6*RND(0)+1) + INT(6*RND(0) + 1)
   f. INT(3*RND(0)+1)*(INT(3*RND(0))+1)
4. If two coins are tossed, two heads, two tails, or one of each may result. The following program was written to simulate tossing two coins a total of 50 times. If it is run, the output will not reflect what would happen if the coins were actually tossed. Explain why, and then write a correct program.

```
100 FOR I=1 TO 50
110    LET R=INT(3*RND(0))
120    IF R=0 THEN 160
130    IF R=1 THEN 180
140    PRINT "ONE OF EACH"
150    GO TO 190
160    PRINT "TWO HEADS"
170    GO TO 190
180    PRINT "TWO TAILS"
190 NEXT I
200 END
```

Write a program to perform each task specified in Problems 5–16.

5. Print a sequence of 20 letters that are selected randomly from the word RANDOM.
6. Simulate tossing a pair of dice 1000 times, and count the number of 2s, 3s, 4s, ..., 12s.
7. Randomly select and print an integer from 1 to 100 and then another from the remaining 99.
8. Create a list B of exactly 20 different integers from 1 to 100. The integers are to be chosen randomly. The list should be printed, but only after it is completely determined.
9. Read 20 different names into a list L$. Randomly select and print a name from L$; then select and print another from the remaining 19 names.

10. Read a list L$ as described in Problem 9. Then create a second list M$ containing exactly 10 different names chosen randomly from list L$. List M$ should be printed, but only after it has been completely determined.

11. A retail store will soon carry a new product. A preliminary market analysis indicates that between 300 and 500 units will be sold each week. (The survey is no more specific than this.) Assuming that each unit costs the store $1.89, write a program to simulate sales for the next 16 weeks. The store management is to be allowed to specify the selling price to obtain a printout showing the week, the estimated sales in number of units, the total revenue, the income (revenue – cost), and the cumulative income. The user should be allowed to try many different selling prices during a single program run.

12. Juanita Fernandes is offered the opportunity to transfer to another sales territory. She is informed that, for each month of the past year, sales in the territory were between $18,000 and $30,000, with sales of $25,000 or more being twice as likely as sales under $25,000. A 4% commission is paid on all sales up to $25,000 and 8% on all sales above that figure. Simulate the next six months' sales, and print the monthly sales and commission to give Juanita some information on which to base her decision to accept or reject the transfer.

13. The IDA Production Company will employ 185 people to work on the production of a new product. It is estimated that each person can complete between 85 and 95 units each working day. Previous experience shows that the absentee rate is between 0% and 15% on Mondays and Fridays and between 0% and 7% on the other days. Simulate the production for one week. The results of this simulation are to be printed in four columns showing the day of the week, the number of workers present, the number of units produced, and the average number produced per worker.

14. Jones and Kelley are to have a duel at 20 paces. At this distance Jones will hit the target on the average of two shots in every five and Kelley will hit one in every three. Kelley shoots first. Who has the best chance of surviving? Use a FOR/NEXT loop to run the program 20 times and print the results.

15. (Drunkard's Walk) A poor soul, considerably intoxicated, stands in the middle of a 10-foot-long bridge that spans a river. The inebriate staggers along, either toward the left bank or toward the right, but fortunately cannot fall off the bridge. Assuming that each step taken is exactly one foot long, how many steps will be taken before the drunkard reaches either bank of the river?

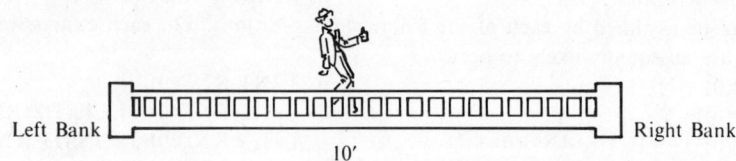

Left Bank   10'   Right Bank

It must be assumed that it is just as likely that a step will be toward the left bank as toward the right. You must do three things.
a. Find how many steps are taken in getting off the bridge.
b. Tell which bank is reached.
c. Let the drunkard go out for several nights and arrive at the same point (the center) on the bridge. Find, on the average, how many steps it takes to get off the bridge.

16. Two knights begin at diagonally opposite corners of a chessboard and travel randomly about the board but always making legitimate knight moves. (The knight moves either one step forward or backward and then two steps to the right or left or else two steps forward or backward and one step to the right or left.) Calculate the number of moves before one knight captures the other. However you number the squares, each knight's move should be printed as it is taken.

17. A single trip for a knight is defined as follows. The knight starts in one corner of a chessboard and randomly makes N knight moves to arrive at one of the 64 squares of the chessboard. (See Problem 16 for a description of an admissible knight move.) Write a program to simulate 1000 such trips for a knight to determine counts of how many times each square was reached at the end of a trip. These counts should be presented as an 8-by-8 table displaying the counts for the 64 squares. A value for N is to be supplied by a user who is allowed to obtain such a frequency table for many values of N during a single program run.

13.6 REVIEW TRUE OR FALSE QUIZ

1. If 100 numbers are generated by the instruction LET R = RND(0), then approximately one-half of these numbers will be less than 50.   T F

2. If 100 numbers are generated by the instruction LET R = INT(2*RND(0)), then approximately one-half will be 0 and one-half will be 1.   T F

3. If 100 numbers are generated by the instruction

$$\text{LET R} = \text{INT}(2*\text{RND}(0)) + \text{INT}(2*\text{RND}(0))$$

then each of the values 1, 2, 3, and 4 will be generated approximately 25 times.   T   F

4. RND(0)/RND(0) = 1.   T   F

5. RND(0) – RND(0) is not necessarily zero.   T   F

6. A certain experiment has two possible outcomes, Outcome 1 and Outcome 2. To simulate this experiment on the computer, we can generate a number R = RND(0) and specify that Outcome 1 occurs if R is less than .5 and Outcome 2 occurs otherwise.   T   F

7. Let L$ be a list of 100 different names. If we wish to select *exactly* 20 of these names randomly, we can generate 100 random numbers between 0 and 1 and select the Ith name in the list L$ if the Ith number generated is less than 0.2.   T   F

8. The value of the expression INT(17*RND(0)) + 1 is an integer between 1 and 17, inclusive.   T   F

9. The value of the expression INT(5*RND(0)) + 5 is an integer between 5 and 10, inclusive.   T   F

14 MATRIX OPERATIONS

In the discussion of subscripted variables in Chapter 9, both two-dimensional and one-dimensional arrays were introduced. The 2-by-3 array B with entries B(1,1) = 5, B(1,2) = 3, B(1,3) = 4, B(2,1) = 6, B(2,2) = 7, and B(2,3) = 9 is normally thought of as a rectangular array of numbers

$$\begin{bmatrix} 5 & 3 & 4 \\ 6 & 7 & 9 \end{bmatrix}$$

having two rows and three columns. The one-dimensional array (list) A with entries A(1) = 4, A(2) = 8, A(3) = 2, and A(4) = 1 can also be thought of as a rectangular array

$$\begin{bmatrix} 4 \\ 8 \\ 2 \\ 1 \end{bmatrix}$$

that has four rows and one column.

We define a **matrix** to be any rectangular array of numbers. (The plural of *matrix* is *matrices*.) Thus, lists and arrays are matrices. Because matrices have proven to be a useful aid in the solution of a variety of problems, the most common mathematical operations on matrices have been included in extended versions of BASIC. This chapter will describe and illustrate the BASIC statements used to perform matrix operations.

14.1 ASSIGNING VALUES TO A MATRIX: THE **MAT READ** AND **MAT INPUT** STATEMENTS

The MAT READ and MAT INPUT statements are used to assign values to matrices. The clarity and conciseness with which a program can be written using these two statements are evident in the following examples.

EXAMPLE 1. A program to read six numbers into a 2-by-3 matrix B and print the matrix B.

For purposes of comparison the program is written in two ways: on the left with subscripted variables and on the right with BASIC matrix instructions.

```
10 FOR I=1 TO 2                    10 DIM B(2,3)
20    FOR J=1 TO 3                 20 MAT READ B
30       READ B(I,J)               30 MAT PRINT B;
40       PRINT B(I,J);             40 DATA 5,3,4,6,7,9
50    NEXT J                       50 END
60    PRINT                        RUN
70 NEXT I
80 DATA 5,3,4,6,7,9                 5   3   4
90 END
RUN                                 6   7   9
                                   READY
  5   3   4

  6   7   9
READY
```

The programming lines

10 DIM B(2,3)
20 MAT READ B

cause the computer to read six values from DATA lines. These values are assigned to the matrix B by rows; that is, B(1,1), B(1,2), B(1,3) will be read first, and then B(2,1), B(2,2), B(2,3) will be read. The MAT PRINT statement (line 30) is described in the next section.

Matrices should be dimensioned. If they are not, BASIC assumes that they are 10-by-10 arrays (11 by 11 where zero subscripts are assumed). Thus, if the DIM statement in Example 1 were omitted, the attempt to read more than the six values presented in the DATA lines would result in an OUT OF DATA message, and the run would terminate.

If your system assumes zero subscripts, you can normally change this with the statement

In OPTION BASE 1

or some similar statement as described in your BASIC manual. In what follows, the assumption is that the smallest subscript is 1.

EXAMPLE 2. A program to assign values to a matrix during program execution.

```
10 DIM B(2,3)
20 MAT INPUT B
30 MAT PRINT B;
40 END
RUN

? 5,3,4
? 6,7,9
  5   3   4

  6   7   9
READY
```

In response to the question mark, you must type the proper number of values to fill the first row of the matrix (matrices are always assigned by row) and then type ®. Another question mark will appear. The process should be repeated until the matrix, as defined, has been completely assigned. Only then will program execution continue.

More than one matrix may appear in a MAT READ or MAT INPUT statement.

EXAMPLE 3.

```
10 DIM C(3,4),D(2,2)
20 MAT READ C,D
30 DATA 8,7,6,5,4,3,2,1
40 DATA 8,7,6,5,4,3,2,1
50 END
```

Two matrices C and D are dimensioned in line 10. Line 20 instructs the computer to read the two matrices C and D. C is read completely before D is read to give

$$C = \begin{bmatrix} 8 & 7 & 6 & 5 \\ 4 & 3 & 2 & 1 \\ 8 & 7 & 6 & 5 \end{bmatrix} \qquad D = \begin{bmatrix} 4 & 3 \\ 2 & 1 \end{bmatrix}$$

The general forms of the MAT READ and MAT INPUT statements are

ln MAT READ **a,b,c,**...
ln MAT INPUT **a,b,c,**...

where **a,b,c,**... denote matrices.

14.2 THE **MAT PRINT** STATEMENT

This statement is used to print matrices. The programming line

30 MAT PRINT B;

in Example 1 caused the matrix B to be printed by rows, the semicolon after B indicating that B should be printed using the packed format. One line is automatically skipped between each row of the matrix. If line 30 had been

30 MAT PRINT B,

the matrix would again be printed by rows, but only one number would appear in each print zone.

EXAMPLE 4.

```
10 DIM B(2,3)
20 MAT READ B
30 MAT PRINT B;
40 MAT PRINT B,
50 DATA 5,3,4,6,7,9
60 END
READY
RUN
```

```
5   3   4

6   7   9
```

```
5               3               4

6               7               9
READY
```

If no punctuation follows the matrix in a MAT PRINT statement, the comma is assumed.

More than one matrix may appear in a MAT PRINT instruction.

EXAMPLE 5.

```
10 DIM C(3,4),D(2,2)
20 MAT READ C,D
25 MAT PRINT C,D
30 DATA 8,7,6,5,4,3,2,1
40 DATA 8,7,6,5,4,3,2,1
50 END
RUN
```

```
8               7               6               5

4               3               2               1

8               7               6               5
```

```
4   3

2   1
READY
```

Matrix C is printed first according to its format, followed by matrix D according to its format.

The general form of the MAT PRINT statement is

$$\text{ln MAT PRINT } \mathbf{a}z\mathbf{b}z\mathbf{c}z\dots$$

where $\mathbf{a},\mathbf{b},\mathbf{c},\dots$ denote matrices and $\mathbf{z}$ is either a comma or a semicolon. The second matrix is printed under the first, the third under the second, and so on.

14.3   ONE-DIMENSIONAL MATRICES

When we are using matrix operations, a one-dimensional array is regarded as a matrix with one column. Thus, the two dimension statements DIM A(5) and DIM A(5,1) are equivalent. If a list A with five elements is to be regarded as having one row with five entries, it must be dimensioned with DIM A(1,5).

EXAMPLE 6. Two programs that yield the same results.

```
10 FOR I=1 TO 5            10 DIM A(1,5)
20    READ A(I)            20 MAT READ A
30    PRINT A(I);          30 MAT PRINT A;
40 NEXT I                  40 DATA 3,1,6,5,4
50 DATA 3,1,6,5,4          50 END
60 END                     RUN
RUN
                            3  1  6  5  4
 3  1  6  5  4             READY
READY
```

EXAMPLE 7.

```
10 DIM M(4)
20 MAT READ M
30 MAT PRINT M
40 DATA 4,3,2,1
50 END
RUN

4

3

2

1
READY
```

14.4   MATRIX OPERATIONS

BASIC allows the standard matrix operations of addition, subtraction, multiplication, and scalar multiplication. These operations are defined as follows.

Addition (Subtraction): The sum (difference) of two matrices A and B is formed by adding (taking the difference of) the corresponding entries in A and B. The matrices must have the same dimensions.

Scalar Multiplication: The product cA, where c denotes a scalar (number) and A a matrix, is formed by multiplying each entry in A by c.

Multiplication: The product C = A*B of the row-and-column matrices

$$A = \begin{bmatrix} a & b & c \end{bmatrix} \qquad B = \begin{bmatrix} x \\ y \\ z \end{bmatrix}$$

is the 1-by-1 matrix

$$C = [ax + by + cz].$$

For example,

$$[1 \quad 2 \quad 4] * \begin{bmatrix} 1 \\ 3 \\ 4 \end{bmatrix} = \quad [1 \cdot 1 + 2 \cdot 3 + 4 \cdot 4] = [23]$$

$$[3 \quad 2] * \begin{bmatrix} 1 \\ 5 \end{bmatrix} = \quad [3 \cdot 1 + 2 \cdot 5] \quad = [13]$$

Note that the number of columns of A must equal the number of rows of B. To find the product A*B of matrices other than row-and-column matrices, we consider the rows of A as row matrices and the columns of B as column matrices. Then, the entry in the Ith row and Jth column of A*B is found by taking the product of the Ith row of A and the Jth column of B as described above. The product matrix A*B will have the same number of rows as A and the same number of columns as B. For example,

$$\begin{bmatrix} 2 & 3 & 1 \\ 4 & 1 & 2 \end{bmatrix} * \begin{bmatrix} 1 & 2 \\ 3 & 4 \\ 1 & 5 \end{bmatrix} = \begin{bmatrix} 2 \cdot 1 + 3 \cdot 3 + 1 \cdot 1 & 2 \cdot 2 + 3 \cdot 4 + 1 \cdot 5 \\ 4 \cdot 1 + 1 \cdot 3 + 2 \cdot 1 & 4 \cdot 2 + 1 \cdot 4 + 2 \cdot 5 \end{bmatrix} = \begin{bmatrix} 12 & 21 \\ 9 & 22 \end{bmatrix}$$

The BASIC instructions to perform these operations are as follows.

$$MAT \ S = A + B$$
$$MAT \ D = A - B$$
$$MAT \ S = (C) * A$$
$$MAT \ P = D * E$$

Matrices A and B must have the same dimensions so that A + B and A – B can be calculated. Also, so that the product P = D*E will be defined, the number of columns of D must equal the number of rows of E.

EXAMPLE 8. A program to compute and print A + B, A – B, 2B, and A*B for the following matrices A and B.

$$A = \begin{bmatrix} 2 & 3 & 4 \\ 6 & 7 & 7 \\ 4 & 4 & 3 \end{bmatrix} \qquad B = \begin{bmatrix} 1 & 2 & 1 \\ 1 & 2 & 1 \\ 1 & 0 & 0 \end{bmatrix}$$

```
100 DIM A(3,3),B(3,3),C(3,3)
110 MAT READ A,B
120 MAT C=A+B
130 PRINT "THE MATRIX A+B"
140 PRINT
150 MAT PRINT C;
160 MAT C=A-B
170 PRINT "THE MATRIX A-B"
180 PRINT
190 MAT PRINT C;
200 MAT C=(2)*B
210 PRINT "THE MATRIX 2*B"
220 PRINT
230 MAT PRINT C;
240 MAT C=A*B
250 PRINT "THE MATRIX A*B"
```

```
260 PRINT
270 MAT PRINT C;
280 DATA 2,3,4,6,7,7,4,4,3
290 DATA 1,2,1,1,2,1,1,0,0
300 END
RUN
```

THE MATRIX A+B

```
 3   5   5

 7   9   8

 5   4   3
```

THE MATRIX A-B

```
 1   1   3

 5   5   6

 3   4   3
```

THE MATRIX 2*B

```
 2   4   2

 2   4   2

 2   0   0
```

THE MATRIX A*B

```
 9  10   5

20  26  13

11  16   8
```

Remark 1: The matrix C that is to be calculated must be dimensioned to the exact size in a DIM statement.

Remark 2: Line 200 is typical of assignment statements that multiply a matrix by a scalar. Note that the scalar (2 in this case) is enclosed in parentheses. The instruction is MAT C = (2)*B, not MAT C = 2*B. The scalar may be any expression, variable, or constant.

Remark 3: Matrix operations must be performed in assignment statements as shown in lines 120, 160, 200, and 240. Statements such as MAT PRINT A + B are not allowed.

EXAMPLE 9. A plumbing-supply company has developed the following data over the past quarter.

	April	May	June
Income	20,415	22,355	33,451
Expenses	19,041	20,851	26,152

Write a program to compute the monthly profit for these three months and also the amount that should be put aside for tax purposes if the tax rate is 18% on all profits.

Problem Analysis: Let's read the income into a 1-by-3 matrix I and the expenses into another 1-by-3 matrix E. Then the profit for each month is given by the entries in the matrix P = I – E and the taxes are given in the matrix T = .18P.

The Program

```
100 REM PROFIT AND TAX COMPUTATION FOR ONE QUARTER
110 DIM I(1,3),E(1,3),P(1,3),T(1,3)
120 MAT READ I,E
130 MAT P=I-E
140 MAT T=(.18)*P
150 READ A$,B$,C$
160 PRINT ,A$,B$,C$
165 PRINT
170 PRINT "PROFIT",
180 MAT PRINT P,
190 PRINT "TAXES",
200 MAT PRINT T,
500 DATA 20415,22355,33451
510 DATA 19041,20851,26152
520 DATA APRIL,MAY,JUNE
999 END
RUN
```

	APRIL	MAY	JUNE
PROFIT	1374	1504	7299
TAXES	247.32	270.72	1313.82

The matrix expressions that may be evaluated in matrix-assignment statements are very limited compared with the freedom allowed in forming BASIC expressions with LET statements. At most one operation may be performed in a single matrix-assignment statement. Statements such as

$$\text{MAT } X = Y + Z - (3)*W$$

are not allowed. Furthermore, a matrix may not be used as an operand in a statement assigning values to the same matrix. Thus, statements such as

$$\text{MAT } A = A + B$$
$$\text{MAT } A = (2)*A$$

are not allowed.

14.5 MATRIX FUNCTIONS

Certain matrix functions are included in the BASIC language.

The **CON** Function

The statement

$$10 \text{ MAT D} = \text{CON}(4,7)$$

will generate a 4-by-7 matrix D, all of whose entries are 1s.

The **ZER** Function

The statement

$$20 \text{ MAT E} = \text{ZER}(5,6)$$

will generate a 5-by-6 matrix E, all of whose entries are 0s. The ZER function is useful when initializing all values of an array to 0.

The **IDN** Function

The statement

$$30 \text{ MAT F} = \text{IDN}(3,3)$$

will generate the 3-by-3 identity matrix (1s in the upper-left to lower-right diagonal and 0s elsewhere). The product of the N-by-N identity matrix and any other N-by-N matrix A is A.

The arguments in these three functions need not be positive integers; they may be any BASIC numerical expressions. As illustrated in the following example, they can be used to assign dimensions to matrices other than those given in DIM statements.

EXAMPLE 10. An illustration of the CON, ZER, and IDN functions.

```
100 DIM C(20,20),Z(20,20),I(20,20)
110 INPUT A,B
120 MAT C=CON(A,B)
130 MAT Z=ZER(B,A)
140 MAT I=IDN(A+B,A+B)
150 MAT PRINT C;Z;I
160 END
RUN

? 3,2

 1  1

 1  1

 1  1


 0  0  0
```

```
0   0   0


1   0   0   0   0

0   1   0   0   0

0   0   1   0   0

0   0   0   1   0

0   0   0   0   1
```

READY

Remark: The matrices C, Z, and I are initially dimensioned as 20-by-20 arrays in line 100. They are redimensioned in lines 120, 130, and 140 using the functions CON, ZER, IDN. If values other than 3 and 2 are input, this program will print matrices of different dimensions. The only restriction is that you cannot redimension a matrix so that it requires more memory locations (the product of its dimensions) than those reserved in the initial DIM statement (20 × 20 = 400 in this example).

BASIC contains the matrix functions **TRN** and **INV** to determine the *transpose* and *inverse,* respectively, of a matrix A. The transpose is the matrix whose rows are the columns of A. Thus, the transpose of

$$\begin{bmatrix} 1 & 2 \\ 3 & 4 \\ 5 & 6 \end{bmatrix} \quad \text{is} \quad \begin{bmatrix} 1 & 3 & 5 \\ 2 & 4 & 6 \end{bmatrix}.$$

The inverse of a matrix A is the matrix B for which A*B = B*A = I, the identity matrix. Only certain square matrices (same number of rows as columns) can have inverses. You may check that

$$\begin{bmatrix} 1 & 1 \\ 0 & 1 \end{bmatrix} * \begin{bmatrix} 1 & -1 \\ 0 & 1 \end{bmatrix} = \begin{bmatrix} 1 & -1 \\ 0 & 1 \end{bmatrix} * \begin{bmatrix} 1 & 1 \\ 0 & 1 \end{bmatrix} = \begin{bmatrix} 1 & 0 \\ 0 & 1 \end{bmatrix}$$

so that the inverse of

$$\begin{bmatrix} 1 & 1 \\ 0 & 1 \end{bmatrix} \quad \text{is} \quad \begin{bmatrix} 1 & -1 \\ 0 & 1 \end{bmatrix}.$$

The functions TRN and INV are used in assignment statements as follows.

ln MAT **a** = TRN(**b**)
ln MAT **a** = INV(**b**)

where **a** and **b** denote different matrices.

The function TRN can sometimes be used to enhance the output of a program. For example, suppose that a 4-by-6 matrix A is to be printed. The instruction

MAT PRINT A,

cannot be used, since A has 6 columns; at most 5 values will be printed on a line. If the instruction

MAT PRINT A;

is used, the six columns may not "line up" because of the packed format. However, if the two instructions

$$\text{MAT T = TRN(A)}$$
$$\text{MAT PRINT T,}$$

are used, there are only 4 columns to be printed and the difficulty vanishes.

Neither the inverse nor the transpose of a matrix may be calculated in place. Hence, statements such as

$$\text{100 MAT B = D*INV(C)}$$
$$\text{200 MAT M = TRN(A) + E}$$

are not allowed.

EXAMPLE 11. A program to read and print a 3-by-3 matrix C and then to calculate and print both the inverse of C and the product of C and its inverse.

```
100 DIM A(3,3),B(3,3),C(3,3)
110 MAT READ C
120 PRINT "MATRIX C"
130 PRINT
140 MAT PRINT C
150 MAT B=INV(C)
160 PRINT "INVERSE OF C"
170 PRINT
180 MAT PRINT B
190 MAT A=C*B
200 PRINT "MATRIX C TIMES INVERSE OF MATRIX C"
210 PRINT
220 MAT PRINT A
230 DATA 1,2,3,9,8,7,-2,5,-7
240 END
RUN

MATRIX C

1               2               3

9               8               7

-2              5               -7


INVERSE OF C

-.478947         .152632        -5.26316E-2

 .257895        -5.26316E-3      .105263

 .321053        -4.73684E-2     -5.26316E-2


MATRIX C TIMES INVERSE OF MATRIX C
```

1.	0	-1.24345E-14
0	1.	3.55271E-15
-4.44089E-16	-3.55271E-15	1

READY

14.6 PROBLEMS

1. What will be printed when each program is run?

a.
```
10 DIM A(4,1)
20 MAT READ A
30 MAT PRINT A;
40 DATA 2,4,6,8,1,3,5
50 END
```

b.
```
10 MAT D=CON(3,3)
20 FOR I=1 TO 3
30    LET D(I,2)=D(I,2)+4
40 NEXT I
50 MAT PRINT D;
60 END
```

c.
```
10 DIM H(4,4),I(8,8)
20 MAT I=IDN(4,4)
30 FOR J=1 TO 4
40    MAT H=(J)*I
50 NEXT J
60 MAT PRINT H;
70 END
```

d.
```
10 DIM A(4,3)
20 FOR I=1 TO 4
30    FOR J=1 TO 3
40       LET A(I,J)=I+J
50    NEXT J
60 NEXT I
70 MAT PRINT A
80 END
```

e.
```
10 DIM A(5,5)
20 MAT A=ZER(5,5)
30 FOR K=1 TO 5
40    READ A(K,K)
50 NEXT K
60 MAT PRINT A;
70 DATA 7,9,1,3,5
80 END
```

f.
```
10 DIM M(8,8)
20 MAT M=ZER(5,5)
30 FOR I=1 TO 5
40    LET M(I,I)=M(I,I)+I
50 NEXT I
60 MAT PRINT M;
70 END
```

2. Each of the following programs contains at least one error. Make corrections to ensure that all programs will run to completion.

a.
```
10 DIM A(8,1),B(8,1)
20 MAT READ A
30 MAT B=4*A
40 MAT PRINT B
50 DATA 4,3,2,1,3,5,7,9
60 END
```

b.
```
10 DIM M(2,2),D(2,2)
20 MAT M=CON(2,2)
30 MAT D=(M+M)+M
40 MAT PRINT D
50 END
```

c.
```
10 DIM A(2,3),B(3,2),C(2,2)
20 MAT READ A,B
30 LET C=A*B
40 MAT PRINT C
50 DATA 3,1,7,2,6,3
60 DATA 5,9,1,8,-3,0
70 END
```

d.
```
10 DIM A(2,3),B(2,3)
20 MAT READ A,B
30 MAT PRINT A+B
40 DATA 2,4,6,5,7,9
50 DATA 3,5,8,2,7,3
60 END
```

Write a program to perform each task specified in Problems 3–13.

3. Read a 2-by-3 matrix A from DATA lines, and print both A and the transpose of A.
4. Read a 2-by-3 matrix A from DATA lines to determine its transpose B and the product A∗B of A and its transpose. Print the three matrices A, B, and A∗B.
5. Read two 3-by-2 matrices from DATA lines, and print the two matrices, the sum of the two matrices, and the transpose of this sum.
6. Input nine values for the 3-by-3 matrix A. Then print the matrices A and $A^2 = A*A$.
7. Print the cube $A^3 = A*A*A$ of any 3-by-3 matrix A whose entries are input at the terminal.
8. Read a 3-by-3 matrix A from DATA lines, and then print the matrices $A, A^2, A^3, \ldots, A^N$ where N is a positive integer input at the terminal. Try your program for the value N = 6 and the matrix

$$A = \begin{bmatrix} .2 & .4 & .4 \\ .01 & .02 & .97 \\ .8 & .05 & .15 \end{bmatrix}$$

9. Often when we are using the computer to manipulate matrices whose entries are integers, we generate matrices with entries that are not actually integers as desired but are very close to integers. For instance (see Example 11), the product of a matrix and its inverse, which should be the identity matrix, often has entries very close to 0 and 1 that should actually be 0 or 1. Write a subroutine to convert all such matrices to their correct integer form.
10. DATA line 500 contains the current salaries of the eight employees of a small business. Line 510 contains the individual merit increases to be given to each employee. In addition, each person is to receive a cost-of-living adjustment of 2.5% of the current salary. Calculate and print the new salaries using only the matrix instructions.
11. Last year's budgets for the seven departments in a retail store appear in DATA lines. Because of inflation, it is decided to increase each budget by 3.4%. Using only matrix instructions, print the new budgets and also the total amount that must be budgeted for all seven departments.
12. A list of allowable medical-insurance claims for the preceding year is given in DATA lines. Because of a $50-deductible clause, each claim is to be reduced by $50. The amount actually paid on each claim is 80% of this reduced amount. Using only matrix instructions, print the amount paid on each claim and the total amount paid.
13. An investment club owns shares in seven different companies. The first seven figures in the following DATA lines give the number of shares owned, and the second seven figures give the respective current values of these seven stocks.

        300 DATA 100,275,350,65,840,975,355
        310 DATA 37.50,12.125,42.75,87.375,125.25,8.75,34.375

Using only matrix instructions, print the total paper value of this stock portfolio.

14.7 REVIEW TRUE OR FALSE QUIZ

1. Once a matrix B has been read from DATA lines, the entries of B may not be changed during program execution.   T F
2. In BASIC, *one-dimensional arrays* are considered to be *matrices* having one column.   T F
3. If a program contains the statement DIM A(10,10), the matrix A can be given different dimensions by using the CON, ZER, or IDN functions.   T F
4. If an 8-by-8 matrix B has been dimensioned in a DIM statement, it may be redimensioned during program execution only if both dimensions are kept less than or equal to 8.   T F
5. In some programs it may be necessary to dimension a matrix more than once by using more than one DIM statement.   T F
6. The statement MAT A = A + C is not allowed.   T F
7. If A and B are both M-by-N matrices, their sum will be printed by the instruction MAT PRINT A + B.   T F
8. Matrices must be assigned values by using matrix instructions.   T F
9. The statement MAT B = A∗INV(C) is not allowed.   T F
10. The two statements MAT A = (3)∗B and MAT A = B + B + B are equivalent.   T F

15 STRING FUNCTIONS AND STATEMENTS

String variables, as described in Chapter 10, provide the means to process data that include strings as well as numerical values. Extended versions of BASIC include special *string functions* and *statements* to assist you in such tasks. These items greatly simplify the task of examining the contents of strings and also allow you to modify strings and build new strings from old ones. BASIC statements and functions to perform these tasks are described in this chapter. However, systems that include these extended features differ in their implementation; hence, a precise description of how they work must be gleaned from your BASIC manual.

15.1   STRING FUNCTIONS

Four of the most useful **string functions** are described in this section. The first determines the length of a string, and the other three are used to examine the individual characters.

The STRING Function **LEN**

The value of LEN(A$) is the number of characters in the string A$. For this reason it is called the LENGTH function.

EXAMPLE 1.

```
10 LET Z$="JOHN AND MARY"
20 LET A=LEN(Z$)
30 PRINT A
40 END
RUN

 13
READY
```

As always, blanks contained in quoted strings are counted as characters.

EXAMPLE 2. A program to print only those strings that contain exactly three characters.

```
10 FOR I=1 TO 6
20    READ X$
30    IF LEN(X$)<>3 THEN 50
40    PRINT X$
50 NEXT I
60 DATA "THE","I DO","ONE","OLD ","THREE","127"
70 END
RUN

THE
ONE
127
READY
```

Note that "I DO" has four characters, three letters and an embedded blank. Similarly, "OLD " has a trailing blank character.

The STRING Function **LEFT**

The value of LEFT(A$,N) is the string consisting of the first N characters of A$. (Some systems use the form SUBSTR(A$,1,N) instead of LEFT(A$,N).)

EXAMPLE 3.

```
10 LET Y$="SEVEN"
20 FOR N=1 TO LEN(Y$)
30    PRINT LEFT(Y$,N)
40 NEXT N
50 END
RUN

S
SE
SEV
SEVE
SEVEN
READY
```

(On systems using SUBSTR, write 30 PRINT SUBSTR(Y$,1,N) in place of line 30.)

EXAMPLE 4. A program to print only those words that begin with whatever prefix is input by a user.

```
100 PRINT "TYPE A PREFIX";
110 INPUT P$
120 PRINT
130 FOR K=1 TO 10
140    READ A$
150    IF LEFT(A$,LEN(P$))<>P$ THEN 170
160    PRINT A$
170 NEXT K
```

```
180 DATA ENABLE,ENACT,ENGAGE,ENSURE,ENDORSE
190 DATA OBCLUDE,OBDURATE,OBJECT,REACT,RECISION
200 END
RUN

TYPE A PREFIX? OB

OBCLUDE
OBDURATE
OBJECT
READY
```

(On systems using SUBSTR, LEFT (A$,LEN(P$)) would be replaced by SUBSTR(A$,1,LEN(P$)).)

The STRING Function **RIGHT**

The value of RIGHT(A$,N) is the string consisting of all characters in A$ from the Nth character on. (Some systems use the form SUBSTR(A$,N).)

EXAMPLE 5.

```
10 LET Y$="SEVEN"
20 FOR N=1 TO LEN(Y$)
30    PRINT RIGHT(Y$,N)
40 NEXT N
50 END

N
EN
VEN
EVEN
SEVEN
READY
```

(On systems using SUBSTR, write 30 PRINT SUBSTR(Y$,N) in place of line 30.)

The STRING Function **MID**(DLE)

The value of MID(A$,I,J) is the string of J characters from A$ beginning with the Ith character of A$. (Some systems use SUBSTR(A$,I,J).)

EXAMPLE 6.

```
10 LET Y$="ABCD"
20 FOR I=1 TO LEN(Y$)
30    PRINT MID(Y$,I,1)
40 NEXT I
50 END
RUN

A
```

```
        B
        C
        D
      READY
```

(On systems using SUBSTR, write 30 PRINT SUBSTR(Y$,I,1).)

EXAMPLE 7. A program to count the number of As in a string A$ of any length.

```
      100 LET C=0
      110 INPUT A$
      120 FOR I=1 TO LEN(A$)
      130    IF MID(A$,I,1)<>"A" THEN 150
      140      LET C=C+1
      150 NEXT I
      160 PRINT "NUMBER OF A'S IS";C
      170 END
      RUN

      ? ABACADABRA
      NUMBER OF A'S IS 5
      READY
```

(On systems using SUBSTR, write 130 IF SUBSTR(A$,I,1)<>"A" THEN 150.)

15.2   COMBINING STRINGS (CONCATENATION)

The **concatenation operator +** allows you to combine two or more strings into a single string. Thus, the statement

$$LET \ X\$ = \text{"PARA"} + \text{"MEDIC"}$$

assigns the string "PARAMEDIC" to the variable X$. Similarly, if A$ = "PARA" and B$ = "MEDIC", the statement

$$LET \ X\$ = A\$ + B\$$$

does exactly the same thing.

EXAMPLE 8. A program to illustrate the concatenation operator.

```
      10 LET X$="BIOLOGY"
      20 LET Y$="ELECTRONICS"
      30 LET Z$=LEFT(X$,3)+RIGHT(Y$,8)
      40 PRINT Z$
      50 END
      RUN

      BIONICS
      READY
```

(On systems using SUBSTR, write 30 LET Z$ = SUBSTR(X$,1,3) + SUBSTR(Y$,8).)

Using only the functions LEFT and RIGHT, we could have caused BIONICS to be printed at the terminal, but we could not have assigned the string "BIONICS" to the variable Z$.

EXAMPLE 9. A program to interchange the first and last names given in the string "EMILY DICKINSON".

```
10 LET A$="EMILY DICKINSON"
20 FOR I=1 TO LEN(A$)
30    IF MID(A$,I,1)=" " THEN 50
40 NEXT I
50 LET L$=RIGHT(A$,I+1)
60 LET A$=L$+" "+LEFT(A$,I-1)
70 PRINT A$
80 END
RUN

DICKINSON EMILY
READY
```

(On systems using SUBSTR, write SUBSTR(A$,I,1) in line 30, SUBSTR(A$,I + 1) in line 50, and SUBSTR(A$,1,I – 1) in line 60.)

The technique illustrated in this example has two immediate applications: it gives you additional control over the precise form of your printed output, and it allows you to alphabetize a list of names, even if first names are given first (simply interchange first and last names and then use a standard sorting algorithm such as the bubblesort to alphabetize your list).

15.3 CONVERSION BETWEEN STRINGS AND NUMERIC CODES: THE **CHANGE** STATEMENT

There are two forms of the CHANGE statement. The first is

ln CHANGE s TO a

where **s** denotes a string variable and **a** denotes a numerical list name. It is used to convert the characters in a string to a list of their numeric codes. The length of the string becomes the first entry in the list, and successive entries are assigned the numeric codes of the individual characters.

EXAMPLE 10.

```
10 LET A$="MARY"
20 CHANGE A$ TO B
30 FOR I=1 TO 5
40    PRINT B(I);
50 NEXT I
60 END
RUN

 4  7  65  82  89
READY
```

"MARY" contains four characters; hence, 4 is assigned to B(1). The numeric code 77 of "M" is assigned to B(2), the code 65 of "A" is assigned to B(3), and so on. As noted in Section 10.2, the numeric codes vary from system to system. This program was run on a system using the ASCII codes shown in Table 10.1 (page 128).

EXAMPLE 11. A program to print the numeric codes used by any BASIC system.

In the following program the characters whose numeric codes are desired are included in DATA lines. Each of these is read into A$, and the statement

CHANGE A$ to B

is used to assign its numeric code to B(2). (B(1) will always be assigned the value 1, since only single-character strings are being converted.) The final DATA value "END" is used to terminate the run.

To conserve paper, we use the TAB function in a FOR/NEXT loop to print the column headings and also in a second FOR/NEXT loop to print the numeric codes in tabular form.

The Program

```
100 FOR I=0 TO 2
110    PRINT TAB(20*I+1);"CHAR.        CODE";
120 NEXT I
130 PRINT
140 PRINT
150 FOR J=0 TO 2
160    READ A$
170    IF A$="END" THEN 290
180    CHANGE A$ TO B
190    PRINT TAB(20*J+3);A$;TAB(20*J+10);B(2);
200 NEXT J
210 PRINT
220 GO TO 150
230 DATA A,B,C,D,E,F,G,H,I,J,K,L,M
240 DATA N,O,P,Q,R,S,T,U,V,W,X,Y,Z
250 DATA "0","1","2","3","4","5","6","7","8","9"
260 DATA ":",";","<","=",">","?","@","!","#","$"
270 DATA "&","'","(",")","*","+",",","-",".","/"
280 DATA " ","↑",END
290 END
RUN
```

CHAR.	CODE	CHAR.	CODE	CHAR.	CODE
A	65	B	66	C	67
D	68	E	69	F	70
G	71	H	72	I	73
J	74	K	75	L	76
M	77	N	78	O	79
P	80	Q	81	R	82
S	83	T	84	U	85
V	86	W	87	X	88
Y	89	Z	90	0	48
1	49	2	50	3	51
4	52	5	53	6	54
7	55	8	56	9	57
:	58	;	59	<	60
>	62	=	61	?	63

!	33	#	35	$	36
&	38	'	39	(	40
)	41	*	42	+	43
,	44	–	45	.	46
/	47		32	↑	94

READY

The second form of the CHANGE statement reverses the process just described. The form is

ln CHANGE a TO s

where **a** denotes a numerical list name and **s** denotes a string variable. The first entry in the list determines the length of the string to be constructed and assigned to the string variable. The BASIC character corresponding to the numeric code in the second entry of the list becomes the first character of the string, the character corresponding to the numeric code in the third entry becomes the second character, and so forth. Of course, the length must be a valid string length. That is, it must be no larger than the maximum-length string assignable to a string variable on the system being used.

EXAMPLE 12.

```
10 FOR I=1 TO 6
20    READ N(I)
30 NEXT I
40 CHANGE N TO S$
50 PRINT S$
60 DATA 5,72,79,87,68,89
70 END
RUN

HOWDY
READY
```

Here, $N(1) = 5$; hence, a string of five characters is created by line 40. $N(2) = 72$ is the numeric code for "H", so this is the first character of the string. The other four characters are assigned similarly.

EXAMPLE 13.

```
100 LET A$="RORRIM"
110 CHANGE A$ TO L
120 FOR I=2 TO 4
130    LET T=L(I)
140    LET L(I)=L(9-I)
150    LET L(9-I)=T
160 NEXT I
170 CHANGE L TO B$
180 PRINT B$,A$
190 END
RUN

MIRROR          RORRIM
READY
```

15.4   PROBLEMS

1. Write a single program statement to perform each of the following tasks. (Use only the functions described in Section 15.1.)
   a. Print the first character of A$.
   b. Print the second character of A$.
   c. Print the last character of A$.
   d. Print the first three characters of A$.
   e. Print the last three characters of A$.
   f. Print the first and last characters of A$.
   g. Transfer control to line 70 if A$ and B$ have the same number of characters.
   h. Transfer control to line 95 if the first character of A$ equals the last character of B$.
   i. Transfer control to line 160 if the first two characters of A$ are the same.
   j. Assign the first N characters of A$ to B$.

2. Write a single program statement to perform each of the following tasks. (Use the concatenation operator but not the CHANGE statement.)
   a. A$ is a two-letter string. Interchange these letters to obtain the string B$.
   b. Interchange the first two characters in S$ to obtain T$.
   c. Create a string F$ consisting of the first three characters of G$ and the last three characters of H$.
   d. Transfer control to line 150 if the first character of A$, the second character of B$, and the third character of C$, spell "YES".

3. What will be printed when each program is run?

a.
```
10 LET A$="BASIC-PLUS"
20 CHANGE A$ TO N
30 LET N(1)=5
40 CHANGE N TO A$
50 PRINT A$
60 END
```

b.
```
10 LET X$="AM"
20 CHANGE X$ TO A
30 LET T=A(2)
40 LET A(2)=A(3)
50 LET A(3)=T
60 CHANGE A TO Y$
70 PRINT Y$+"D"+X$
80 END
```

c.
```
10 LET N$="TEA CUP"
20 CHANGE N$ TO A
30 LET A(1)=A(1)-1
40 FOR I=5 TO 7
50    LET A(I)=A(I+1)
60 NEXT I
70 CHANGE A TO N$
80 PRINT N$
90 END
```

d.
```
10 LET S$="RED"
20 CHANGE S$ TO M
30 FOR I=5 TO 7
40    LET M(I)=M(9-I)
50 NEXT I
60 LET M(1)=M(1)+3
70 CHANGE M TO S$
80 PRINT S$
90 END
```

Write a program for each task specified in Problems 4–12.

4. Any five-character string input at the terminal is to be printed in reverse order. If the string does not contain exactly five characters, nothing is to be printed. A user should be allowed to try many strings, and the program should halt when the user types "DONE".

5. Any string input at the terminal is to be printed in reverse order. The program should halt only when the user types "DONE".

6. For any string input at the terminal, two columns are to be printed. The first column is to contain the characters in the string and the second their numeric codes.

7. All strings appearing in DATA lines are to be examined to determine and print those that begin with whatever letter is input at the terminal. A user is to be allowed to try different letters during a single run.

8. Two five-letter words are to be input at the terminal. They are to be compared, letter by letter. If two corresponding letters are different, a dollar sign should be printed. Otherwise, the letter should be printed. For example, if "CANDY" and "CHIDE" are input, the output should be C$$D$.

9. Two words are to be input to obtain a listing of those letters in the second word that are also in the first. For example, if "STRING" and "HARNESS" are typed, the output should be RNSS, since these four letters in the second word HARNESS are also in the first.

10. A string containing two words separated by a comma is to be input. The two words are to be printed in reverse order without the comma. For example, if "GARVEY, STEVE" is typed, the output should be STEVE GARVEY.

11. A program is to contain the following DATA lines.

```
800 DATA 9
810 DATA "MARIAN EVANS","JAMES PAYN","JOSEPH CONRAD"
820 DATA "EMILY DICKENSON","HENRY THOREAU","JOHN PAYNE"
830 DATA "JOHN FOX","MARY FREEMAN","GEORGE ELIOT"
```

The names are to be read twice. On the first pass, only those names with a last name beginning with a letter from A to M are to be printed. The remaining names are to be printed in the second pass.

12. Alphabetize the list of names given in Problem 11. (See Example 9, Section 15.2.) Use the following algorithm.

    a. Read the names into a list A$.
    b. Create a new list B$ containing the names in A$ but with last names first.
    c. Use a bubblesort to place B$ in alphabetical order. When a swap is made in B$, make the same swap in A$.
    d. Print the list A$.

15.5   REVIEW TRUE OR FALSE QUIZ

1. If LEN(X$) = LEN(Y$), then X$ = Y$.   T   F
2. If A denotes a number, LEN(A) will give the number of digits in A.   T   F
3. LEN("GO TO")<>LEN("GOTO").   T   F
4. LEN(X$ + Y$) = LEN(X$) + LEN(Y$).   T   F
5. The CHANGE statement is used to convert a string to a numerical list and also a numerical list to a string.   T   F
6. If A$ = "TEA FOR TWO", then the statement CHANGE A$ TO A will assign the value 9 to A(1).   T   F

(For systems using LEFT, RIGHT, MID)

7. B$ = LEFT(B$,LEN(B$)).   T   F
8. Although it may be convenient to use the functions LEFT and RIGHT, they are not necessary. The function MID can always be used in their place.   T   F
9. If X$ = "MADAM", then MID(X$,3,3) has the value "D".   T   F

(For systems using SUBSTR)

10. B$ = SUBSTR(B$,1,LEN(B$)).   T   F
11. If Y$ = "SEVEN", then SUBSTR(Y$,3,3) has the value "V".   T   F
12. If A$ = "CYBER78", then SUBSTR(A$,6) has the value "78".   T   F

APPENDIX A:
A TYPICAL
SESSION
AT THE
COMPUTER
TERMINAL

During a typical session at the computer terminal, you should be able to perform the following tasks.

1. Establish communication between the terminal and the time-sharing system (log- in).
2. Save your program for later use.
3. Retrieve and run a program that was previously saved.
4. Modify a saved program.
5. Break communication between the terminal and the time-sharing system (log-off).

In this appendix, the system commands that allow you to carry out these tasks are described.

A.1   THE LOG-IN PROCEDURE

The log-in procedure differs from system to system. Normally, you will need a **password** and a **project-programmer number** (called a **user number** on many systems). With these in hand, you should follow the log-in procedure described in the User's Guide for your BASIC system. Following is the printout generated at the terminal during the log-in process for two widely used BASIC systems.

Log-in under RSTS (Version 4) Time-Sharing Systems

(Underlined characters are printed by the computer.)

HELLO	(Type this to initiate the log-in procedure.)

RSTS---(System identifies itself)---

# 110,65	(Type your project-programmer number.)
PASSWORD:	(Type your password here. It is not printed.)

    (A message to RSTS users may be printed)

NEW OR OLD: NEW	(Type NEW to indicate that you wish to type in a new program.)
NEW FILE NAME---PROG1	(Type a name for your program.)

204

<u>READY</u>

Log-in under the Kronos Time-Sharing System

(Underlined characters are printed by the computer.)

<u>USER NUMBER</u>: ABC652   (Type your user number.)

<u>PASSWORD</u>   (Type your password. It is printed in the
▨▨▨▨▨▨▨▨   blocked-out positions.)
<u>SYSTEM</u>: BASIC   (Type BASIC to indicate that you will be
                                              using the BASIC language.)
<u>NEW OR OLD FILE</u>: NEW   (Type NEW to indicate that you wish to
                                              type in a new program.)

<u>FILE NAME</u>: PROG1   (Type a name for your program.)

<u>READY</u>

The READY message indicates that the log-in procedure is complete. You may now type in your program or may type any system command. For example, after READY is printed, you may proceed as follows (underlined characters are printed by the computer).

```
READY
100 LET S = 13 * 2 + 9
110 PRINT S
120 END
RUN

 35
READY
LIST

100 LET S = 13 * 2 + 9
110 PRINT S
120 END
READY
```

A.2   SAVING YOUR PROGRAM

A file created under the NEW command is called a **local** or **temporary file.** It continues to exist only as long as you are logged into the system. To preserve such a file for later use, you may issue the SAVE command.

SAVE   (You type this.)
READY   (Printed by the computer.)

The SAVE command creates a permanent copy of the current local file. This permanent copy is called a **permanent file,** for it will continue to exist even after you log off the system.

The following printout shows how you can type in two programs and create a permanent copy of each of them (underlined characters are printed by the computer).

NEW   (Indicates that a new program will be
                                              typed.)
<u>NEW FILE NAME</u>--PROG1   (You name the program PROG1.)
<u>READY</u>   (The local file PROG1 is empty.)

(Type your first program.)

.
.
.

SAVE	(Save PROG1 as a permanent file.)
READY	(PROG1 also exists as the local file.)
NEW	(Indicates that a new program will be typed.)
NEW FILE NAME--PROG2	(You name the program PROG2.)
READY	(The new local file PROG2 is empty.)

(Type your second program.)

.
.
.

SAVE	(Save PROG2 as a permanent file.)
READY	(PROG2 also exists as the local file.)

If you now log-off the system, the permanent files PROG1 and PROG2 will not be lost and can be used again at another time.

A.3   RETRIEVING A PERMANENT FILE

Let's assume that the files PROG1 and PROG2 have been made permanent by the SAVE command. If at a later session you wish to run these programs, you may proceed as follows (underlined characters are printed by the computer).

(log-in)

.
.
.

NEW OR OLD: OLD	(A previously saved file is wanted.)
OLD FILE NAME--PROG1	(Request PROG1.)
READY	(PROG1 is now the local file.)

RUN

.
.
.

    (PROG1 will be executed.)

.
.
.

READY

LIST

.
.
.

    (PROG1 will be listed.)

.
.
.

READY

OLD   (Type OLD to request another permanent file.)

OLD FILE NAME--PROG2   (Request PROG2.)
READY   (PROG2 is now the local file.)

At this point, the new files PROG1 and PROG2 continue to exist as permanent files. They can be retrieved as local files by issuing the OLD command, and, as local files, they can be executed or listed using the commands RUN and LIST. They can also be modified as described in the next section.

A.4   MODIFYING A PERMANENT FILE

It is often the case that a program is saved before it is completely debugged. Let's assume that a permanent file named POWER2 contains such a program. To modify POWER2, you must first use the OLD command to retrieve it as the local file. Having done this, you can modify the local file POWER2 just as you could when creating it under the NEW command. After making the necessary modifications, you may replace the permanent copy of POWER2 with the modified version by typing

REPLACE

The modified version is now the permanent file and can be retrieved at any subsequent session at the terminal.

The following printout illustrates what has just been described (underlined characters are printed by the computer).

OLD   (Request a permanent file.)
OLD FILE NAME--POWER2
READY   (POWER2 is now the local file.)

LIST

100 LET A=5   (Contents of POWER2.)
110 LET B=A↑2
120 PRINT B
130 END
READY

100 LET A=7   (Change line 100.)
LIST

100 LET A=7   (Updated POWER2.)
110 LET B=A↑2
120 PRINT B
130 END
READY

REPLACE   (Updated version of POWER2 is now
READY   permanent.)

RUN   (The local file POWER2 is executed.)
49
READY

If in this example you type SAVE instead of REPLACE, the system will print a message such as

FILE EXISTS   or   POWER2 ALREADY PERMANENT

and will leave the permanent file POWER2 unchanged. If you really mean to replace the old version with the new one, you must type REPLACE. However, if you wish to preserve the permanent file POWER2 and also save the modified version that now exists as the local file POWER2, you must first rename the local file. This can be accomplished by typing

RENAME POWER3

where POWER3 is chosen as the new name for the local file. (You should consult the User's Guide for your system to find the precise form of the RENAME command.)

Having renamed the local file as POWER3, and assuming that you had not previously saved a file under that name, you may type the command SAVE to create a permanent copy of POWER3.

A.5   LOG-OFF PROCEDURE

Before you log off, be sure that all permanent files no longer needed are excised from permanent storage. Each BASIC system that allows you to SAVE programs also allows you to remove them from permanent storage. On some systems the command

UNSAVE PROG7

will remove PROG7 from permanent storage, whereas another system may require that you type

PURGE, PROG7

The precise form to be used will be described in the User's Guide for your system. Normally, a listing of all your permanent files can be obtained with the system command CATALOG.

To break the communication link between your terminal and the time-sharing system, type

BYE

Should this command not log you off of your system, you should consult your User's Guide.

IMPORTANT: At this time turn your terminal off.

APPENDIX B:
ANSWERS
TO
SELECTED
PROBLEMS

SECTION 1.4

1. 5% discount   **2.** Calculate discount only if total is greater than $500.   **3.** $693.50   **4.** $250.00
5. G denotes gross pay; B denotes overtime pay.   **6.** $4.00   **7.** $6.00   **8.** Determine whether overtime
applies.
10. a. Read an employee's 3-by-5 card.
   b. If years of service is not greater than ten years, skip the next step.
   c. Write employee's name, job classification, and years of service on the report form.
   d. If there is another card, go to step (a). Otherwise, stop.
12. a. Depress the CLEAR key.
   b. Insert your ID card into reader as shown.
   c. Enter your four-digit code and depress ENTER.
   d. Enter amount of check (2500 or 5000) and depress ENTER.
   e. Place check in punch unit, blank side toward you.
   f. Remove check when READY light comes on.

SECTION 1.5

1. T   **2.** T   **3.** T   **4.** F   **5.** F   **6.** F   **7.** F   **8.** T   **9.** F   **10.** T   **11.** F   **12.** T

SECTION 2.3

1. a. 17   b. 33   c. −2   d. −6   e. −15   f. −9   g. 17   h. 9   i. 0.25   j. −9   k. 64
   l. 3
2. a. 3.5   b. 5   c. 0.75   d. 0.75   e. 10   f. 25   g. 4.5   h. 1.6667   i. 10   j. 3
   k. −8   l. −8
3. a, c, d, e, f, g, and j are not admissible.
4. a. admissible; −12.3   b. admissible; 4   c. 4*(−3); −12
   d. admissible; 10   e. admissible; −12   f. 5E1; 50
   g. admissible; 9   h. admissible; −9   i. 7/(−14); −0.5
   j. admissible; −5   k. admissible; 2   l. admissible; −2
5. a. 0.06*P   b. 5*X+5*Y   c. A↑2+B↑2   d. 6/(5*A)
   e. A/B+C/D   f. (A+B)/(C+D)   g. A*X↑2+B*X+C   h. (B↑2−4*A*C)↑0.5
   i. (X↑2+4*X*Y)/(X+2*Y)

SECTION 2.7

1. a. 10 LET M=7   b. 20 LET B=B+7   c. 30 LET H=2*H
   d. 40 LET C2=(A−B)/2   e. 50 LET A=(1+R)↑10   f. 60 LET X=X−2*Y

2. a. 50 LET X=(A+B)*C   **b.** Correct   **c.** 100 LET R=M–N
d. Correct   **e.** 15 LET X1=2+3*X   **f.** 100 LET S=A+B
g. Correct   **h.** 40 LET Y=4*10↑0.5   **i.** 5 PRINT "SUMMING PROGRAM"
j. Correct

3. a. 12   **b.** AMOUNT=108   **c.** –2   **d.** 5

4. a.

	A	B	C
100	1	–	–
110	1	2	–
120	1	2	1
130	1	2	3
140	4	2	3
150	4	5	3
160	4	5	2
170	4	20	2
180	2	20	2
190	2	20	11

b.

	N	Output
100	1	
110	1	1
120	2	
130	2	2
140	6	
150	6	6
160	42	
170	42	42

c.

	X	Y	Z	Output
100	0	–	–	
110	0	7	–	
120	0	7	7	
130	0	7	7	7
140	7	7	7	
150	7	343	7	
160	7	343	7	343

5. a.

	S	A	Output
100	0	–	
110	0	25	
120	25	25	
130	25	25	25
140	50	25	
150	50	25	50
160	25	25	
170	25	25	25

b.

	X	Y	Output
100	1.5	–	
110	1.5	0.6	
120	1.5	0.6	0.6
130	–1.5	0.6	
140	–1.5	0.6	–1.5
150	–1.5	0.6	0.6

c.

	N	C	S	G	P	Output
100	130	–	–	–	–	
110	130	3	–	–	–	
150	130	3	3.6	–	–	
160	130	3	3.6	468	–	
170	130	3	3.6	468	78	
180	130	3	3.6	468	78	SALES 468
190	130	3	3.6	468	78	PROFIT 78

d.

	A	P	Output
100	–	–	NTH POWERS OF 7
110	7	–	
120	7	7	
130	7	49	
140	7	49	FOR N=2 49
150	7	343	
160	7	343	FOR N=3 343
170	7	2401	
180	7	2401	FOR N=4 2401
190	7	2401	

SECTION 2.8

1. F   **2.** F   **3.** T   **4.** T   **5.** F   **6.** F   **7.** F   **8.** T   **9.** T   **10.** F   **11.** T   **12.** F
13. F   **14.** T   **15.** F

SECTION 3.7

1.
```
100 LET A=14
110 LET B=30
120 LET S=A+B
```

2.
```
100 LET X=5
120 LET Y=20
125 LET S=X+Y
```

```
130 PRINT "SUM IS",S            130 PRINT "X+Y=",S
140 END                         140 END
```

output: SUM IS   44   output: X+Y=   25

3.
```
110 LET P=120
120 LET D=0.1*P
130 LET C=P-D
140 PRINT "DISCOUNT",D
150 PRINT "COST",C
160 END
```

output: DISCOUNT   12
         COST   108

4. Syntax: 30 LET D=23000
   Programming: 40 LET R=.06
   Syntax: 50 LET A=R*D
   Output: ANSWER IS   1380

5. Programming: 50 LET A=(N1+N2)/2
   Syntax: 60 PRINT "AVERAGE IS",A
   Output: AVERAGE IS   19.5

6. Syntax and programming: 40 LET T=0.05
   Syntax: 70 PRINT "TOTAL COST=",S
   Output: TOTAL COST = 126

7. Syntax and programming: 60 LET X=-B/A
   Output: SOLUTION IS -6.28571

8. Syntax: 150 PRINT "B=",B
   Programming: 165 LET T=A
                 180 LET B=T
   Output: A =   5
            B =   8
            A =   8
            B =   5

9. Syntax: quotes missing in lines 170 and 190
   Programming: 185 LET T=V*R
   Output: TAX ON FIRST CAR IS   297
            TAX ON SECOND CAR IS   376.2

SECTION 3.8

1. T   2. F   3. T   4. F   5. T   6. T   7. F   8. T   9. T

SECTION 4.2

1. 120 LET A=100*(1.06)↑X
5. 120 LET A=X/19.2
9. 120 LET A=(4*X/3.14159)↑0.5

3. 120 LET A=X+0.045*X
7. 120 LET A=X/(52*40)

SECTION 4.4

1. a. Output: b. Output: c. Output: d. Output:
      1   1 2 3   1 1   5
      1   1 3 2   2 2   -1
      2   2 3 1   3 6   4
      3   2 1 3   4 24   -2
      5   3 1 2   5 120   3
      8   3 2 1   .   .
      .   .   .   .
      .   .   .   .
      .

2. a. 60 GO TO 40   **b.** 40 LET D=B–A. Interchange lines 50 and 60.
   c. 40 LET T=0.08*X. Change line number 50 to 25.   **d.**   50 LET R=N↑(1/2)
                                                                       80 GO TO 50

SECTION 4.5

1. T   **2.** F   **3.** T   **4.** F   **5.** F   **6.** F   **7.** T   **8.** T

SECTION 5.3

1. a. T   **b.** T   **c.** F   **d.** T   **e.** F   **f.** T   **g.** F   **h.** F

2. a. (A–B)*(A+B) is not a relational expression. Error message.
   b. The comma will cause an error message.
   c. 2<Y<4 is not an admissible relational expression. Error message.
   d. If A<B, control is transferred to line 70. Infinite loop.
   e. Line 51 will be executed next whether or not X<X–B.
   f. Improper use of IF statement. Error message.

3. 150 IF A>0 THEN 180
   160 PRINT "A IS NEGATIVE"
   170 STOP
   180 PRINT "A IS POSITIVE"
   190 END

4. a. –1   **b.** 5   **c.** 1.75   **d.** 225
                                          15

5. a.

	B	I	A	Output
100	0	-	-	
110	0	0	-	
120	0	0	11	
130	2	0	11	
150	2	1	11	
160	2	1	10	
130	5	1	10	
150	5	2	10	
160	5	2	9	
130	9	2	9	
150	9	3	9	
160	9	3	8	
180	9	3	8	3

b.

	B	A	I	Output
100	0	-	-	
110	0	1	-	
120	1	1	-	
170	1	2	-	
180	1	–2	-	
120	–1	–2	-	
140	–1	–2	5	
150	–1	–3	5	
180	–1	3	5	
120	2	3	5	
170	2	4	5	
180	2	–4	5	
120	–2	–4	5	
140	–2	–4	5	
150	–2	–5	5	
180	–2	5	5	
200	–2	5	6	
210	–2	5	6	–2 6 5

6. a. 20 IF N<50 THEN 50
      Delete line 30.
   c. 20 IF X<=0 THEN 10
      40 IF Y<=0 THEN 10
      Delete lines 30 and 50.

   b. 30 IF A<=0 THEN 60
      Delete line 40.
   d. 10 INPUT A,B
      20 IF A<=B THEN 60
      30 LET T=A
      40 LET A=B
      50 LET B=T
      60 PRINT "SMALLEST IS",A
      70 PRINT "LARGEST IS",B
      80 END

SECTION 5.6

1. F   **2.** F   **3.** T   **4.** F   **5.** F   **6.** T   **7.** T   **8.** F   **9.** T   **10.** F   **11.** F   **12.** T

SECTION 6.4

1. a. BASEBALL'S HALL OF FAME   COOPERSTOWN,N.Y.   U.S.A.

b. 0   5   10   15   20

25   30   35   FINI

c. 5 TIMES 8 = 40   d. HAPPY

HAPPY

HOLIDAY

e. 1 2 3 4 5 6 7   f. IF A= 5 THEN A+2= 7

1 2 3 4 5 6 7   IF A= 10 THEN A+2= 12

.   .   .   IF A= 15 THEN A+2= 17

.   .   .

.   .   .

2. a. 10 PRINT X;"/";Y;"=";X/Y   c. 30 PRINT "X–";Y;"=";–X

e. 50 PRINT "DEPT.NO.";Y+Y+X

3. a. 145 PRINT   b. 120 PRINT "7";   c. Prints TEAFORTWO

150 PRINT X;

160 LET X=X+1

SECTION 6.6

1. a.   0   b. 7777777

–1   7

–2   7

–3   7

–4   7

THAT'S ENOUGH   7

7

c.   *   d. X   X↑2

*

*   1   1

*   2   4

*   3   9

*   4   16

.   .

.   .

.   .

2. a. 10 PRINT TAB(6);"B";TAB(9);3

b. 20 PRINT X;TAB(18);0.04*X;TAB(36);0.06*X;TAB(54);0.08*X

c. 90 PRINT 0;TAB(12);0;TAB(24);0;TAB(36);0;TAB(48);0;TAB(60);0

d. 25 PRINT TAB(34);"NAME"

SECTION 6.8

1. a. 1/8=12.5 CENTS   b. TIME 1 A= 0.00

3/8=37.5 CENTS   TIME 2 A= 0.01

5/8=62.5 CENTS   TIME 3 A= 0.01

7/8=87.5 CENTS

c. 01234567890
23.60
23.6

d. RIVERBOAT
BOATSWAIN

SECTION 6.9

1. F   **2.** T   **3.** F   **4.** T   **5.** F   **6.** F   **7.** T   **8.** T   **9.** F   **10.** T   **11.** F

SECTION 7.2

1. a. 4   b. 6   c. 7   d. 3
    7   4   3   11
    1   18
             4

2. a. 140 READ X
    150 LET S=S+X
c. 105 LET N=0
    107 LET S=0
    130 LET N=N+1
    150 GO TO 110

b. 130 READ A
    160 IF N<=4 THEN 130
d. 160 IF X=999 THEN 190
    170 LET S=S+X
    200 GO TO 130

SECTION 7.5

1. a. 9   b. 3
    3   3
    5

2. a. Delete lines 150 and 160. Insert REM in 110 and 120.

    135 RESTORE
    160 IF I>4 THEN 130

SECTION 7.6

1. T   **2.** F   **3.** F   **4.** F   **5.** T   **6.** T   **7.** F   **8.** F   **9.** T   **10.** F   **11.** F   **12.** T

SECTION 8.3

1. a. 4   b. 5   c. TIMES THROUGH LOOP= 2   d. +++///
    5   1   3
    6   −3

2. a. Syntax error:
    50 NEXT N

c. Programming error:
    40 READ Y
    50 LET S=S+Y
    60 PRINT "SUM IS";S

b. Programming error:
    25 LET C=0
    Delete line 40.
d. Programming error:
    STEP S is admissible but the step value
    cannot be changed within the loop.
    30 LET S=0
    40 FOR N=1 TO 5
    50 LET S=S+N
    60 PRINT S

SECTION 8.5

1. a. 2   b. 13 16 11 14   c. 1 1 1 1 1
    3   2 2 2 2 2
    2   3 3 3 3 3
    3
    2
    3

```
d. 2 3 4 5            e. 108            f.  *       *
   3 4 5                                    *     *
   4 5                                        * *
   5                                           *
                                             * *
                                           *     *
                                         *     . *
```

2. a. Syntax error: interchange lines 50 and 60.
  b. Programming error: include STEP –1 in lines 20 and 30.
  c. Programming error: 30 IF I>=J THEN 50
  d. Programming error: 30 IF R<=C THEN 60

3. a.
```
10 FOR R=1 TO 5
20    FOR C=1 TO R
30       PRINT R;
40    NEXT C
50    PRINT
60 NEXT R
70 END
```
c.
```
10 FOR R=1 TO 7
15    FOR C=1 TO 7
20       IF R=3 THEN 50
25       IF R=5 THEN 50
30       IF C=3 THEN 50
35       IF C=5 THEN 50
40       PRINT " ";
45       GO TO 60
50       PRINT "*";
60    NEXT C
65    PRINT
70 NEXT R
75 END
```

SECTION 8.6

1. F   **2.** T   **3.** T   **4.** F   **5.** T   **6.** F   **7.** T   **8.** F   **9.** T   **10.** F   **11.** T

SECTION 9.3

1. a. 5   b. 3 1 5   c. 8   d. 8   8
           4   3   3
2. a. Cannot dimension an array using a variable as in line 20.
  b. DIM statement needed.   c. Values of L(6) through L(10) are lost.
  d. 425 LET S=L(1)
     430 FOR J=2 TO N
     450 LET S=L(J)

SECTION 9.7

1. a. 1 4 9 16   b. 2 4 6   c. 1 1 2   d. 1 1 1 1
                                                           0 1 1 1
                                                           0 0 1 1
                                                           0 0 0 1
2. a. Interchange lines 220 and 230.   b. 230 FOR J=I+1 TO 5

SECTION 9.8

1. T   **2.** F   **3.** F   **4.** F   **5.** F   **6.** F   **7.** T   **8.** T   **9.** T   **10.** F   **11.** F   **12.** F
13. F   **14.** F

SECTION 10.3

1. a. JULY 4, 1776   b. CATWOMAN   c. ROBINHEAD   d. ALBERT
ROBERT

2. a. Use quotes in lines 20 and 30.
b. Use Y$ for Y, or remove the quotes from "42".
c. 60 DATA "LEXINGTON,MA ","02173"
d. Use Y$ for X, or remove quotes from "1".
e. HELLO in line 20 must be quoted.
f. OFFON in line 20 must be quoted. Also, an extra numerical value must be placed after OFFON in line 50.

SECTION 10.6

1. F   **2.** F   **3.** T   **4.** T   **5.** T   **6.** T   **7.** T   **8.** F   **9.** T   **10.** F

SECTION 11.3

1. a. 30 INPUT#1,N,A$,S
Displays the contents of file ABC1 but not the line numbers included in ABC1.
b. 30 READ#2,A$,S
Displays the contents of file ABC2.
c. 20 INPUT#3,N,A$,S
40 INPUT#3,N,B$,T
Displays the name and score of the person with the largest score. If two persons had this largest score, only the first would be displayed.
d. The pointer for file #1 must be reset prior to the loop in lines 70 to 90. The program merges the two files into a single file ABC1. Line numbers are not included in this new file.

SECTION 11.4

1. T   **2.** T   **3.** F   **4.** F   **5.** F   **6.** T   **7.** T   **8.** F   **9.** F

SECTION 12.2

1. a. 9   b. 6   c. 18   d. 26   e. –43   f. 2.4   g. 1200   h. 4   i. 3
2. a. 4   b. 5   c. 6   d. –4   e. 2865   f. 2860   g. 2900   h. 3000   i. 2864.714
3. a. 0   8   b. 1.1   1
1   8   1.21   1
2   6   1.331   1
3   2   1.4641   1
4   4
c. 13.99   13.99   d. 3
13.993   13.99   7
13.996   14.   9
13.999   14.   21
4. a. 10 LET X=INT(10*X+0.5)/10   c. 30 LET X=INT(1000*X+0.5)/1000
e. 50 LET X=1000*INT(X/1000+0.5)

SECTION 12.4

1. a. Programming error: 50 LET V=FNZ(X)
b. Programming error: 20 DEF FNS(X)=X↑2
c. Syntax error: use FNC for FCN.
d. Programming error: 30 DEF FNR(I)=X/I
2. a. 200   b. .5 2 .5   c. 1 2 3 4   d. 10
1400   .5 1 1.5 2   15
0   20
25

3. a. 10 DEF FNF(C)=9/5*C+32
    c. 30 DEF FNM(F)=F/5280
    e. 50 DEF FNK(M)=1.6093*M
    g. 70 DEF FNS(D,T)=D/T
    i. 90 DEF FNC(X,Y)=X/15*Y

    b. 20 DEF FNC(F)=5/9*(F–32)
    d. 40 DEF FNM(K)=K/1.6093
    f. 60 DEF FNA(X,Y)=(X+Y)/2
    h. 80 DEF FNS(X,Y)=X–Y/100*X

SECTION 12.6

1. a.

1	3	5	8
2	8	6	14
3	–2	1	–1

b. 343

c.
1
3
6
10

d.
2
–2

SECTION 12.7

1. F   **2.** F   **3.** T   **4.** F   **5.** F   **6.** T   **7.** T   **8.** F   **9.** T   **10.** T   **11.** F   **12.** T
13. F   **14.** F   **15.** T   **16.** F   **17.** F   **18.** F   **19.** F   **20.** F

SECTION 13.5

1. a. 10 PRINT 4*RND(0)
    c. 30 PRINT 8*RND(0)–5
    e. 50 PRINT 2*INT(5*RND(0))

    b. 20 PRINT 6*RND(0)+5
    d. 40 PRINT INT(7*RND(0))+6
    f. 60 PRINT 2*INT(5*RND(0))+1

2. a. T   b. T   c. T   d. T   e. either   f. T   g. T   h. either (but most likely false)

3. a. 1,2 (equally likely)
    c. –2,–1,0,1,2 (equally likely)

    b. 0
    d. 2,3,4 (3 about half the time; 2 and 4
        each about one-fourth the time)

    e. 2,3,4,...,12 (not equally likely—simulates rolling a pair of dice)
    f. 1,2,3,4,6,9 (not equally likely)

4. ONE OF EACH, TWO HEADS, and TWO TAILS will be printed about the same number of times. In practice, ONE OF EACH will occur about half the time. A better approach is to use

LET A=INT(2*RND(0))
LET B=INT(2*RND(0))

and let 0 denote a head and 1 a tail.

SECTION 13.6

1. F   **2.** T   **3.** F   **4.** F   **5.** T   **6.** F   **7.** F   **8.** T   **9.** F

SECTION 14.6

1. a.
2
4
6
8

b.

1	5	1
1	5	1
1	5	1

c.

4	0	0	0
0	4	0	0
0	0	4	0
0	0	0	4

d.

2	3	4
3	4	5
4	5	6
5	6	7

e.

7	0	0	0	0
0	9	0	0	0
0	0	1	0	0
0	0	0	3	0
0	0	0	0	5

f.

1	0	0	0	0
0	2	0	0	0
0	0	3	0	0
0	0	0	4	0
0	0	0	0	5

2. a. 30 MAT B=(4)*A   b. 30 MAT D=(3)*M
   c. 30 MAT C=A*B   d. 15 MAT S=ZER(2,3) or 15 DIM S(2,3)
                                       30 MAT S=A+B
                                       35 MAT PRINT S

SECTION 14.7

1. F   **2.** T   **3.** T   **4.** F   **5.** F   **6.** T   **7.** F   **8.** F   **9.** T   **10.** F

SECTION 15.4

1. a. 10 PRINT LEFT (A$,1) or 10 PRINT SUBSTR(A$,1,1)
   b. 15 PRINT MID(A$,2,1) or 15 PRINT SUBSTR(A$,2,1)
   c. 20 PRINT RIGHT(A$,LEN(A$)) or 20 PRINT SUBSTR(A$,LEN(A$))
   d. 25 PRINT LEFT(A$,3) or 25 PRINT SUBSTR(A$,1,3)
   e. 30 PRINT RIGHT(A$,LEN(A$)–2) or 30 PRINT SUBSTR(A$,LEN(A$)–2)
   f. 35 PRINT LEFT(A$,1);RIGHT(A$,LEN(A$))
                     or
      35 PRINT SUBSTR(A$,1,1);SUBSTR(A$,LEN(A$))
   g. 40 IF LEN(A$)=LEN(B$) THEN 70
   h. 45 IF LEFT(A$,1)=RIGHT(B$,LEN(B$)) THEN 95
                     or
      45 IF SUBSTR(A$,1,1)=SUBSTR(B$,LEN(B$)) THEN 95
   i. 50 IF LEFT(A$,1)=MID(A$,2,1) THEN 160
                     or
      50 IF SUBSTR(A$,1,1)=SUBSTR(A$,2,1) THEN 160
   j. 55 LET B$=LEFT(A$,N) or 55 LET B$=SUBSTR(A$,1,N)
2. a. 10 LET B$=RIGHT(A$,2)+LEFT(A$,1) or 10 LET B$=SUBSTR(A$,2)+SUBSTR(A$,1,1)
   b. 15 LET T$=MID(S$,2,1)+LEFT(S$,1)+RIGHT(S$,3)
                     or
      15 LET T$=SUBSTR(S$,2,1)+SUBSTR(S$,1,1)+SUBSTR(S$,3)
   c. 20 LET F$=LEFT(G$,3)+RIGHT(H$,LEN(H$)–2)
                     or
      20 LET F$=SUBSTR(G$,1,3)+SUBSTR(H$,LEN(H$)–2)
   d. 25 IF LEFT(A$,1)+MID(B$,2,1)+MID(C$,3,1)="YES" THEN 150
                     or
      25 IF SUBSTR(A$,1,1)+SUBSTR(A$,2,1)+SUBSTR(A$,3,1)="YES" THEN 150
3. a. BASIC   b. MADAM   c. TEACUP   d. REDDER

SECTION 15.5

1. F   **2.** F   **3.** T   **4.** T   **5.** T   **6.** F   **7.** T   **8.** T   **9.** F   **10.** T   **11.** F   **12.** T

INDEX

219